T0008206

# Thrilling Cities

## Also by Ian Fleming

*Fiction*

Casino Royale
Live and Let Die
Moonraker
Diamonds are Forever
From Russia with Love
Dr No
Goldfinger
For Your Eyes Only
Thunderball
The Spy Who Loved Me
On Her Majesty's Secret Service
You Only Live Twice
The Man with the Golden Gun
Octopussy and The Living Daylights

Chitty Chitty Bang Bang

*Non-fiction*

The Diamond Smugglers
Thrilling Cities

# Thrilling Cities

## IAN FLEMING

IAN FLEMING PUBLICATIONS

WILLIAM MORROW
*An Imprint of* HarperCollins*Publishers*

THRILLING CITIES. Copyright © 1963 by Ian Fleming Publications Ltd.

All rights reserved. Printed in the United States of America. No part of this book may be used or reproduced in any manner whatsoever without written permission except in the case of brief quotations embodied in critical articles and reviews. For information, address HarperCollins Publishers, 195 Broadway, New York, NY 10007.

HarperCollins books may be purchased for educational, business, or sales promotional use. For information, please email the Special Markets Department at SPsales@harpercollins.com.

Originally published in Great Britain in 1963 by Jonathan Cape

First William Morrow paperback published 2024

James Bond and 007 are registered trademarks of Danjaq LLC, used under license by Ian Fleming Publications Ltd.

The Ian Fleming signature and the Ian Fleming logo are both trademarks owned by The Ian Fleming Estate, used under license by Ian Fleming Publications Ltd.

www.ianfleming.com

Library of Congress Cataloging-in-Publication Data has been applied for.

ISBN 978-0-06-329914-6

24 25 26 27 28  LBC  5 4 3 2 1

# Contents

# Author's Note

There is very little to say as an introduction to this book that is not self-evident from its title, but there are one or two comments I would like to make on its origins.

These are thirteen essays on some of the thrilling cities of the world written for the *Sunday Times* in 1959 and 1960 Seven of them are about cities round the world, and six round Europe.

They are what is known, in publishing vernacular, as 'mood pieces'. They are, I hope – or were, within their date – factually accurate, but they do not claim to be comprehensive, and such information as they provide is focused on the bizarre and perhaps the shadier side of life.

All my life I have been interested in adventure and, abroad, I have enjoyed the *frisson* of leaving the wide, well-lit streets and venturing up back alleys in search of the hidden, authentic pulse of towns. It was perhaps this habit that turned me into a writer of thrillers and, by the time I made the two journeys that produced these essays, I had certainly got into the way of looking at people and places and things through a thriller-writer's eye.

The essays entertained, and sometimes scandalized, the readers of the *Sunday Times*, and the editorial blue pencil scored through many a passage which has now been impurgated (if that is the opposite of expurgated) in the present text. There were suggestions that I should embody the two series in a book, but I was too busy, or too lazy, to take the step until now, despite the warning of my friends that the essays would date.

I do not think they have dated to any serious extent and, rereading them, they seem, to me at any rate, to retain such freshness as they ever possessed. The cities may have changed minutely, this or that restaurant may have disappeared, a few characters have died, but I stick to the validity of the landscapes, painted with a broad and idiosyncratic brush, and I have embellished each chapter with stop-press indices of 'Incidental Intelligence' which should, since they were provided for the most part by foreign correspondents of the *Sunday Times*, be of value to the traveller of today.

Nothing remains but to dedicate this biased, cranky but at least zestful hotchpotch to my friends and colleagues on the *Sunday Times* in London and abroad, and particularly to a man called 'C.D.', who pulled the trigger, and to Mr Roy Thomson who cheerfully paid for these very expensive and self-indulgent peregrinations.

I.L.F.

# 1

# Hong Kong

If you write thrillers, people think that you must live a thrilling life and enjoy doing thrilling things. Starting with these false assumptions, the Editorial Board of the *Sunday Times* repeatedly urged me to do something exciting and write about it and, at the end of October 1959, they came up with the idea that I should make a round trip of the most exciting cities of the world and describe them in beautiful, beautiful prose. This could be accomplished, they said, within a month.

Dubiously I discussed this project with Mr Leonard Russell, Features and Literary Editor of the paper. I said it was going to be very expensive and very exhausting, and that one couldn't go round the world in thirty days and report either beautifully or accurately on great cities in approximately three days per city. I also said that I was the world's worst sightseer and that I had often advocated the provision of roller-skates at the doors of museums and art galleries. I was also, I said, impatient of lunching at Government Houses and of visiting clinics and resettlement areas.

Leonard Russell was adamant. 'We don't want that

sort of thing,' he said. 'In your James Bond books, even if people can't put up with James Bond and those fancy heroines of yours, they seem to like the exotic backgrounds. Surely you want to pick up some more material for your stories? This is a wonderful opportunity.'

I objected that my stories were fiction and the sort of things that happened to James Bond didn't happen in real life.

'Rot,' he said firmly.

So, wishing privately to see the world, however rapidly, while it was still there to see, I purchased a round-the-world air ticket for £803 19s. 2d., drew £500 in travellers' cheques from the Chief Accountant and had several 'shots' which made me feel sore and rather dizzy. Then, on November 2nd, armed with a sheaf of visas, a round-the-world suit with concealed money pockets, one suitcase in which, as one always does, I packed more than I needed, and my typewriter, I left humdrum London for the thrilling cities of the world – Hong Kong, Macao, Tokyo, Honolulu, Los Angeles, Las Vegas, Chicago, New York.

On that soft, grey morning, Comet G/ADOK shot up so abruptly from the north–south runway of London Airport that the beige curtains concealing the lavatories and the cockpit swayed back into the cabin at an angle of fifteen degrees. The first soaring leap through the overcast was to ten thousand feet. There was a slight tremor as we went through the lower cloud base and another as we came out into the brilliant sunshine.

We climbed on another twenty thousand feet into that world above the cotton-wool cloud carpet where it is always a beautiful day. The mind adjusted itself to the prospect of twenty-four hours of this sort of thing – the hot face and rather chilly feet, eyes that smart with the outside brilliance, the smell of Elizabeth Arden and Yardley cosmetics that B.O.A.C. provide for their passengers, the varying whine of the jets, the first cigarette of an endless chain of smoke, and the first conversational gambits exchanged with the seatfellow who, in this instance, was a pleasant New Zealander with a flow of aboriginal jokes and nothing else to do but talk the whole way to Hong Kong.

Zürich came and the banal beauty of Switzerland, then the jagged sugar-icing of the Alps, the blue puddles of the Italian lakes and the snow melting down towards the baked terrazza of the Italian plains. My companion commented that we had a good seat 'viewwise', not like the other day when he was crossing the Atlantic and an American woman came aboard and complained when she found herself sitting over the wing. 'It's always the same,' she had cried. 'When I get on an aircraft all I can see outside is wing.' The American next to her had said, 'Listen, Ma'am, you go right on seeing that wing. Start worrying when you can't see it any longer.'

Below us Venice was an irregular brown biscuit surrounded by the crumbs of her islands. A straggling crack in the biscuit was the Grand Canal. At six hundred miles an hour, the Adriatic and the distant jagged line of Yugoslavia were gone in thirty minutes.

Greece was blanketed in cloud and we were out over the Eastern Mediterranean in the time it took to consume a cupful of B.O.A.C. fruit salad. (My neighbour told me he liked sweet things. When I got to Los Angeles I must be sure and not forget to eat poison-berry pie.)

It was now two o'clock in the afternoon, G.M.T., but we were hastening towards the night and dusk came to meet us. An hour more of slow, spectacular sunset and blue-black night and then Beirut showed up ahead – a sprawl of twinkling hundreds-and-thousands under an Arabian Nights new moon that dived down into the oil lands as the Comet banked to make her landing. Beirut is a crooked town and, when we came to rest, I advised my neighbour to leave nothing small on his seat, and particularly not his extremely expensive camera. I said that we were now entering the thieving areas of the world. Someone would get it. The hatch clanged open and the first sticky fingers of the East reached in.

'Our Man in the Lebanon' was there to meet me, full of the gossip of the bazaars. Beirut is the great smuggling junction of the world. Diamonds thieved from Sierra Leone come in here for onward passage to Germany, cigarettes and pornography from Tangier, arms for the sheikhs of Araby and drugs from Turkey. Gold? Yes, said my friend. Did I remember the case brought by the Bank of England in the Italian courts against a ring that was minting real gold sovereigns containing the exactly correct amount of gold?

The Bank of England had finally won their case in Switzerland, but now another ring had gone one better. They were minting gold sovereigns in Aleppo and now saving a bit on the gold content. These were for India. Only last week there had been a big Indian buyer in Beirut. He had bought sacks of sovereigns and flown them to a neighbouring port where he had put them on board his private yacht. Then he sailed to Goa in Portuguese India. From there, with the help of conniving Indian frontier officials, the gold would go on its way to the bullion brokers in Bombay. There was still this mad thirst for gold in India. The premium was not what it had been after the war, only about sixty per cent now instead of the old three hundred per cent, but it was still well worth the trouble and occasional danger. Opium? Yes, there was a steady stream coming in from Turkey; also heroin, which is refined opium, from Germany via Turkey and Syria. Every now and then the American Federal Narcotics Bureau in Rome would trace a gang back to Beirut and, with the help of local police, there would be a raid and a handful of prison sentences. But Interpol, he urged, really should have an office in Beirut. There would be plenty to keep them busy. I asked where all the drugs were going to. To Rome and then down to Naples for shipment to America. That's where the consumption was, and the big prices. Arms smuggling wasn't doing too well now that Cyprus was more or less settled. Beirut had been the centre of that traffic – mostly Italian and Belgian arms – but now there was sir. But have you red hairs on your chest?' I said that I was sorry but I simply must read my book as I had to review it. The lie was effective and my companion went off to sleep hogging more than his share of the arm-rest.

Bahrain is, without question, the scruffiest international airport in the world. The washing facilities would not be tolerated in a prison and the slow fans in the ceilings of the bedraggled hutments hardly stirred the flies. Stale, hot air blew down off the desert and there was a chirrup of unknown insects. A few onlookers shuffled about with their feet barely off the ground, spitting and scratching themselves. This is the East one is glad to get through quickly.

Up again over the Arabian Sea with, below us, the occasional winking flares of the smuggling dhows that hug the coast from India down past the Aden Protectorate and East Africa, carrying cargoes of illegal Indian emigrants on their way to join fathers and uncles and cousins in the cheap labour markets of Kenya and Tanganyika. Without passports, they are landed on the African continent anywhere south of the Equator and disappear into the bidonvilles that are so much more hospitable than the stews of Bombay. From now on, we shall be in the lands of baksheesh, squeeze and graft, which rule from the smallest coolie to the Mr Bigs in government.

Ten thousand feet below us a baby thunderstorm flashed violet. My neighbour said he must get a picture of it, groped under his seat. Consternation! A hundred and fifty pounds' worth of camera and lenses had been filched! Already the loot would be on its way up the pipeline to the bazaars. The long argument with the chief steward about responsibility and insurance went on far across the great black vacuum of India.

More thunderstorms fluttered in the foothills of the Himalayas while B.O.A.C. stuffed us once again, like Strasbourg geese, with food and drink. I had no idea what time it was or when I was going to get any sleep between these four- or five-hour leaps across the world. My watch said midnight G.M.T. and this tricked me into drinking a whisky and soda in the pretentious airport at New Delhi where the sad Benares brassware in unsaleable Indian shapes and sizes collects dust in the forlorn showcases. Alas, before I had finished it, a pale dawn was coming up and great flocks of awakened crows fled silently overhead towards some distant breakfast among the rubbish dumps outside India's capital.

India has always depressed me. I can't bear the universal dirt and squalor and the impression, false I am sure, that everyone is doing no work except living off his neighbour. And I am desolated by the *outward* manifestations of the two great Indian religions. Ignorant, narrow-minded, bigoted? Of course I am. But perhaps this extract from India's leading newspaper, boxed and in heavy black type on the back page of the *Statesman* of November 21st, 1959, will help to excuse my prejudices:

## 10 YEARS' PRISON FOR KIDNAPPING
*New Delhi, Nov. 16*

A bill providing deterrent punishment for kidnapping minors and maiming and employing them for begging, was introduced in the Lok Sabha today by the Home Minister, Pandit Pant.

The bill seeks to amend the relevant sections of the Indian Penal Code, and provides for imprisonment extending up to 10 years and fine in the case of kidnapping or obtaining custody of minors for employing them for begging, and life imprisonment and fine in the case of maiming. – P.T.I.

Back on the plane, the assistant stewardess wore the Siamese equivalent of a cheong sam. Five hours away was Bangkok. One rejected sleep and breakfast for the splendour below and away to port where the Himalayas shone proudly and the tooth of Everest looked small and easy to climb. Why had no one ever told me that the mouths of the Ganges are one of the wonders of the world? Gigantic brown meanderings between walls and islands of olive green, each one of a hundred tributaries seeming ten times the size of the Thames. A short neck of the Bay of Bengal and then down over the rice fields of Burma to the heavenly green pastures of Thailand, spread out among wandering rivers and arrow-straight canals like some enchanted garden. This was the first place of really startling beauty I had so far seen and the temperature of ninety-two degrees in the shade on the tarmac did nothing to spoil the impact of the country where I would advise other travellers to have their first view of the true Orient. The minute air hostess, smiling the first true smile, as opposed to an air-hostess smile, since London, told us to 'forrow me'.

In spite of the mosquitoes as large as Messerschmitts and the wringing humidity, everyone seems to agree that Bangkok is a dream city, and I blamed myself for hurrying on to Hong Kong. In only one hour, one still got the impression of the topsy-turvy, childlike quality of the country and an old Siamese hand, a chance acquaintance, summed it up with a recent cutting from a Bangkok newspaper. This was a plaintive article by a high police official remonstrating with tourists for accosting girls in the streets. These street-walkers were unworthy representatives of Siamese womanhood. A tourist had only to call at the nearest police station to be given names and addresses and prices of not only the most beautiful, but the most respectable, girls in the city.

Back in the Comet that, after six thousand miles, seemed as fresh and trim as it had at London Airport, it was half an hour across the China Sea before one's clothes came unstuck from one's body. Then it was only another hour or so before the Chinese communist-owned outer islands of Hong Kong showed up below and we began to drift down to that last little strip of tarmac set in one of the most beautiful views in the world. It was nearly five o'clock and just over twenty-six hours and seven thousand miles from London. Twenty minutes late! Take a letter please, Miss Trueblood.

*

'Is more better now, Master?' I grunted luxuriously and the velvet hands withdrew from my shoulders. More Tiger Balm was applied to the finger tips and then the hands were back, now to massage the base of my neck with soft authority. Through the open french windows the song of bulbuls came from the big orchid tree covered with deep pink blossom and two Chinese magpies chattered in the grove of casuarina. Somewhere far away turtle doves were saying 'coocoroo'. Number One Boy (Number One from among seven in the house) came in to say that breakfast was ready on the veranda. I exchanged compliments with the dimpling masseuse, put on a shirt and trousers and sandals and walked out into the spectacular, sun-drenched view.

As, half-way through the delicious scrambled eggs and bacon, a confiding butterfly, black and cream and dark blue, settled on my wrist, I reflected that heaven could wait. Here, on the green and scarcely inhabited slopes of Shek-O, above Big Wave Bay on the south-east corner of Hong Kong island, was good enough.

This was my first morning in Hong Kong and this small paradise was the house of friends, Mr and Mrs Hugh Barton. Hugh Barton is perhaps the most powerful surviving English *taipan* (big shot) in the Orient, and he lives in discreet accordance with his status as Chairman of Messrs Jardine Matheson, the great Far Eastern trading corporation founded by two energetic Scotsmen one hundred and forty years ago. They say in Hong Kong that power resides in the Jockey Club, Jardine Mathesons, the Hong Kong and Shanghai Bank, and Her Majesty's Government – in that order. Hugh Barton, being a steward of the Jockey Club, Chairman of Jardine's, Deputy Chairman of the Hong Kong and Shanghai Bank and a member of the Governor's Legislative Council, has it every way, and when I complained of a mildly stiff neck after my flight it was natural that so powerful a *taipan*'s household should conjure up a comely masseuse before breakfast. That is the right way, but alas how rare, for powerful *taipans* to operate. When, the night before, I had complimented Mrs Barton for having fixed a supremely theatrical new moon for my arrival, I was not being all that fanciful.

Apart from being the last stronghold of feudal luxury in the world, Hong Kong is the most vivid and exciting city I have ever seen, and I recommend it without reserve to anyone who possesses the fate. It seems to have everything – modern comfort in a theatrically Oriental setting; an equable climate except during the monsoons; beautiful country for walking or riding; all sports, including the finest golf course – the Royal Hong Kong – in the East, the most expensively equipped racecourse, and wonderful skin-diving; exciting flora and fauna, including the celebrated butterflies of Hong Kong; and a cost of living that compares favourably with any other tourist city. Minor attractions include really good Western and Chinese restaurants, exotic night life, cigarettes at 1s. 3d. for twenty, and heavy Shantung silk suits, shirts, etc., expertly tailored in forty-eight hours.

With these and innumerable other advantages it is, therefore, not surprising that the population of this minute territory is over three million, or one million more than the whole of New Zealand. The fact that six hundred and fifty million communist Chinese are a few miles away across the frontier seems only to add zest to the excitement at all levels of life in the colony and, from the Governor down, if there is an underlying tension, there is certainly no dismay. Obviously China could take Hong Kong by a snap of its giant fingers, but China has shown no signs of wishing to do so, and when the remaining forty years of our lease of the mainland territory expire, I see no reason why a reduced population should not retreat to the islands and the original territory which we hold in perpetuity.

Whatever the future holds, there is no sign that a sinister, doom-fraught count-down is in progress. It is true that the colony every now and then gets the shivers, but when an American bank pulled up stumps during the Quemoy troubles in 1958, there was nothing but mockery. The government pressed on inside the leased territory with the building of the largest hospital in the Orient and with the erection of an average of two schools a month to meet the influx of refugees from China. The private Chinese and European builders also pressed on, and continue to press on today, with the construction of twenty-storey apartment houses for the lower and middle classes. Altogether it is a gay and splendid colony humming with vitality and progress, and pure joy to the senses and spirits.

Apart from my host, my guide, philosopher and friend in Hong Kong, and later in Japan, was 'Our Man in the Orient', Richard Hughes, Far Eastern correspondent of the *Sunday Times*. He is a giant Australian with a European mind and a quixotic view of the world exemplified by his founding of the Baritsu branch of the Baker Street Irregulars – Baritsu is Japanese for the national code of self-defence which includes judo, and is the only Japanese word known to have been used by Sherlock Holmes.

On my first evening he and I went out on the town.

The streets of Hong Kong are the most enchanting night streets I have trod. Here the advertising agencies are ignorant of the drab fact, known all too well in London and New York, that patterns of black and red and yellow have the most compelling impact on the human eye. Avoiding harsh primary colours, the streets of Hong Kong are evidence that neon lighting need not be hideous, and the crowded Chinese ideograms in pale violet and pink and green with a plentiful use of white are entrancing not only for their colours but also because one does not know what drab messages and exhortations they spell out. The smell of the streets is sea-clean with an occasional exciting dash of sandalwood from a joss-stick factory, frying onions, and the scent of sweet perspiration that underlies Chinese cooking. The girls, thanks to the cheong sams they wear, have a deft and coltish prettiness which sends Western women into paroxysms of envy. The high, rather stiff collar of the cheong sam gives authority and poise to the head and shoulders, and the flirtatious slits from the hem of the dress upwards, as high as the beauty of the leg will allow, demonstrate that the sex appeal of the inside of a woman's knee has apparently never occurred to Dior or Balmain. No doubt there are fat or dumpy Chinese women in Hong Kong, but I never saw one. Even the men, in their spotless white shirts and dark trousers, seem to have better, fitter figures than we in the West, and the children are a constant enchantment.

We started off our evening at the solidest bar in Hong Kong – the sort of place that Hemingway liked to write about, lined with ships' badges and other trophies, with, over the bar, a stuffed alligator with an iguana riding on its back. The bar belongs to Jack Conder, a former Shanghai municipal policeman and reputed to have been the best pistol shot there in the old days. His huge fists seem to hold the memory of many a recalcitrant chin. He will not allow women in the bar downstairs on the grounds that real men should be allowed to drink alone. When the Japanese came in 1941, Conder stayed on in Shanghai, was captured and escaped. He took the long walk all the way down China to Chungking, sleeping during daylight hours in graveyards, where the ghosts effectively protected him. He is the authentic Hemingway type and he sells solid drinks at reasonable prices. His bar is the meeting place of 'Alcoholics Synonymous' – a group of lesser Hemingway characters, most of them local press correspondents. The initiation ceremony requires the consumption of sixteen San Migs, which is the pro name for the local San Miguel beer – to my taste a very unencouraging brew.

After fortification with Western poisons (I gather that

no self-respecting Chinese would think of drinking before dinner, but that the fashion for whisky is invading the Orient almost as fast as it has invaded France) we proceeded to one of the finest Chinese locales, the Peking Restaurant. Dick Hughes, a hard-bitten Orientalogue, was determined that I should become Easternized as soon as possible and he missed no opportunity to achieve the conversion. The Peking Restaurant was bright and clean. We consumed seriatim:

> shark's fin soup with crab,
> shrimp balls in oil,
> bamboo shoots with seaweed,
> chicken and walnuts,

with, as a main dish,

> roast Peking duckling,

washed down with mulled wine. Lotus seeds in syrup added a final gracious touch.

Dick insisted that then, and on all future occasions when we were together, I should eat with chopsticks, and I pecked around with these graceful but ridiculous instruments with clumsy enthusiasm. To my surprise the meal, most elegantly presented and served, was in every respect delicious. All the tastes were new and elusive, but I was particularly struck with another aspect of Oriental cuisine – each dish had a quality of gaiety about it, assisted by discreet ornamentation, so that the basically unattractive process of shovelling food into one's mouth achieved, whether one liked it or not, a kind of elegance. And the background to this, and to all my subsequent meals in the East, always had this quality of gaiety – people chattering happily and smiling with pleasure and encouragement. From now on, all the meals I ate in authentic, as opposed to tourist, Chinese or Japanese restaurants were infinitely removed from what, for a lifetime, had been a dull, rather unattractive routine in the sombre eating-mills of the West, where the customer, his neighbours and the waiters seem subtly to resent each other, the fact that they should all be there together, and very often the things they are eating.

Dick Hughes spiced our banquet with the underground and underworld gossip of the colony – the inability of the government to deal drastically with Hong Kong's only real problem, the water shortage. Why didn't they hand it over to private enterprise? The gas and electricity services were splendidly run by the Kadoorie brothers, whose record had been equally honourable in Shanghai. There was a grave shortage of hotels. Why didn't Jardines do something about it? Japanese mistresses were preferable to Chinese girls. If, for one reason or another, you fell out with your Japanese girl, she would be dignified, philosophical. But the Chinese girl would throw endless hysterical scenes, and probably turn up at your office and complain to your employer. Servants? They were plentiful and wonderful, but too many of the English and American wives had no idea how to treat good servants. They would clap their hands and shout 'Boy!' to cover their lack of self-confidence. This sort of behaviour was out of fashion and brought the Westerner into disrepute. (How often one has heard the same thing said of English wives in other 'coloured' countries!)

The latest public scandal was the massage parlours and the blue cinemas (with colour and sound!) that flourished, particularly across the harbour in Kowloon. The *Hong Kong Standard* had been trying to clean them up. The details they had published had anyway been good for circulation. He read out from the *Standard*: 'Erotic dailies circulate freely here. Blue films shown openly. Hong Kong police round up massage girls.' The *Standard* had given the names and addresses: 'Miss Ten Thousand Fun and Safety at 23 Stanley Street, 2nd floor. Business starting at 9 a.m. . . . Miss Soft and Warm Village . . . Miss Outer Space, and Miss Lotus of Love at 17 Cafe Apartments, Room 113, ground floor. (Opposite the French Hospital. Room heated) . . . Miss Chaste and Refined, Flat A, Percival Mansion, 6th floor (lift service).' And more wonderful names: 'Miss Smooth and Fragrant . . . Miss Emerald Parsley . . . Miss Peach Stream Pool (satisfaction guaranteed),' and so forth.

The trouble, explained Dick, was partly the traditional desire of Oriental womanhood to please, combined with unemployment and the rising cost of living. Increase in the number of light industries, particularly the textile mills, the bane of Lancashire and America, might help.

Would I like to visit the latest textile mill? I said I wouldn't.

It was a natural step from this conversation to proceed from the Peking Restaurant to the world of Suzie Wong.

Richard Mason, with his splendid book *The World of Suzie Wong*, has done for a modest waterfront hotel what Hemingway did for his very different Harry's Bar in Venice. The book, though, like *A Many-Splendoured Thing* by Han Suyin, read universally by the literate in Hong Kong, is small-mindedly frowned upon, largely I gather because miscegenation with beautiful Chinese girls is understandably an unpopular topic with the great union of British womanhood. But the Suzie Wong myth is in Hong Kong to stay, and Richard Mason would be amused to find how it has gathered depth and detail.

It seems to be fact, for instance, and perhaps the only known fact, that when he was in Hong Kong Richard Mason did live in a waterfront establishment called the Luk Kwok Hotel, transformed in his book into the Nam Kok House of Pleasure, where the painter, Robert Lomax, befriended and, after comic, tender, romantic and finally tragic interludes, married the charming prostitute Suzie Wong.

As a result of the book, the Luk Kwok Hotel, so conveniently placed near the Fleet landing stage and the British Sailors' Home, has boomed. Solitary girls may still not sit unaccompanied in the spacious bar with its great and many-splendoured jukebox. You must still bring them in from outside, as did Lomax, to prevent the hotel becoming, legally, a disorderly house. But the whole place has been redecorated in deep battleship grey (to remind the sailors of home?) and one of Messrs Collins's posters advertising Richard Mason's book has a place of honour on the main wall. Other signs of prosperity are a huge and hideous near-Braque on another wall, a smart Anglepoise light over the cash register, and a large bowl of Siamese fighting fish. (It is also a sign of fame, of which the proprietor is very proud, that the totally respectable Prime Minister of Laos and his Foreign Minister stayed at the Luk Kwok on a visit to Hong Kong.) If you inquire after Suzie herself, you are answered with a melancholy shake of the head and the sad, dramatic news that Suzie's marriage failed and she is now back 'on the pipe'. When you ask where you could find her, it is explained that she will see no other man and waits for Lomax one day to return. She is not in too bad a way, as Lomax sends her regular remittances from London. But there are many other beautiful girls here just as beautiful as Suzie. Would you care to meet one, a very particular friend of Suzie's?

I don't know how much the sailors believe this story, but I suspect they are all quite happy to put up with 'Suzie's friend', and I for one greatly enjoyed exploring the myth that will forever inhabit the Luk Kwok Hotel with its neon slogans: 'GIRLS, BUT NO OBLIGATION TO BUY DRINKS! CLEAN SURROUNDINGS! ENJOY TO THE MAXIMUM AT THE LEAST EXPENSE!'

Dick Hughes misunderstood one author's delighted

interest in the brilliance of another author's myth, and protested that there were far better establishments awaiting my patronage. But by now it was late and the after-effects of jet travel – a dull headache and a bronchial breathlessness – had caught up with me, and we ended our evening with a walk along the thronged quays in search of a taxi and home.

On the way I commented on the fact that there is not a single seagull in the whole vast expanse of Hong Kong harbour. Dick waved towards the dense flood of junks and sampans on which families of up to half a dozen spend the whole of their lives, mostly tied up in harbour. There hadn't used to be any seagulls in Shanghai either, he said. Since the communists took over they have come back. The communists have put it about that they had come back because they no longer have to fight with the humans for the harbour refuse. It was probably the same thing in Hong Kong. It would taken an awful lot of seagulls to compete for a living with three million Chinese.

On this downbeat note I closed my first enchanted day.

## INCIDENTAL INTELLIGENCE

### Hotels

By tradition and probably correctly, the *Peninsula* (the '*Pen*'), on the Kowloon peninsula, is regarded as the Number 1 hotel for visitors to the colony. It now has an annexe, *Peninsula Court*. Rates are from HK$70 (single) to HK$100 (double). Very colonial, comfortable, proper. It is generally booked fully for months in advance. Next come the *Miramar* (behind the *Peninsula* geographically, but livelier and overtaking it by enterprise and expansion) and the *Gloucester* (on the island). *Miramar* rates range from HK$36 to 75; the *Gloucester*, HK$40 to 75.

If you are holidaying, the *Repulse Bay Hotel*, across the island and fronting a reasonable beach, is recommended. (HK$30 to 95.) This is set in lovely gardens and the local beauties, wives and concubines offer a dazzling display at the Sunday afternoon tea-dances. The food is better than at the *Peninsula* or the *Miramar*. But it takes half an hour to cross the island to the business, shopping and social centre of Hong Kong (officially called Victoria).

The *Luk Kwok*, Suzie Wong's original official address, encourages a livelier clientele. Single room (an interesting aspiration), HK$11; double (virtually *de rigueur*), up to HK$35.

(For comparison, a Chinese can get a bed of a sort in a wooden hut or 'garage', shared with half a dozen companions, in the industrial areas for HK$8 (10s.) a *month*.)

*Eating*

For Western food, the *Marco Polo* in the *Peninsula Court* is the most expensive restaurant and can sometimes be the best. *Gaddi's*, off the *Peninsula* ground-floor marble lobby, is also recommended. On the island, the

*Parisian Grill* (the 'P.G.') is the oldest and best-known restaurant, jam-packed at lunch; but standards and prices at *Jimmy's Kitchen* and the *Gloucester* (now operating a rejuvenated kitchen) are roughly equivalent. *Maxim's* and the *Café de Paris* charge slightly more. More Chinese go to *Maxim's* than to the 'P.G.', and there is dancing in the evening; Hong Kong's feminine elegance glitters at *Maxim's* at the cocktail hour. You can get bear's paw – overrated – at the *Gloucester.* (N.B. The best and biggest martinis in the colony are served in the Mexican bar in the *Gloucester.*)

All visitors want to eat on the floating restaurants at Aberdeen. As this venture involves a forty-minute taxi haul from Victoria, the earnest diner might care to break his journey at the *Repulse Bay Hotel* and brace himself with a few shots on the veranda around sunset before tackling the next fifteen minute stage to reach the floating restaurants at twilight.

Dinner at the *Carlton,* four miles out of Kowloon on the main road to the New Territories, unfolds one of the world's most memorable panoramas: the jewelled lights of Kowloon, the harbour and the island.

## Chinese food

The range and quality of Chinese cuisine in Hong Kong are matched only in Taipeh. Beggar's chicken at the *Tien Hong Lau* in Kowloon is incomparable; if possible, it should be ordered the day before. Peking duck is the speciality of the *Princess Garden* in Kowloon and the *Peking Restaurant* on the island. The *Ivy* (on the island) serves exotic Szechuanese-style food. The *Café de Chine* serves Cantonese-style dishes in two huge connecting dining-rooms on the top floor of a ten-storey building in the heart of Victoria. A regular wealthy Chinese visitor from San Francisco always goes to the *Tai Tung* for one special dish which he claims is unequalled anywhere else: roast sucking pig *à la Cantonese*. Everyone has his favourite. You can feast cheaply at the lot.

## Night Life

Generally, night life in Hong Kong is much as anywhere else. There are twenty-five registered night-clubs, some of which tolerate second-rate floor shows on the dreary Asian circuit (Singapore – Kuala Lumpur – Bangkok – Hong Kong – Manila – Tokyo). None are in the same class as the Tokyo night-clubs, and chauvinistic Hong Kong apologists, with desperate parochialism, are compelled to find compensation in the proud boast that the local night-clubs don't close until two a.m., while the lights go out reluctantly in the Tokyo cabarets (but not the bars) at midnight.

The dance-hostesses are on call which does not mean by telephone, but by personal arrangement at seventy-six 'ballrooms'. The prettiest girls and the best bands tend to be in places like the *Tonnochy Ballroom* and the *Golden Phoenix* (on the island) and at the *Oriental* (in Kowloon), where most of the patrons are Chinese and no hard liquor is served, only tea, soft drinks and melon seeds.

There are 8,000 registered hostesses, whose company

(financed by a coupon system) ranges from 60 cents to HK$5.50 per twenty minutes. At the *Tonnochy* or the *Metropole* (where you should ask to study the telephone-directory-like album, which shows the photographs and names of available hostesses), an hour's dancing will thus cost HK$16.50 (just over £1). Most of the girls in the higher-priced ballrooms are glamorous and English-speaking and, subject to financial adjustment with the proprietor, will gladly leave the ballroom and accompany a visitor to a night-club; this invitation, of course, gives them great face. The tourist has the patriotic satisfaction of knowing that the colony's government collects ten per cent tax on every dance-girl's coupons.

There are scores of brash and noisy bars along Lockhart Street and in Wanchai and North Point (on the island) and throughout the back lanes of Kowloon, some of which, when the navies are in port, are a dim echo of Shanghai's old Blood Alley.

Although not featured in the prim official tourist handbooks, small sampans at Causeway Bay (on the island) offer a mild variation of the old Shanghai and Canton flower-boat entertainment as once available in the dear dead days before the coming of Mao Tse-Tung. A curtain gives the passengers privacy from the pilot, and the sampan either drifts with wind and current in seclusion, or moves, as desired, to floating markets and teashops and rafts of singers and musicians. (Tariff: about HK$1 an hour or up to HK$10 for the night.)

# 2

# Macao

Gold, hand in hand with opium, plays an extraordinary secret role through the Far East, and Hong Kong and Macao, the tiny Portuguese possession only forty miles away, are the hub of the whole underground traffic.

In England, except between bullion brokers, nobody ever talks about gold as a medium of exchange or as an important item among personal possessions. But from India eastwards gold is a constant topic of conversation, and the daily newspapers are never without their list of gold prices in bullion, English sovereigns, French Napoléons and louis d'or, and rarely a day goes by without there being a gold case in the Press. Someone has been caught smuggling gold. So-and-so has been murdered for his gold hoard. Someone else has been counterfeiting gold. The reason for this passionate awareness of the metal is the total mistrust all Orientals have for paper money and the profound belief that, without one's bar or beaten leaf of gold concealed somewhere on one's person or kept in a secret place at home, one is a poor man.

The gold king of the Orient is the enigmatic Doctor

Lobo of the Villa Verde in Macao. Irresistibly attracted, I gravitated towards him, the internal Geiger-counter of a writer of thrillers ticking furiously.

Richard Hughes and I took the S.S. *Takshing,* one of the three famous ferries that do the Macao run every day. These ferries are not the broken-down, smoke-billowing rattletraps engineered by whisky-sodden Scotsmen we see on the films, but commodious three-decker steamers run with workmanlike precision. The three-hour trip through the islands and across Deep Bay, brown with the waters of the Pearl River that more or less marks the boundary between the leased territories and Communist China, was beautiful and uneventful. The communist gunboats have given up molesting Western shipping and the wallowing sampans chugging with their single diesels homewards with the day's catch, the red flag streaming from the insect-wing sails, were the only sign that we were crossing communist waters. At the northern extremity of Deep Bay lies Macao, a peninsula about one-tenth the size of the Isle of Wight that is the oldest European settlement in China. It was founded in 1557 and is chiefly famous for the first lighthouse built on the whole coast of China. It also boasts the graves of Robert Morrison, the Protestant missionary who compiled the first Chinese–English dictionary in 1820, of George Chinnery, the great Irish painter of the Oriental scene, and of the uncle of Sir Winston Churchill, Lord John Spencer Churchill. It is also noted for the gigantic ruins of St Paul's Cathedral built in 1602 and burned down in 1835; and finally

– save the mark! – for the largest 'house of ill-fame' in the world.

So far as its premier citizen, Dr Lobo, is concerned, the most interesting features of Macao are that there is no income tax and no exchange control whatever, and that there is complete freedom of import and export of foreign currencies; and all forms of bullion. To take only the case of gold bullion, it is, therefore, perfectly easy for anyone to arrive by ferry or seaplane or come across from Communist China, only fifty yards away across the river, buy any quantity of gold, from a ton down to a gold coin, and leave Macao quite openly with his booty. It is then up to the purchaser, and of no concern whatsoever to Dr Lobo or the chief of the Macao police, to smuggle his gold back into China, into neighbouring Hong Kong or, if he has a seaplane, fly off with it into the wide world. These considerations make Macao one of the most interesting marketplaces in the world, and one with many secrets.

As we came into the roadstead, we were greeted by a scene of great splendour. The sun was setting and in its pathway lay a spectacular fleet of many hundreds of junks and sampans at anchor. This caused much excited chattering amongst our fellow-passengers and it was only on the next morning, when this fleet and other fleets from the outer islands were spread all over the sea, now under the *rising* sun, all heading for the mouth of the Pearl River, that we learnt the answer. The Sea Fishing Co-operative of Communist China had ordered all fishermen to a great meeting at which new fishing laws were to be promulgated – matters such as that the smaller junks should fish home waters within a certain radius, while the larger junks and sampans would be confined to the more distant fishing grounds. It all sounded very orderly and sensible, and very un-Chinese.

The Portuguese Navy, represented by a small Kiplingesque gunboat with one gun behind a square shield (surely a gatling!), stood guard over the interior harbour, but no courtesies were exchanged with the *Takshing,* nor could there have been, for the signal halyard had been run from the short mast to the muzzle of the main armament and was now hung with the crew's variegated washing, from which it was discernible that Persil appeared to have been but sparingly used for the Navy's big wash.

The waterfront was an astonishing mixture of rotting godowns announcing in sun-faded letters that they were, for instance, FABRICIA DE AGUAS GASOSAS or the KWONG HUNG TAI FIRECRACKER MANUFACTURING COMPANY, interspersed with the ruined facades of once grandiose private houses ornamented with the most exquisite, though dilapidated, baroque plaster and stonework. The whole town is like this, a jumble of eighteenth- and early nineteenth-century highly ornamented European styles, gimcrack modern ferro-concrete, and spruce, hideous villas. Half the streets are cobbled alleys and half wide, empty modern highways at whose pretentious crossings an occasional rickshaw waits for the otiose traffic lights to change to green. In short, the place is as picturesque as, and deader than, a beautiful graveyard.

We repaired to the Macao Inn on the junction of the waterfront and the Travessa do Padre Narciso. There we met 'Our Man in Macao' and drank warm gins and tonics under a banyan tree while I enlightened myself about the four Mr Bigs – who, with the Portuguese Government in the background, control pretty well everything that goes on in this enigmatic territory. In America these four men would be called the Syndicate, but here they are just friendly business partners who co-operate to keep trade running along the right channels. They were at that time, in order of importance, the aforesaid Dr P. J. Lobo, who looks after gold; Mr Foo Tak Yam, who concerns himself with gambling and associate activities, which may be broadly described as 'entertainment', and who owns the Central Hotel, of which more later; Mr C. Y. Leung, a silent partner; and Mr Ho Yin, the chief intermediary for trade with Communist China.

The fortunes of these four gentlemen rose during and after the war – during the war through trade with the Japanese who then occupied the mainland, and, after the war, during the golden days when the harbour of Macao was thronged with ships from Europe smuggling arms to Communist China. Those latter days had turned Macao into a boom town when a single street running half the length of the town, the 'Street of Happiness', had been one great and continuous street of pleasure and when the nine-storey-high Central Hotel, the largest house of gambling and self-indulgence in the world, had been constructed by Mr Foo to siphon off the cream of the pleasure-seekers. Those golden days had now passed. Communist China was manufacturing her own weapons, the Street of Happiness had emptied through lack of roistering sailors, and now pleasure, devoted only to the relaxation of Hong Kong tourists, was confined to the Central Hotel.

Having got all this straight in our minds, it was obvious to Dick and me that only one question remained: where to have dinner before repairing to the Central Hotel? We were advised to choose between the Fat Siu Lau, the 'Loving Buddha', in the Street of Happiness, noted for its Chinese pigeon, or the Long Kee, famous for its fish. We chose the Loving Buddha, dined excellently and repaired to the Central Hotel, whose function and design I recommend most warmly to the attention of those concerned with English morals.

The Central Hotel is not precisely a hotel. It is a nine-storey skyscraper, by far the largest building in Macao, and it is devoted solely to the human so-called vices. It has one more original feature. The higher up the building you go, the more beautiful and expensive are the girls, the higher the stakes at the gambling tables, and the better the music. Thus, on the ground floor, the honest coolie can choose a girl of his own class and gamble for pennies by lowering his bet on a fishing-rod contraption through a hole in the floor on to the gaming tables below. Those with longer pockets can progress upwards through various heavens until they reach the earthly paradise on the sixth floor. Above this are the bedrooms. In the pursuit of information which would be in accordance with the readership of the *Sunday Times*, it was a matter of course that, very soon after our arrival at the Central Hotel, Dick Hughes and I should take the lift to the sixth floor.

The sixth floor was spacious and well-lit with the sort of pseudo-modern decor you would find in a once-expensive French cafe that is on the way downhill. Across the entrance hall was the gambling hell to which we were drawn by the rattle of dice and the cries of the attractive, as it turned out, feminine croupiers. Here we found fan-tan being played, and a rather complicated dice game known as hi-lo. Having read about fan-tan in my Doctor Fu-Manchu days, when I had assumed that this must be the most sinful game on the face of the earth, I made straight for the fan-tan table, changed a hundred Hong Kong dollars (about £6 5s. 0d.) into counters and sat firmly down at the sparsely occupied table next to the 'dealer', an almond-eyed witch in a green cheong sam. On the other side of the table, beside the rack of chips, stood a similarly dressed girl with an air of authority. It was she who ran the game, while the girl on my right went through the necessary motions.

I must say that the adventure books of one's youth do give one false impressions. Fan-tan is simply a rather pretty, childlike way of inevitably losing your money. To begin with, the odds are 10 per cent in favour of the house compared with about 1.35 at roulette, and anybody who gambles at those odds is either off his head or a Chinaman.

The game proceeds as follows: in the centre of the

table is a square of painted wood divided into four compartments, marked 1, 2, 3 and 4, and you place your bet on one of these numbers. The croupier has in front of her a large pile of two or three hundred small white plastic buttons, a species of inverted brass goblet, and a thin wooden wand about two feet long. When the bids have been placed, she muddles the inverted goblet around in the pile of buttons, pushes it out in front of her, well away from the original mass of buttons, and lifts it away. She then takes her wand and delicately separates the buttons, four by four, from the pile heaped in the middle of the table. The winner is he who has guessed that at the end of her separating of these buttons, four by four, she will leave either one, two, three or four buttons behind. If you have bet on the correct remainder you are paid two to one, less 10 per cent. The girl then rakes in the central pile of buttons to join the mass in front of her, muddles them all together and squashes her goblet once again down in amongst them.

It is a pretty, restful game containing only one point of interest. A third, or not later than halfway, through the separating of the pile of buttons, the experienced fan-tan player, or certainly the organizing croupier, will hold up one, two, three or four fingers to predict the winning figure although perhaps fifty buttons have still to be separated and these are still piled up in an apparently unfathomable muddle, some on top of others and most of them overlapping. While I duly and happily lost my hundred dollars, enjoying the gentle ritual, the authoritative girl opposite was never wrong in divining the winning number from the piled-up jumble. It was quite uncanny, and the girl smiled appreciatively at my polite applause.

After Dick and I had had enough of this dainty piracy, we repaired to the neighbouring hell to try our fortunes at the more adult game of hi-lo. This is a game played at a long table with a green baize board marked out in various sections rather in the fashion of American craps. Behind this sits the usual beautiful *croupière* (if that is the feminine for croupier) with, in front of her, a shining aluminium contraption which looks like a cross between a pressure-cooker and an atomic warhead but is, in fact, a locked container containing three dice. When, after a good deal of mumbo-jumbo, she shakes the apparatus and removes the lid, the game is completed and up to a maximum of three sixes, or eighteen, and a minimum of three ones, will be displayed by the dice. So far as the even chances are concerned, you can either bet on the numbers three to eight inclusive, which is 'lo', or ten to fifteen, which, is 'hi', the number nine in the middle being zero. On these you get even money odds. You can also bet on single numbers from three to eighteen and various combinations, such as three of a kind, or a sequence. If you have bet on 'hi' or 'lo' and three of a kind turned up, you have lost. These nuances are complicated and I could not work out the odds in favour of the house. It seemed easier to stick to 'hi' or 'lo', which I did until a further hundred dollars of the *Sunday Times*'s money had gone down the drain.

An interesting feature of the hi-lo gambling hell is that halfway up the wall behind the players there is a crow's-nest in which a small Macaon sits. When the *croupière* is about to raise the fateful lid, she presses an electric bell which rings in the room and also in the various nether gambling hells down the building. In these, gamblers of lesser degree have been staking on similar tables. When the lid is lifted, the man in the crow's-nest relays the winning number down to these tables and also to electric indicators in the dance halls where gamblers can place their bets with the hostesses. Thus the dice I was watching on the sixth floor were vital for the many games being played throughout the Central Hotel.

Having educated ourselves in these matters, Dick Hughes and I repaired to our sixth-floor dance hall to see how Mr Foo was handling the second human vice. The place had a central, well-lit dance floor and a well-disciplined eight-piece 'combo' playing good but conventional jazz. In the shadows round the walls sat some twenty or thirty 'hostesses'. Dick and I arranged ourselves at a comfortable banquette in the sparsely frequented room and ordered gins and tonics and two hostesses. Mine was called Garbo, 'same like film star', she explained. She wore a pale-green embroidered cheong sam and a 'Mamie Eisenhower' bang rather low on the forehead. She had the usual immaculate ivory skin and the conventional 'almond' eyes which were bright with intelligence and a desire to please. Rather startlingly, she appeared to have black lipstick but, as my eyes grew accustomed to the light, this turned crimson. Dick's girl was a trifle older, perhaps thirty-five, wore a beige cheong sam, and was more forward and vivacious than Garbo. They asked for lemonades and, for a while, we made the usual rattling, gay, and highly artificial night-club conversation. When, in my case, the springs threatened to run dry, I fell back on that hoary gambit of reading my partner's hand.

Through experience in this science, dating back to my teens, I have acquired a crude expertise in palmistry and, with my first pronouncement that Garbo had three children, I hit a lucky jackpot. The two girls chattered excitedly and, realizing with awe that her hand was being held by a great soothsayer from the West, perspiration rose in Garbo's palm and she was hard put to it to keep this dew at bay with a paper napkin. In the reverent hush that ensued, looking alternately into the dewy palm and the reverent almond eyes, I solemnly warned her that her heart was not ruled by her head, that she had artistic leanings which had not yet come to fruition, that she would have a serious illness when she was about fifty, and finally, provocatively, that she was inclined to be under-sexed. This last pronouncement was greeted with much hilarious protestation which drew two more girls to our table and involved me in a further hour of miscellaneous prognostication and consumption of gins and tonics.

We then danced for a further hour, during which Garbo told me that I looked like Stewart Granger and danced like Fred Astaire. She also said that I was the perfect type of English gentleman and very 'humourlous' which, thinking she had said 'humourless', came as a dash of the good old Western cold water to which the Englishman is accustomed. But the small cloud was soon dispersed by further happy-talk and, by the end of the evening, I felt that I was the greatest factor in Anglo-Oriental relations since Lieutenant Pinkerton.

The evening, the reader will be relieved to learn, ended decorously in a minor snowstorm of twenty-dollar notes and protestations of undying love, and Dick and I left the magnificent Central Hotel on a wave of virtue and euphoria, showering blessings on Mr Foo and his much maligned nine-storey palace of ill-fame.

This was my first experience of Oriental Woman, and this, and my subsequent investigations, confirmed the one great advantage she possesses for Western Man. Oriental ladies have an almost inexhaustible desire to please. They also have the capacity to make the man not only suspect, but actually believe, that he is in every respect a far more splendid fellow than in his wildest dreams he had imagined. Not only that, but the women of the East appear, and in fact actually are, grateful for one's modest favours, with the result that every meeting with them leaves one in good humour and with a better opinion of oneself. However ill-founded this feeling may be, how very different from the knocking we all get in the West where women – and this applies particularly to America – take such a ferocious delight in cutting the man down to size! 'All you want is slaves,' I hear the friends expostulate. 'Well, er . . .' one mumbles, 'not absolutely. It's not exactly slavishness. It's just well, er, the desire to please.'

But I must not allow impious comment to get mixed up with sacred fact.

The next morning I was awakened by a European clang of cathedral bells and a thin, distant tucket of military bugles, and we girded ourselves for luncheon with Dr Lobo. Ever since *Life* magazine cast a shining light on Macao in 1949, the Doctor has been very wary of writers and journalists, but the magical name of a friend in Hong Kong had opened even this door for us, and in due course we were picked up by a powerful-looking 'secretary' in a battered brown Austin. We had spent the morning observing a communist co-operative hard at work across the river, admired the awe-inspiring facade of St Paul's Cathedral upon which the Japanese Christian stonemasons had sprinkled plenty of dragons and flying skeletons amongst the angels, and taken note of the hospital founded by Sun Yat-sen in 1906.

Neither the Austin nor the battered Chevrolet in which we later left to catch our ferry, nor the Villa Verde, which belonged to some tropical Wimbledon, suggested that Dr Lobo was worth the five or ten million pounds with which he is credited. At first sight, the Doctor, in his trim blue suit, stiff white collar and rimless glasses, looked like the bank manager or dentist (in fact he started life as an oculist) one would have found in the more benign Wimbledon. Dr Lobo is a small, thin Malayan Chinese with a pursed mouth and blank eyes. He is in his early seventies. He greeted us carefully in a sparsely furnished suburban living-room with a Roman Catholic shrine over the doorway, a large, nineteenth-century oleograph depicting heaven and hell, and a coloured reproduction of a famous picture I could not place – a woman with bowed head swathed in buttermuslin, who was either Faith, Hope or Charity. A powerfully built butler, who looked more like a judo black-belt than a butler, offered us Johnny Walker and we launched into careful conversation about the pros and cons of alcohol and cigarettes, neither of which, Dr Lobo said, appealed to him.

A spark of animation came into Dr Lobo's eyes when I said I heard that he was an amateur composer of note. The Doctor said he had been a violinist and had given concerts in Hong Kong. But he was certainly, he vouch-safed, no Menuhin or Heifetz. Nowadays, when he had time, he did indeed try his hand at composing. I asked if we might hear something. Readily Dr Lobo handed us a gramophone record entitled 'Gems of the Orient', privately recorded by His Master's Voice. Meanwhile he busied himself with a large gramophone. The titles of Dr Lobo's compositions were 'Souls in Sorrow', 'Passing Thoughts', 'Waves of the South Seas', 'Lilies of the Mountains' and 'Lasting Memories'.

The Doctor put 'Waves of the South Seas' on the gramophone and turned various knobs, which resulted only in a devastating roar of static from a concealed loudspeaker. More knobs were turned and still the static hooted and screamed. Dr Lobo shouted through the racket that there was something wrong. The secretary was sent off to fetch the house engineer. Dick and I sipped our whisky and avoided each other's eye. The engineer arrived and repeated Dr Lobo's previous motions. Identical hullabaloo. The engineer conjured with the back of the machine while we looked on politely. Dr Lobo adopted the familiar expression of the rich man whose toy is kaput.

In due course the thin, wavering strains of a tune containing vague echoes of 'Tales of the Vienna Woods', 'In a Monastery Garden' and 'Rose Marie' fixed expressions of rapt attention on all our faces. I shifted my posture to the bowed stance with eyes covered which I adopt for concert and opera. There was nothing to do but think of other things until both sides of the longest player I have ever heard had been completed. Dick and I made appreciative grunts as if we had come back to earth, speechless, from some musical paradise. I muttered something about 'remarkable virtuosity' and 'many-sided talent'. And then, blessedly, luncheon was served.

Dr Lobo's dining-room was lined from floor to ceiling with cabinets of cut glass that winked painfully from all sides as if one was sitting in the middle of a giant chandelier. The tepid macaroni and vegetable soup promised an unmemorable meal, so I politely got on to the topic of gold. Yes, indeed, it was an interesting business. Did I know the Bank of England and Messrs Samuel Montague? Such nice, correct people to deal with. No, he hadn't actually got an office in Europe. A manufacturer of baby powder represented him in those parts. The Doctor himself had never been farther abroad than Hong Kong.

I pressed on about gold. As I understood it, I said, Macao had been excluded by Portugal from the Bretton Woods monetary agreement which tied most of the other countries in the world to a gold price of $35 an ounce. Since, for instance, the Chinese price is around $50 an ounce, there was obviously a handsome profit to be made somewhere. Was I correct in thinking that Dr Lobo bought gold from, say, the Bank of England, at $35 an ounce and then sold it at a premium to anyone who cared to buy; how it then left Macao for the outside world being none of his business? Yes, agreed Dr Lobo, that was more or less the position. Nowadays the business was difficult. Before, when the premium over the official gold price had been higher, it had been more interesting. Smuggling? Yes, no doubt such a thing did take place. Dr Lobo smiled indulgently. The people in these parts liked to have a small piece of gold. If they bought gold in Macao, I insisted gently, how did they get it out? Dr Lobo's face went blank. These were matters of which he knew little. He had heard that they sewed single coins into their clothes and hammered thin plates of gold which they could carry in their belts. There had also been a case where some cows had been found to contain gold. The bamboo that is so much a part of sampans, for instance, is conveniently hollow. Was I interested in cut glass? All this glass had been a hobby of his late wife's. It was Stuart glass, the best.

How, I persisted, was the Indian market in gold

nowadays? 'I hear it is not so good,' said Dr Lobo. Nowadays the Indians were poor. They had no foreign exchange with which to buy gold and nobody wanted the rupee. Previously, he understood, large fortunes had been made from selling gold to India, but nowadays, the eyes twinkled frostily, it was perhaps more profitable to buy newspapers. Yes? This neat reference to the change of ownership of the *Sunday Times* showed that Dr Lobo had his wits about him.

I allowed myself also to become personal. Dr Lobo was reputed to be a very rich man. Was he not frightened of being kidnapped? I had heard that much of this had been going on in Singapore and also in Hong Kong. Had there not been a recent case . . . ? This was clearly a subject which had had Dr Lobo's close attention. He became more animated. 'I have precautions,' he said. 'I take care. We have excellent police in Macao.' The business in Hong Kong had been foolish. The family had received an ear and had gone to the police. This was an error. They should have paid the ransom money. As it was, the head of the family had never been seen again. Very foolish! Had this, I asked, been anything to do with the Tongs or Triads, criminal brotherhoods that operate in every Oriental town? That was possible, thought Dr Lobo. He had heard that these people were very powerful, particularly in the opium traffic. Opium was a very sad business. Dr Lobo became eloquent.

'It is a terrible thing, Mr Fleming. These people give all their money for opium. Soon they lose their interest in food and then in women. They become sexless, neuter, and waste away. It would be much better if they drank beer, even too much beer, as I believe is sometimes the case in your country. But what do you think of my coffee? This is my own coffee from my estate in Timor.'

The conversation petered away into polite inanity and it was nearly time for Dick and me to take the ferry. But first, said Dr Lobo, we must see his radio station. We went out into the garden and there indeed was a concrete building the size of a squash court, which is Radio Villa Verde, dispensing, amongst other things, entertainment to the inhabitants of Macao. We went in and saw the operator on the other side of the big glass window putting a record on. The Chinese girl at the control desk jumped up and bowed, her earphones still on her ears. The radio station seemed to me a wonderful adjunct to a man dealing in the bullion markets of the world. Good communications are the sinews of successful business. I said so.

Dr Lobo looked pained. 'This station is only for entertainment, Mr Fleming.' I said, yes, of course, and we stepped out and turned our backs on the innocent building to have our photographs taken with Dr Lobo by the secretary, and a copy of 'Gems of the Orient', inscribed with best compliments, presented to us.

My last sight of the enigmatic Dr Lobo, as we rattled away in the ancient Chevrolet, was of a small, trim figure cutting short the last wave of his hand as he turned and, flanked by the powerful secretary and powerful butler, disappeared back into the villa. What had I learned of Dr Lobo, the gold king whose name is whispered with awe throughout the East? Absolutely nothing at all. What do I think of Dr Lobo? I think that while there may be unexplained corners in his history, as there are in the histories of many a successful millionaire, he is what he appears to be: a careful, astute operator who has chosen an exotic line of business which may have caused a good deal in its retail outlets to the regret, no doubt, of the wholesaler. The respectability of all ageing millionaires is now his, together with the laurels of good citizenship – a doctorate of sciences unspecified and, two weeks after I left him, his appointment as Chairman of the Municipal Council of Macao, a post equivalent to mayor.

Commenting on his last appointment, the *China Morning Post* spoke of him as:

Probably the best known local man who retired from public service about three years ago as head of the Economics and Statistics Department of Macao. It was thought then that Dr Lobo would at last be able to enjoy a well merited rest. On the contrary he has been recalled to public duty . . . Dr Lobo's long experience in administrative matters and his natural knack for getting things done, should see him through with flying colours.

Good show!

Dr Lobo's fellow-member of the Syndicate, Mr Foo, has not fared so well. Since I left his establishment of a thousand pleasures, the Tongs have been after him. As the local press reports:

A group of terrorists, calling itself the Fa Mok Lang Group, after writing blackmailing letters to Mr Foo, placed three bombs in the lavatories of the mezzanine restaurants of the Central Hotel, having previously thrown leaflets from the roof of the hotel urging gamblers and pleasure seekers not to go into the hotel any more 'because the hotel was menaced by bomb explosions'.

There are always interfering busybodies around when someone tries to give the common people a bit of fun.

On our way back to Hong Kong, and in the ferry, recalling Dr Lobo's mention of the Tongs, now known as Triads, and musing over their possible connection with the smuggling of gold and opium which are more or less interconnected, I asked Dick Hughes, who knows the answer to everything in the Far East, what the Triads really amounted to, and this is the gist of what he told me.

There are scores of Triads, or secret Chinese blood societies, in Hong Kong, mostly concentrated in the Kowloon district, and their members, ranging from pimps and shoe-shine boys to businessmen and teachers, run into tens of thousands. Originally the aims of the Triads were laudable and patriotic. Members were rigorously tested, sworn to unselfish brotherhood and dedicated to moral and religious principles. But the process of degeneration has been profound. Politics, then squeeze and conspiracy, and finally crime, rackets, extortion, blackmail and smuggling have debased the high ideals of the early Tongs, just as the semi-religious Society of Harmonious Fists (*I Ho Chuan*) of A.D. 1700 became the horrendous Boxers of 1900.

The Triads are not banned in Macao, and Dick hazarded the suggestion that Dr Lobo and other members of the Syndicate were probably forced to pay them protection money. (No doubt Mr Foo failed to pay up and was punished with bombs in the lavatories of his Central Hotel.) But they are illegal in Hong Kong, where they flourish underground with secret signs and passwords and iron rules of punishment and vengeance. The old membership identifications, a cash coin or a cotton badge, have gone, but nowadays one member can distinguish another by the manner, perhaps, in which he lights a cigarette or sets the teacups before a visitor.

The largest and most powerful of the Hong Kong Triads today is the formidable '14 K', so called because the ancient Canton address was Number 14 in Po-wah Road, with the 'K' added later for 'karat' of gold in memory of a bloody pitched battle over 'protection' – against a rival Triad whose members likened their strength to local but softer gold. '14 K' dates from the seventeenth century, but was rejuvenated and developed by General Kot Sui Wong as a secret agency of the Kuomintang. He was deported from Hong Kong to Formosa in 1950, but returned incognito to the colony and, before he died in 1953, re-activated all eighteen groups of the redoubtable '14 K' which now has an estimated membership of eighty thousand divided into mellifluously named sub-branches.

For instance, Dick Hughes explained, the 'Sincere' sub-branch of '14 K' is a strong-arm gang who protect squatter areas in Kowloon. The 'Filials' have about fifteen thousand members who specialize in the drug and prostitution traffic. These two gangs were chiefly responsible for the rioting, bloodshed, looting and arson in the recent Kowloon riots.

The initiation ceremony into '14 K' lasts all night and involves the novices in an elaborate ritual handed down through the centuries. The 'Ten Precious Articles', which figure in the initiation, include a red lamp (to distinguish true from false), a red pole (for punishment), a white paper fan (to strike down traitors) and a peach-wood sword (representing a magical blade which has the power to decapitate enemies when merely flourished in the air). Joss-sticks are lighted on an altar before which the aspirants swear thirty-six death-binding oaths and drink from a bowl containing sugar, wine, cinnabar, blood from a beheaded rooster and a drop of blood from the middle finger of the novice's left hand. After election, the new members hurl their joss-sticks to the floor with the demand that their own lives be similarly extinguished if they break their oaths. There is a picturesque variety of death-penalty methods, ranging from the meticulous 'ten thousand knife cuts' to the imponderable 'exposure to thunderclaps'. The rivalry, terrorism and intrigues of the different Triads are the explanation for nearly all the mysterious stories of officially motiveless murder and assault in the Hong Kong press. Recently there was unusual cooperation between the Hong Kong police and the communist authorities following a Triad murder in the colony. An elderly Triad leader was stabbed in the back after a friendly game of mahjong. The killer, from a rival Triad, timed the murder so that he could catch the midnight ferry to Macao. The Hong Kong police vainly pursued the ferry in a motor launch and then alerted the Macao police, but the man managed to cross over into Communist China for sanctuary. Within a week, the communists, having seen the man's photograph in the Hong Kong press, located him and returned him to Macao, where the murderer committed suicide.

Like the Mafia, Dick explained, the Triad member never squeals and thus, for the running of smuggling channels, the Triads provide an almost limitless army of reliable couriers for the dispersal, through Hong Kong to the rest of the Orient, of the gold bullion quite legally purchased from Dr Lobo. Only a couple of years ago, one of Jardine Matheson's most respectable cargo and passenger ships had been arrested in Calcutta where the police found £200,000 worth of solid gold neatly inset and over-painted by a passenger in the woodwork of a cabin. The gold was on its way into India. Although arrests were made, the highly indignant firm of Jardines (or rather their insurance company) was fined £100,000 by the Indian Government for inadequate protective devices and for acting as a carrier, at however many removes, of smuggled gold. As a result, Jardines have had to organize their own security service to supplement the incredibly active and ingenious Hong Kong Customs and Police Department.

I asked Dick how Dr Lobo, in the face of the Triads, managed to bring his gold bullion into Macao without its being hi-jacked in transit, and Dick explained about Len Cosgrove and his ancient Catalina amphibian. I was later to meet Len Cosgrove (in Jack Conder's bar, of course) and I was greatly taken with him. He is a Scot, another Hemingway character, generally known as 'Cos', a small, tough, cheerful individual who can stand your hair on end with his stories of authentic derring-do. He was in the R.A.F. during the war and drifted into civil aviation and then into this perilous job of ferrying fortunes in gold bullion from Singapore to Dr Lobo's vaults in Macao, expecting to be cracked on the head by a crew member or shot down by communist planes on each trip. And with these lone jobs, as he explained to me, things could go wrong. An Australian friend of his, also flying a Catalina, had been paid by a Chinese syndicate to fly a huge cargo of opium from Singapore to Macao for onward smuggling into Communist China. At the point of no return from Singapore he had flown into the edge of a monsoon and had had to keep going. With his fuel almost exhausted, he came over the islands to find Macao harbour completely obscured by low cloud. He came down through it and found himself almost on top of one of the neighbouring communist islands with a bad swell running. At this moment one of his engines failed and he decided to ditch, got the angle wrong and buried his nose in the sea. The plane slowly broke up and, as the communist gunboat appeared, he was horrified to see the canisters of raw opium bobbing about in the waves. He and his navigator spent two years in a communist jail, came out, and died of their experiences. Cos was very matter-of-fact about the hazards of his profession, but also understandably tight-lipped – not necessarily because of the secrets he knows, but because, when the last five years of his contract have run out, he wants to write his memoirs. I shall look forward to them.

The next few days in Hong Kong were more respectable than the Macao interlude – golf at the Royal Hong Kong Club a few miles from the communist frontier, where the rattle of Bren-guns at the ranges and the occasional passage of a tank are apt to disturb one's swing, and where the huge cartwheel hats of the Haka women, plucking weeds out of the greens with their finger-nails, form a useful back wall for the topped approach; a morning in Cat Street, the Portobello Road of Hong Kong, where I found no difficulty in rejecting the assorted chinoiserie of ten centuries; dinner one night in an enchanting Sea Palace amidst the myriad sampans that pave the fishing port of Aberdeen; and a final fling on the Hong Kong racecourse from the luxurious fastness of the Jardine box. This must be one of the most splendidly equipped racecourses in the world, with overall closed-circuit television coverage giving instantaneous photographs of the entire race, the latest totalizator (at least £30,000 is bet on each race) and modern moving staircases to each floor. There, with the help of Jardine's know-how and a place accumulator, I recovered my and the *Sunday Times*'s losses in the gambling hells of Macao.

And then it was time to go, on an evening of brilliant stars, to make the next leap, in Comet G/APDO, over Formosa and Okinawa, to Tokyo.

I have seldom left a town with more regret.

## INCIDENTAL INTELLIGENCE

The *Bella Vista* is the best hotel to stop at. Ask for a double room with veranda overlooking the wide sea-approaches to the Pearl River, which are alive day and night with fishing-junks hastening to and from Canton. (Tariff: HK$45 a day.)

Best place for eating: the *Macao Inn* on the Avenue of the Republic, not far from the British Consulate and the residence of Mr Foo Tak Yam, the gambling king of the colony. Ask for the special baked or grilled Macao pigeon, or select from a wide range of peppery Portuguese dishes, including African chicken (baked in coconut). Excellent cheap, light, dry Portuguese wines.

The gambling tables are open day and night at the *Central Hotel*. The cricket-fighting season is held in the autumn. There is a Grand Prix motor-race early in November.

(Travel agencies at the leading Hong Kong hotels will

buy your return ferry ticket to Macao and will also secure your passport visa for you. There is no need to change your Hong Kong dollars for Macao patacas; Hong Kong money has the same exchange rate and is as interchangeable as English money in Dublin.)

# 3

# Tokyo

I was full of reservations about Japan. Before and during the war they had been bad enemies and many of my friends had suffered at their hands. But many other friends whose opinions I value love the country and its people, and my comprador, Richard Hughes, who came with me in the Comet and who, being an Australian, should have been predisposed against Japan, was totally enamoured of it. There was nothing to do but clear my mind of the splendours of Hong Kong and prepare myself for a great deal of hissing and bowing.

We had a happy landing. Japanese friends of Dick Hughes were at the airport to meet him and I was at once taken with 'Tiger' Saito, editor-in-chief of *This is Japan,* the massive and beautifully produced annual which the privileged receive through the Japanese Embassy around Christmas time. He was a chunky, reserved man with considerable stores of quiet humour and intelligence, and with a subdued but rather tense personality. He looked like a fighter – one of those war-lords of the Japanese films. He had, in fact, been a judo black-belt, one rank below the red-belt elite, and there was a formidable quality about him which I enjoyed. We crowded ourselves into some kind of a car and hurtled off into the night. It was an hour's run through endless and very depressing suburbs (Tokyo, with a population of nine million, is the largest, and incidentally the most expensive, city in the world). It had been a four-and-a-half hour flight from Hong Kong. It was one o'clock in the morning and everyone was chattering about people I didn't know. I began to long for bed and solitude.

Dick had tried to get us into a Western hotel, but on top of hordes of American tourists attending the fashionable autumn or Chrysanthemum Season, six hundred delegates for a G.A.T.T. conference had descended on the town and Dick had finally had to accept rooms in a Japanese inn. 'They're wonderful,' he enthused. 'Much better than those ghastly Western hotels. You'll really be seeing the Japanese way of life.'

We bumped and clattered through darkened side-streets, stopping every now and then to verify our whereabouts and consult about the next turning. My depression grew. In due course, down a rutted lane, there was a glimmer of light coming from a pagoda-form entrance. We piled out. Immediately there were two wide-awake, bowing women in full traditional dress on the doorstep. A polite rattle of Japanese ensued. Behind the porte cochère were the dwarf shrubs and firs of a tiny Japanese garden and the outlines of some kind of a villa. My companions seemed excessively cheerful. I fixed a Japanese grin on my face and followed them to the front door and, for the first of many times, took off my shoes at the threshold and tried to stuff my feet into Japanese-size slippers.

Inside, it was very light and gleaming with polish and cleanliness. I slip-slopped up a short shiny staircase and was shown, with many smiles and bows, through a sliding partition into one of those rooms you see in Japanese prints. There I was left alone, staring at my suitcase, while Dick's voice boomed happily down the corridor and the rustling sound of awakened sleepers reached me through the walls.

I hate small, finicky, breakable things, and I am slightly over six feet tall.

My room appeared to be made of plywood and rice-paper. The floor was carpeted with black-edged oblongs of rush matting that reminded me of unin-scribed mourning cards. In the centre of the floor, or rather on it, was the spotless bedding, a thin feather mattress, sparkling sheets and a silken eiderdown. Behind the small, hard pillow was a child's teapot, a glass with a wooden cover, a small lacquer box containing toothpicks and a bed light. Next to this, against one wall, was a very broad red lacquer table about one foot off the floor. Above this hung a scroll depicting a wispy landscape and opposite, in the corner, was what appeared to be a large earthenware waste-paper basket filled to the top with fine grey ash in which were stuck two iron styluses and a kind of iron comb. In the corner opposite on the floor stood a tall rough pottery vase containing a spindly branch encrusted with small red berries and a much shorter branch of dwarf chrysanthemums. Having read a B.O.A.C. leaflet about Japanese flower arrangement, I assumed that these twigs held some gracious message which was hidden from me. The only other furniture was a narrow shelf against one wall which held a lacquered box containing a stylus and a bottle of sepia ink and, on the floor, a telephone balanced precariously on a black lacquered mushroom.

I moved gingerly round the walls looking for cupboards amongst the anonymous maze of what turned out to be plastic rice-paper and thin battens of three-ply. One of these revealed a wardrobe containing one coat hanger and an extra roll of bedding. Another partition concealed a blessed basin with running water. I looked again at my bulky round-the-world suitcase standing obscenely in the midst of this delicate chamber and, aching with the gorilla stance that was necessary because of the low ceiling, I slumped down on the exquisite red lacquer table and cursed gently but fluently.

Dick appeared, happy and boisterous. 'Where the hell do I put my clothes?' I said. 'What the hell's that waste-paper-basket full of ash for? And, anyway, where's the lavatory?' Dick looked grieved at this Western outburst. He meekly showed me across the corridor to an odd-looking hole-in-the-floor contraption. 'But there's a Western one downstairs,' he said. 'Next to the Japanese bath.'

'What the hell's a Japanese bath?'

'Oh, haven't I told you? You've got to wash outside and then get into the bath. There may be other people in it but you don't have to bother about them.'

'Thanks very much.'

'Perhaps you'd better put your clothes on the table. The barrel with the ash in it is for a charcoal fire.'

I said, 'Thanks very much,' again, furiously, and we parted for the night.

I will pass over the further tribulations I suffered in my dainty, willow-pattern bird-cage. I took a sleeping-pill, composed my aching limbs amongst the bedding on the floor and went to sleep trying to remember the full details of Saki's 'Barbary Apes Wrecking a Boudoir'. Dick had told me to clap my hands if I wanted anything. The next morning, awakened by a mild earth-quake that rattled the hotel like a dice-box, I did this until I got bored with it and then padded downstairs and, in sign language and pidgin English, extracted a promise of breakfast from the bowing and giggling maid. She was so amused and happy about everything that I was at once filled with a good humour which remained with me for the rest of my stay in Japan. I even got to like my idiotic, damnably pretty little room, and somehow learned to contort my limbs into a painful approximation to the lotus position on the many occa-sions when I had to eat meals off foot-high tables. All in all, I can warmly recommend the Fukudaya Inn (it means, for what that is worth, 'Rich Ricefield'), not far from the British Embassy. May its dwarf pine trees never grow smaller!

With only three days in Japan, I decided to be totally ruthless. I told Dick that there would be no politicians, museums, temples, Imperial palaces or Noh plays, let alone tea ceremonies. I wanted, I said, to see Mr Somerset Maugham, who had just arrived and was receiving a triumphal welcome; visit the supreme Judo Academy; see a Sumo wrestling match; explore the Ginza; have the most luxurious Japanese bath; spend an evening with geishas; consult the top Japanese sooth-sayer; and take a day trip into the country. I also said that I wanted to eat large quantities of raw fish, for which I have a weakness, and ascertain whether sake was truly alcoholic or not. Thanks to Dick and Tiger Saito, I achieved all these ambitions to the full, with the exception of the Sumo wrestling bout which I was only able to see on television.

We started off with Mr Maugham. We happen to be friends.

Our friendship is largely based on the fact that he also wishes to be married to my wife, and he is always pleased to see me if only to hear news of her. We met at the Imperial Hotel and had a cheerful and excellent luncheon, through which Mr Maugham alternately crackled with malice about our friends in London and purred with pleasure at his first visit to the East for thirty years. After luncheon we repaired to the Kodo Kan gymnasium and judo academy for a most memo-rable experience.

Briefly, judo is a philosophy, or way of life, and ju-jitsu is an art of self-defence based on judo. I have

always been vaguely interested in the subject since, at
Eton, two vast sergeant majors used to give exhibitions
of throwing each other about with flicks of the wrist.
Tiger Saito, who is an excellent photographer, accompanied us, and the head of the establishment showed
us round – Mr Maugham, Mr Alan Searle, his secretary, Dick Hughes and myself. The Academy is a very
large and imposing building. The ground floor is
devoted to miscellaneous classes. There was a room
where fifty young men were practising break-falls,
another where foreigners, four Americans, a Frenchman
and a Turk, were trying various holds while awaiting
their teacher, and another room for the girls, who
obligingly staged a mock fight, which was not as
exciting as it sounds.

Then up to the next floor and to an astonishing
scene. Here, in one vast hall, upwards of two hundred
individual bouts and classes were in progress. Black-
belts were two a penny, but what fascinated us all was
the class for children between eight and ten being
conducted by a famous red-belt aged about sixty. As
it might have been at some sporting event in an English
school, half a dozen doting mothers sat on a bench
and watched their sons with a mixture of pride and
anxiety as they wrestled together or had lessons from
their teachers.

But what held our whole attention was the wise
old red-belt teaching leg and kick routines to a tough,
lively little boy of ten. Between these two all the
traditions were strictly adhered to – the courteous

bow before the lesson and after each surrender, and the smiling concentration. For perhaps ten minutes the red-belt tried to teach the little boy one particular backward hack which sweeps the legs of the opponent from under him and can only be defeated by various counter-moves. Again and again the red-belt swept the little boy's legs from underneath him and, while holding the lapels of his wrestling robe, collapsed him gently, but not too gently, on the floor. And again and again the little boy was up and trying again, hacking bravely at the back of the red-belt's bulging calves with the inside of his own small leg. At last he got it right and, in acknowledgment, and by no means with false theatricality, the red-belt measured his length, got to his knees, bowed to his vanquisher and they started again.

What was so splendid about this scene was its entire seriousness. The old champion, without mockery, fell to the ground because the little boy had got the gambit absolutely right. He wanted to demonstrate to the little boy that, in ju-jitsu, no matter how inferior your size, Jack can bring down the Giant-killer. It was an exquisite scene, and Tiger Saito took a photograph which caught Mr Maugham exclaiming at its beauty.

The fag end of the afternoon I spent with Japan Air Lines, whom I had chosen to carry me on to Hawaii because I was already reluctant to embrace the West again and wished to leave myself in Oriental hands for as long as possible. It was only as my ticket was being made out that I realized I would be flying the 'Willow

Pattern' route on Friday the 13th. But what matter! In a book of mine, *From Russia With Love,* when my hero, James Bond, arranged to fly to Istanbul, there is the following passage:

The day before, when he had left M and had gone back to his office to arrange details of his flight, his secretary had protested violently at the idea of his travelling on Friday the 13th.

'But it's always best to travel on the 13th,' Bond had explained patiently. 'There are practically no passengers and it's more comfortable and you get better service. I always choose the 13th when I can.'

I felt I must try and keep up with my hero and it was not until dinner that night, when I mentioned the coincidence to Dick Hughes, that he looked thoughtful. 'I suppose you realize,' he said, 'that you'll be crossing the international date-line and running into another Friday the 13th. Double Friday the 13ths don't sound so good.' I laughed the detail away and forgot about it until the next morning at ten o'clock when I was waiting in the ante-room of the most famous fortune-teller in Japan, Seki Ryushi, with a charming interpreter friend of Tiger Saito's called Chin Chan.

I am not particularly interested in having my fortune told, but I am rather intrigued by fortune-telling and all matters connected with extra-sensory perception. Moreover, Dick had fascinated me with true stories of

Oriental soothsaying and I was determined to see what it was all about. We were waiting in the sitting-room of Mr Seki Ryushi's house. There were no tokens of his trade except a vast reading-glass in a wooden frame and one of those china skulls you find in junk shops with the brain-pan marked off in segments entitled Love, Future, Intelligence, etc. When, after a polite interval to show how busy he was, the soothsayer appeared, I was not greatly impressed. He looked far too happy and well-fed for a man who should be in communion with the spirits of darkness, and his eyes twinkled merrily from behind rimless glasses. We squatted down opposite each other across the inevitable low table and bowed as if we were about to start a wrestling match. I was asked to write down my name and age, and did so. The soothsayer gave the script a cursory glance and went into a long conversation with Chin Chan about how clever he was. He had forecast Eisenhower's successes at the last two elections and also the outcome of his various illnesses. When the Duke of Windsor married Mrs Simpson he had prophesied that they would have a long and happy marriage. I said a mental 'humph', rearranged my already aching limbs and waited for him to start on me.

In due course he picked up the large reading-glass, asked me to approach my face and examined it, inch by inch. At the same time, I examined his and saw nothing but happy birdlike eyes and evidence of a rather hasty shave in those difficult corners just below the nose. There was a lengthy exchange with Chin

Chan, which in due course was interpreted, to the effect that I was a man of very independent spirit who should always walk alone and never go into partnership. This sounded rather like the sort of stuff I had told Garbo in the night-club in Macao. There was to be no improvement.

It took nearly an hour and a half for the great seer to tell me that I was in a particularly golden period which would end around the middle of March, but that the whole of the next ten years was going to be quite splendid for me. I would live happily until I was eighty. I would certainly be back in Japan before next May (most unlikely, and I wasn't), I must not be so 'obstinate' towards my wife, and I looked more like my mother than my father. There was absolutely nothing else that I can remember and the only piece of information for which I was grateful, with my double Friday the 13th round the corner, was the prognostication about the wonderfully lucky period I was now traversing.

Rather pointedly perhaps, I asked Mr Seki Ryushi if he could tell his own fortune. He said he couldn't. When he wanted to know anything he asked his close rival, Sozan Takashima, who always gave him the correct answer. I should have asked him if he could tell Mr Takashima's fortune with equal success, because the fates were already plotting the terrible end to Takashima's life which was just approaching. About two weeks after my interview, the following story appeared in the local press and I quote it in its entirety:

# FORTUNE-TELLER COULD NOT FORESEE OWN DEATH

*Tokyo, November 25th*

A famous Japanese fortune-teller could not foresee his own fate. He was surprised this morning by an assassin who stabbed him to death with a knife.

Sozan Takashima, 71, Japan's most famous fortune-teller, who has been doing a thriving business, was slain by a young colleague in the same profession, Toshiyuki Domoto, 24. The motive was professional jealousy.

Domoto also stabbed the old diviner's 40-year-old son, who is also practising the arts of divination, injuring him critically. – France-Presse.

This curious coincidence, in retrospect, adds point to what was otherwise a rather wasted morning.

The night before, Dick and I had consumed large quantities of raw fish in a restaurant off the Ginza, which is one of the great pleasure streets of the world, and even larger quantities of sake, a heated rice-spirit to which I took rather too enthusiastically, and now, nursing something of a hangover, I was looking forward to the healing properties of the most famous Japanese bath-house, the Tokyo Onsen. We went there after another delicious meal which included quails cooked in raw quail's egg (Mrs Elizabeth David, please note!) and it was indeed a remarkable experience.

Many Japanese have no baths in their houses and

the two or three bath-days a week at the public baths are great occasions. I can now well understand why. At the desk on the first floor of the large, rather drab, building, I paid fifteen shillings and was then taken in hand by the prettiest Japanese girl I was to see during the whole of my stay. Her name was Baby and she was twenty-one. She had the face of a smaller, rather neater, Brigitte Bardot, with black hair in a B.B. cut. She wore nothing but the shortest and tightest of white shorts and a white brassière.

She led me by the hand down a corridor to a small room divided in two. The ante-room contained a dressing-table laden with various oils, powders and unguents and a chair for my clothes, which she prettily asked me to remove. It was obviously no good being demure about this, so I obeyed her and she took my suit and brushed it and hung it up on a hanger. She then took me by the hand into the interior half of the room, where there was a large wooden box with a hole in the top – a one-man Turkish bath – into which she placed me. She then closed the top and, after some pleasant but rather stilted conversation, coquetted with her hair-do in a looking-glass. After a quarter of an hour in the very hot box, she raised the lid and helped me down on to the spotless tiled floor, and bade me sit beside a sunken blue-tiled bath on a small stool, when she proceeded to give me an energetic shampoo and scrubbed me with soap and a loofah from top to toe. Well, almost, that is. She avoided the central zone and handed me the loofah with a dimpling, 'You do body.' She then poured wooden pitchers of water over me to clean off the soap and guided me down the two steps into the deep, oval bath, the very hot water in which comes from natural hot springs.

Ten minutes of this and then, when she had towelled me down, I was bidden to lie on a high massage table where she proceeded to massage me thoroughly and expertly – none of that *effleurage,* but the really deep massage for which the Japanese are famous. I may say that any crude Western thoughts I might have entertained during these processes were thoroughly washed from my mind by the general heat and exertions I was put through, but that is not to say that I was not vastly stimulated and intrigued by the whole performance. Thinking that she might find my reserve rather ungallant, I asked her if she didn't occasionally have 'bad men' who suggested 'bad things' to her. The message, not perhaps unexpected, got through. She answered with a bewitching but quite neutral politeness that such people went to other places, places on the Ginza. The Onsen was only for 'gentlemen'. There was no hint of a rebuke in her attitude.

In the East, sex is a delightful pastime totally unconnected with sin – a much lighter, airier affair than in the West, where I fear that this account of my Japanese bath may shock. But in fact there was nothing in the least shocking about it, and when we went to the desk and said a happy and friendly goodbye, there was already a slim, serious-looking Japanese waiting to take my place. It was really rather like going to the dentist. Pleasanter, of course.

I spent the afternoon walking the length of the Ginza, window-shopping and wondering, as I do whenever I walk down a great shopping street, who buys all the cameras, sun glasses, wristwatches and fountain pens that seem to infest the world. But I hate taking photographs and, having taken them, hate looking at them, and since I already possess a wristwatch and a fountain pen, my purchases were confined to one dramatic Kabuki print of a man being beheaded. Mostly I just walked and looked at the people, and repelled the ubiquitous pimps offering me a variety of pleasures down to one or two that I couldn't even understand.

The first thing that struck me was how gay and purposeful the young Japanese are, and how healthy a rice diet must be. They move at an astonishing speed compared with the easy stroll you will normally see in the comparable Piccadilly or Champs-Elysées crowds. And how bright all their eyes are, with the sort of intelligent brightness you see in small animals! Very few of the men wear hats and would look rather foolish if they did so, and yet you never see a man with a hair out of place or with curly or unruly hair. It is all a sea of black shiny heads upon which, Gulliver-like, the Westerner looks down. They are rude and rough to each other on the streets, in sharp contrast with their good manners when at rest. They bump and jostle without apology and apparently without offence. The eyes of the women are not almond-shaped. It is the tautness of the Mongolian fold of the upper eyelid that appears to slant the eye, and I learnt later, from Tiger Saito, that facial surgery to remove the Mongolian fold and widen the eye is immensely popular all over the country. The girls are aping the West in countless other fashions. Long legs have become desirable, and those hideous wooden clogs have been exchanged for stiletto heels. The Eastern hair-dos, which I find enchanting, are going out in favour of permanent waves and other fuzzy fashions. Traditional dress – the kimono and the obi, the complicated bundle of silk in the small of the back – is disappearing fast and is now worn, so far as the towns are concerned, only in the family circle, together with the giant cake of hair and monstrous hair-pins in the Madame Butterfly fashion.

The Japanese are not, in fact, yellow-skinned. The colour ranges from ivory to a light sunburnt brown, and many of the women have natural pink in their cheeks. The men and women are specklessly clean and so are their houses and belongings, though how they manage it in Tokyo, amidst the blown dust of the ubiquitous construction work, I cannot imagine.

The endless taxis drive like hell, particularly the small Renaults, known as Kamikazes. But the taxis are well driven and I never saw one even graze another. They are the only taxi-drivers in the world who do not expect, or get, tips, and, in fact, there is practically no tipping whatsoever in Japan, though in hotels ten per cent is added to your bill. Dick Hughes was firm with me about this and insisted that we should always tip modestly. The tip, he said, was, in most cases, the difference between whether a man could have one or two meals a day, for in Japan the fight for existence is quite terrifying. Walking down the Ginza and occasionally going into a shop was evidence of this – a plethora of shop assistants. At least one, and often three, bell-boys to open the doors in hotels. Ten pimps where, in Paris, there would be one. This is due to the appalling over-crowding in the country, which has a population of ninety million with the lowest death-rate in the world – a population that increases at the rate of a million and a half a year, despite the number of recorded abortions (which are legal) of about the same number annually. This density of population was certainly brought home to me that afternoon on the Ginza, and finally, battered and exhausted, I repaired to my dainty inn to complete my toilet for a night out with the geishas.

I should at once make a point clear about geishas and I will quote from an official guide-book to make it: 'Most foreigners do not have a correct understanding of the geisha,' says the guide. 'They are not prostitutes.' I will quote again, this time from Dick Hughes, who warned me, 'To tell you the truth, the whole of this geisha business is a bit of a bore.'

'Gei' means art and 'sha' person, and a geisha is, in fact, a form of artist, meticulously trained in dancing, playing a kind of flute and drum, conducting tea ceremonies and arranging flowers. In addition, she should be good-looking, vivacious and an expert conversationalist.

She usually has a wealthy protector, whose mistress she may be, but she lives in a geisha house, which is a kind of seminary in which half a dozen girls live, supervised by a kind of Mother Geisha. You do not go to a geisha house to be entertained by geishas. You go to a private room in a restaurant – in our case a fish restaurant hard by the Shinbashi Bridge over the Sumida River, which, to my surprise, as I did not know Tokyo was on a river, bisects the town.

Tiger Saito, our host, had chosen a beautiful room, similar in most respects to my hotel room, looking over the river and, shortly after Dick and I had groaned and creaked ourselves into a near-lotus position, the three geishas trooped in in full regalia, knelt in turn at the head of the table and bowed first to our host and then to us. Then they sat down between us and set to pouring egg-cup-sized bowls of hot sake for us in a never-ending succession. I say 'never-ending' because, as soon as you put your little bowl down, it has to be filled again. Short of throwing the bowl out of the window, there is no way of halting this chain delivery until the flagon is empty or you fall over.

My geisha was called Masami, an enchanting girl of about thirty with straightforward good looks lit with that sincere delight in your presence and in the evening that, as I have said, one finds in Eastern girls. Dick's geisha had neater limbs but was otherwise similar, whereas Tiger's neighbour was a woman of an entirely different quality. She was perhaps forty years old, with an oval, heavily made-up face and the tower of black hair one knows from Japanese prints. She had a queenly poise, hooded eyes, and features of almost reptilian impassivity which occasionally dissolved into expressions of surpassing wit and malice. She was the most formidable feminine personality I think I have ever encountered. One's eyes were constantly attracted away from one's more conventional neighbour, for all her pretty ways, to this glittering she-devil across the table. She spoke no English, although she seemed to understand it, and I suspect that most of her rapier-like asides to Tiger, which always dissolved him in laughter, consisted of scathing comments on the boorish manners, uncultured habits and loathsome appearance of the two hulking red-faced pigs on the other side of the table.

We consumed, in between gallons of sake, various enchanting fish courses, including a kind of thick eel soup that was out of this world. All Oriental dishes are made to look as delightful as they taste, and very often it seemed desecration to disturb the still-life arrangement on one's plate with its minute attention to colour and arrangement. Needless to say, I had no hesitation in desecrating the lot.

I am not usually considered to be a great hand at tossing the conversational ball around, but I think on this occasion I can justly claim to have made the party go. I achieved this miracle by challenging my geisha to choose from her limitless repertory, which, I told her, her intricate education must have furnished, one really brilliant remark. 'That is what I have always understood geishas are for,' I teased her. 'I've come halfway round the world to hear what you are going to say.' At this, our two geishas burst into peals of laughter and even the Empress opposite allowed herself a wry titter. 'Come, come,' I urged. 'Just *one* brilliant aphorism.'

I knew what was coming and my mind was working furiously. Sure enough, after a great deal of badinage, I was challenged to say something brilliant first. I held up a hand and composed my features into what I hoped was a Confucian pattern. 'The only good chrysanthemum is a dead chrysanthemum,' I intoned weightily. The giggles were doubtful and the eyes round and rather uncertain. In Japan, the winter is known as the Season of the Chrysanthemum and what I had said was a slap in the face to a great slice of Japan's myth. The Empress, her eyes glittering, spat out some words at Tiger who translated: 'She asks why you say this?' I looked benignly at the Empress. 'Because,' I pronounced, 'until the chrysanthemums die, the roses cannot begin to bloom.' At this, I admit, rather elephantine profundity, there was a moment's pause for station identification with the Empress and then, at her reluctant nod of approval, excited applause and expressions of admiration which culminated in my geisha seizing my hand and saying I might kiss her, which I did.

Much gratified by a social success which had previously evaded me, I commanded our two geishas that they should now go through their paces, upon which they rose giggling and disappeared out of the room, Dick's to return quickly with a drum and some sort of a triangle which she proceeded to clonk and ping in a corner of the room, while mine brought in a drawing-block and paints with which she executed a bamboo sketch. I asked her to balance the black bamboo with some profound saying in the blank space on the right. 'You must paint it in your own blood,' I said. 'The red will complement the black.' After more screams and giggling protestations she used a pale crimson to write in the ideograms which translate as follows: 'The younger bamboo grows higher than the older bamboo, but the younger will sustain the older.' We all applauded vigorously, but I privately judged myself the winner by a nostril.

As a compliment to my dictum about the roses, Masami then painted a rose for me, upon which she wrote the pretty, if rather forward conceit: 'My garden faces East but it is open to all.'

All this, what with compliments and other miscellaneous graciousness, had taken longer than it sounds, and it was now time for the party to break up with expressions of esteem and affection and giggling kisses given and returned. (The Empress's cheek was like ice, and the peck she returned was somewhere outside my right ear.) And then, as the fans fluttered prettily from the three butterfly figures, the elephantine Westerners, exuding sake and beautiful thoughts, were borne happily off into the night.

There remained only our expedition into the countryside, and since our route was a conventional one and almost ruined by rain, I will be brief about it.

Accompanied by Tiger Saito, we left by a routine

express for Yugawara, about ten miles south-east of Mount Fujiyama, which was invisible in the low cloud. Our objective was a modest Japanese inn, frequented only by Japanese, and the conventional Japanese bath, the three of us together in the small, roastingly hot, round pool. We then drove over the mountains in mist and pouring rain to a renowned tourist hotel at Miyanoshita, whose lately-deceased manager had been President of the International Moustaches Club and where I was delighted to find, in a prominent position on the wall, a photograph of a great-uncle of mine whose two-foot moustaches terrified me as a child. Then to Yamato and back to Tokyo by the most beautiful train I have ever travelled in – a streamlined aluminium affair in bright orange that looked as if it belonged to Mars, but in fact was operated by the Odawara Express Train Company, a private enterprise which, with its soft, piped music and its pretty girls in claret uniform dispensing tea and Japanese whisky (very good, though I, a Scot, say it), could teach British Railways a thing or two.

And then it was time to pack and say the fond good-byes, and after a last and, to me, rather melancholy banquet of raw fish and martinis with my Orientalist guide, philosopher and friend, Dick Hughes, the taxi dashed through the suburbs of Tokyo to catch the plane that would take me, in one hop across the Pacific, to Honolulu.

As the travelogue would put it, Sayonara Japan! Aloha Hawaii . . . on double Friday the 13th!

## INCIDENTAL INTELLIGENCE

*Hotels*

Whatever season you visit Tokyo, cable your accommodation reservations well in advance, and reckon on spending double your normal budget while you are in the most expensive city in the world.

The *Imperial Hotel Annexe,* to which the reckless always flock, will cost 6,000 yen (£6) a day, but you can get into the original *Imperial Hotel,* which many people prefer anyway in the autumn and spring, when bedroom air-conditioning is not required, for two-thirds that price. For 3,000 yen you can get a good enough room at the *Shiba Park Hotel,* near by and also operated by the *Imperial.* The *Nikkatsu* is almost as expensive as the *Imperial Annexe* but more liberal and tolerant in – shall we say? – its policies. Because of the demand, there is a take-it-or-leave-it indifference at the reception desks in most of the big hotels.

Recommended compromises may be found within fifteen minutes' taxi drive from the Ginza and the heart of down-town Tokyo. One such is the *Matsudaira* – up to 3,000 yen a day for a small air-conditioned suite. The *Matsudaira* has an elegant swimming-pool, is quiet and discreet and caters for foreign airline crews on overnight stop-overs. Japanese-style inns of good quality like the *Fukudaya* usually require an introduction for a gaijin (foreigner).

With the next Olympic Games in the offing, there is a boom in Tokyo hotel-building, so new names will be

rising and maybe old names will be becoming less
autocratic.

*Eating*

Tokyo, to quote an old Zen proverb, is a veritable
paradise for gourmets. Japanese beef, fish, eels, fruit,
mushrooms and vegetables are unexcelled anywhere,
and Hiroshima oysters are reminiscent of Colchester's.
Eat your fish Western-style in either of the three Prunier
restaurants (in the *Tokyo Kaikan,* the *Imperial,* or opposite the *Asahi* newspaper office), in either of the two
*Tsujitome* restaurants (operated by maestro Kaichi Tsuji
of Kyoto) or in the celebrated *Shin Kiraku* or *Kinsui*
(both at Tsukiji). The *Crescent* is currently the most
fashionable – which is also to say, the most expensive
– Western-style dining-room in the city. That old
Oriental delicacy, smorgasbrod, is served lavishly in the
*Viking Room* at the *Imperial Annexe.* In a city distin-
guished for its peerless Kobe or Matsuzaka beef, the
*Foreign Correspondents' Club* will serve you a superb
steak if a member can get you a seat at lunch-time, but
a visitor may prefer the authentic Japanese *Ogawa-ken*
restaurant, where you are invited to press your finger
into the steak before choosing: if the impression made
by your finger lingers, the steak is ready for the cook
and the table.

Don't confine your experiments in the wide and rich
field of Japanese cuisine to the tourist's stand-bys: sukiyaki and tempura. The first is an indifferent beef stew
which the Japanese seldom bother to eat themselves;

the latter is just deep-fried fish, which is tasty enough but not outstanding. If you must try it, sukiyaki is available at any Japanese-style restaurant; the best place for tempura, among hundreds of good places, is the Hashizen in Shimbashi.

You do not need to be daringly venturesome to try yakitori; which is charcoal-grilled chicken or duck, interspersed with green pimento and Japanese onions, and spiked à la brochette on bamboo needles. There are as many cheap and gay yakitori restaurants and bars in the swarming labyrinth of alleys around the Ginza as there are tempura and noodle shops.

Be certain not to miss the magnificent *supponnabe*, or snapping turtle, which is combined soup and flesh cooked at the table in private rooms at a celebrated restaurant behind the Ginza. (Addresses are almost impossible to give in Tokyo but your hotel will write the location of any of the Tokyo restaurants mentioned for your taxi-driver.) Only the poor in spirit will refuse to taste sashimi (sliced raw fish); only the deficient in taste will refuse to repeat the order. And, as is well known to all Tokyo old hands, no one ever has a hangover, no matter what his excesses have been, if before going home he halts briefly and happily at a reputable bar for some sushi (rice topped with raw fish).

For the truly adventurous, the ancient and famed *Momonjiya* restaurant still serves roast monkey, monkey brains and wild boar; there are haunts near the Tsukiji fish-markets that specialize in the delicious blow-fish, which can be prepared only in registered kitchens because it contains a deadly poison; and, finally, the *Taiko* restaurant (next door to the *Show Boat* cabaret) offers, very frankly: 'Soup with sexual organs of ox and cock; sliced pork ovary with mushrooms; and sweet and sour sexual organs of ox – all 300 yen (6s.).' These last entrées are described delicately as 'Tonic Dishes'.

## Night-clubs and Night Life

Tokyo is a wide-open city – except that there is no gambling. There is an embarrassing choice of night-clubs, embarrassing in price as well as in variety. The Copacabana is probably the best; it is run by the handsome and redoubtable Madam Cherry, who recruits most of her luscious hostesses from Kobe – in Western opinion, the cradle of the most beautiful Japanese girls. (The Japanese say that the most beautiful come from Hokkaido and Niigata.) The company of a hostess in the night-club puts you back 1,000 yen (£1) an hour. A foot-loose visitor will get more incident, value and variety for his money by roaming the colourful legion of little bars in the crowded, lantern-hung lanes around the Ginza. The names are immaterial because these little bars ceaselessly rise, fall and change hands as the shifting coteries of sincere Japanese drinkers lurch to new surroundings and find new bottles and new faces.

Two notable and intimate cabarets which should be visited and compared are *L'Espoir,* controlled by Beautiful Crystal, an elegant former dancer, and *Osome* ('Modesty'), controlled by Dawn of Love, a voluptuous former geisha from Kyoto. Both these cabarets compete for the patronage of Tokyo's smart intellectual set, writers, artists and politicians (men only, of course). Gaijin are discreetly and carefully screened.

## Hints for Sake-drinkers

Don't be fooled by the apparent mildness of good sake. Sake has an alcoholic content of twenty per cent. It should be drunk warm, with food, and is much better for serious drinkers when poured into no-nonsense thick china mugs instead of the conventional porcelain thimbles, which smack of the tea ceremony to good flagon-men. Sake continues to ferment with age and does not keep much longer than a year even when bottled and sealed. Nor does it travel well. So there are no such things as sake cellars or sake vintage years.

There is a delicate sweet sake, *amakuchi,* and also a more robust dry sake, *karakuchi. Tokkyu* means 'special class'; *ikkyu,* 'first class'. Any type of sake from the Okura Company, especially *tokkyu Gekke ikan* ('Laurel Crown'), is excellent; these brewers are purveyors to the Imperial household. Another top brand is the Kikumasamune of Nada (*karakuclu*), which goes well with grilled fish and octopus, but *not* with tempura.

*Tokkyu* Taruhe (*karakuchi*) from Yamagata is the Burgundy of sakes, and has too much body to accompany sashimi (raw fish). With sashimi take very warm *ikkyu* Taiheizan (*amakuchz*), which has a delicate pine tree aroma. *Tokkyu* Ryozeki (also from Akita) is another *amakuchi*-type sake which can be recommended. Order Kembishi sake with tempura. When you sample blow-fish the barkeeper should thrust a fish-fin into your china mug of *karakuchi* sake.

Don't drink sake with Western food and don't drink sake after plain rice has ended a Japanese meal. Officers of the pre-war Imperial Japanese Navy preferred cold sake as a summer drink to beer. Today, young Japanese, to the regret of the old *samurai* class, are turning to Japanese-type whisky instead of sake.

# 4

# Honolulu

'Have a good fright.' The pretty hostess bowed demurely as I left the unfortunately-named 'Final Departure Lounge' of Tokyo Airport and walked out towards the sturdy, four-engined DC-6 of Japan Air Lines, Flight 614, for Honolulu. It was ten-thirty in the evening of Friday the 13th and, thanks to the international dateline, we were due at Honolulu before we had started – at two thirty-five on the afternoon of Friday the 13th. That double Friday the 13th! Here we go!

I rather enjoy flying. I like the comparative privacy and quiet of the hurtling cocoon (now bouncing as well as hurtling as we battled with the fringes of Typhoon Number Twenty, cosily dubbed 'Emma', which at that moment was causing havoc around Okinawa), where one can sit and read books and write up one's notes while people come and cosset you and positively beg you to drink champagne. And Japan Air Lines, as I had expected, had, to an exquisite degree, the desire to please – almost too much of it. With the suspicion born of Scots ancestry, a tiny mite of mistrust built up just above the level of consciousness as gift after gift 'With the compliments of Japan Air Lines' was heaped upon me. The usual travel folder, of course, but also a sandalwood scented fan, an expensive black moiré silk box containing masculine cosmetics, and finally a thing called a Happi Coat. This was a sort of waist-length kimono in black and white with a vast red ideogram on its back, which I assumed meant 'Happiness'. Most of the American passengers put this on, but none of the Japanese, and not I, who decided to save it up as a round-the-world present for somebody. Drinks were brought and a midnight snack, and then it was time to climb into a comfortable bunk and say my thanks and farewells to the Orient before, via a deep sleep, preparing my mind for the impact of the West.

About four hours later we were almost exactly at the point of no return between Tokyo and Honolulu, and around 2,000 miles out across the Pacific. So far as I was concerned, I had just about passed my half-way flight distance of 22,696 miles around the world. I was awoken by the authoritative voice of the captain. 'Ladies and gentlemen, this is your captain speaking. There has been an explosion in number three engine and a fire, which has been got under control. I have no hydraulic pressure. We have altered course for Wake Island where I shall carry out a no-flap landing at an unusual altitude and faster than is the custom. We shall then be towed to the airport. I have made many three-engine landings and also many without hydraulic pressure, so – see you on the ground!'

Thinking, so much for a double Friday the 13th! I dressed and climbed out of my bunk to the ground.

People were sitting very still and looking straight in front of them. The steward and the pretty stewardesses in their kimonos looked as impassive as the Japanese are supposed to look. The steward bustled up and moved a Japanese from my seat and apologized. The passengers from the front of the plane had been moved to the back while the fire-fighting went on. I gazed out of the window at the dead, blackened engine that now drooped somewhat from the horizontal. A beautiful dawn was coming up over the cloudless horizon. We had come down to about ten thousand feet and the flat calm looked positively inviting. I remembered Monsieur Bombard's instructions about survival at sea. One must not struggle, but remain calm and conserve one's energies, floating as much as possible. The salinity of the Pacific, I guessed, would be a help. I had laughed when the steward had demonstrated the inflatable life jackets. 'This is your life vest,' he had said. 'This is your front-side and this is your back-side. There is a whistle to blow and a light to shine.' Now I tried to remember the further instructions and, above all, not to inflate the thing until one was outside the aircraft. We hummed sturdily on, the aircraft vibrating slightly because of the unco-operative number three engine.

Half an hour later and there was suddenly a big, four-engined air-sea-rescue plane with a yellow nose and yellow tail, belonging to the U.S. Air Force from Wake, only fifty yards away to starboard. She stayed there, dead steady, ready to throw out life rafts. A quarter of an hour later, far below us, just above the surface of the sea, two PBY amphibians of the American Navy were shadowing us ready to come down on the surface and pick up the bits. I felt greatly reassured and, remembering my soothsayer's happy predictions and trying to forget the double Friday the 13th, I shaved and had coffee. There was a crackle from the Tannoy and the calm voice of the captain came to us again: 'This is your captain speaking. To lighten the plane, I am about to dump fuel, so there will be *no* smoking please.' (As if she had heard the announcement, the air-sea-rescue plane edged away from us.) 'This aircraft will be unserviceable for many days. I have been in touch with our Tokyo headquarters and a relief plane is already on its way. Not much further to go!' We all continued to stare straight in front of us.

In due course, there was the blessed island of Wake, a tiny coral island fringed with surf and with a big, shallow, palegreen lagoon in its centre. We circled gently several times, losing height, and then, only just above sea level, came in at a good 200 miles an hour. We hit the runway smoothly and the captain juggled with his engines to keep us going straight. We did a few mild zigzags and then came to rest with a screech from the tyres. The fire engines and ambulances swept down on us and then the blessed hatch opened and we were back on terra firma.

The man who achieved this satisfactory climax was Captain Stuart Baird of Balboa, California, a United Air Lines pilot loaned to Japan Air Lines. I salute him.

Wake Island, which is an important aircraft staging-point, is notable for having absolutely no air-conditioning.

I had always assumed that the first civilizing benefits Americans brought to newly acquired overseas territories were CocaCola, corned beef hash, and canned air, in that order. It was about ninety-five degrees in the mosquito-netted Quonsett huts that are the only buildings on Wake, and we spent an exhausting day nodding enthusiastically as successive ground and crew personnel came up and assured us how lucky we had been, Bud. Wake is one of the homes of the Pacific albatross, now so much disturbed, I believe, by the aircraft that they are in danger of extermination, but it was too hot to go and visit their haunts in the mangroves at the other end of the island. Instead, I slept gratefully in the spare crew quarters and gossiped with a man with a spotted dog who was in charge of quarantine animals – mostly monkeys and parrots *en route* for the States after being collected in the East by tourists. He told me that, though he liked life on Wake, there was nothing to do there but skin-dive and teach parrots in transit dirty words to shock their American owners.

At eight o'clock that night, the relief aircraft from Tokyo arrived with a director of Japan Air Lines who was extremely nice and polite and thanked us all 'for our co-operation', though how we were to have done anything but sit tight and co-operate was not made clear. More unguents and scented fans, fresh Happi Coats and then we were out of the second Friday the 13th and drowsily bound for Honolulu.

*

After the zest and delight of Hong Kong and Tokyo, I had been dreading impact with the West, but Honolulu let me down comparatively softly. To begin with, I had always thought those famous leis you see in the Matson Line advertisements in American magazines were made of coloured paper. But I discovered with pleasure that they are not, and when I descended from my aeroplane, I was presented with a handsome and very fragrant garland of white ginger and Vanda orchids. (I later discovered that the tariff for these leis is: orchids $3, frangipani or ginger, $1.50.) Seven o'clock in the morning, dyspeptic and unshaven, with U.S. Immigration and Customs in front of you, is not the best time to be garlanded with flowers, and when, inside the airport, I found the wash-rooms inscribed '*Kane*' for men and '*Wahime*' for women, I anticipated that all this aloha stuff might quickly pall. But I must admit it was a relief to get to the Moana Surf Riders' Hotel, walk again on carpet instead of on the highly polished wood floors of Japan, and rediscover the comforts of a Western hotel bedroom and bath.

The last time I had been in Honolulu had been in 1944 when I had done a brief spell with the Office of Naval Intelligence in Pearl Harbor. Then there had been no leis and the Moana and its neighbouring Royal Hawaiian had been Naval headquarters, camouflaged in black and green. But now, stepping out on to my balcony directly above the centre of Waikiki Beach, with Diamond Head glittering in the sun to my left and, in front, the first surf-riders coming gracefully in towards me on the creaming breakers, it was impossible to recall the days when Honolulu had been a fortress and Pearl Harbor a mass of unsalvaged wrecks. Yet behind this tropical tourist facade, Hawaii is still, after Okinawa, America's forward naval base in the Pacific, the advance post for the Early Warning Defense System and, at this very moment, the centre from which the cones from the latest guided missiles were in the process of attempted recovery. And, since my last visit, Hawaii had come of age. She had become the fiftieth State of the Union and her population of over 600,000 had almost doubled since 1944.

It will certainly double again before long, because the islands, of which there are eight in the group, with an area of 6,500 square miles, are becoming a tourist resort and retirement paradise second only to Florida. This is not surprising. The islands possess real beauty and an average, year-round temperature of 75°. (Half-way through November, the board on the life-saver's cabin on the beach below my room says: 'Air 78°, Water 75°.') And jets do the 2,000 miles from the mainland in about five hours.

For a European, the main disadvantage of the place is the high-pressure tourist atmosphere and the uniformity of the tourist and retired population – the men either bulging or scrawny, the women unshapely, blue-rinsed, rimless-glassed, and all with those tight, rather petulant mouths of the pensioned American. If they were dressed in fashions seemly to their age-group, these elderly hordes would fade into the background; but, to me, there is something infinitely depressing in thousands of sixty-eight-year-olds in Hawaiian or any other fancy dress – the men with aloha shirts and slacks or, worse, knee-length shorts; the women in over-decorated straw hats and ghastly Mother Hubbards known as 'muumuus', or other hideous confections described in the shops as 'holokus', 'flounced holomuus' or, for the cocktail hour, 'sheath tea-timers'. On the beach, as I was later to observe, these elderly ghouls looked even worse without their muumuus – huge, blue-veined, dimpled thighs, scrawny necks and sagging bosoms garlanded with leis, their broken-down, spavined spouses trailing behind carrying the coconut mats, the sun oil, the bath robes and the *Wall Street Journal*. And, alas, in this and in other similar resorts, there are so few young people to relieve the eye and restore one's faith in the human race. The young people cannot afford the fare or the cost of these resorts. If I were a Sheraton or a Hilton, I would reserve a proportion of my hotel space for young and attractive people and put them up for next to nothing, both to gladden the eye of the more hideous customers and perhaps to shame them into dressing their age.

Having had breakfast and thought these harsh thoughts, I decided to get some of the bile out of my system on a surf board. By now the whole sea in front of me, to about half a mile out where the waves began to gather, was crowded with flying figures and, though I had never tried the sport before, the guidebook I had purchased at the airport said that if I could swim and ride a bicycle I could learn to surf. 'South Sea Scotty' Guletz, who wrote the guide, was, in my case, mistaken.

I hired a beautiful pale-blue board. It was the Malibu model, made of balsa wood and coated with fibreglass. It cost one dollar per hour. The board is about ten feet long and weighs thirty-five pounds. I found that even to lie on it and paddle with both hands out towards the distant starting point was no mean feat, and I was several times capsized by the waves before I even got to the fringe of the riders. (I later discovered that the beach-boy should not have hired me a surf board without having some assurance that I could handle it, particularly since the son of an American admiral from Pearl Harbor had been killed the week before in a welter of crashing boards capsized by a particularly gigantic wave.) However, knowing nothing of this, I paddled on through the speeding experts who bore down on me with every wave, and in due course I was the requisite half-mile from the shore. I lay for a while and admired the beautiful distant hills and the whizzing sunburnt nymphets flying laughing by, Venuses on the half-shell, pursued by sleekly fat Hawaiian beach-boys, and tried to keep out of the way of their hurtling boards.

This surf-riding elite, composed of local shop-girls and boys from the town who seem to have nothing else to do from dawn till dusk but ride the waves, reminded me of those other superior beings you admire from afar at other resorts – the aristocracy of ski-teachers, golf and tennis pros and the like, whom the tourist sucks up to and the women tourists pay for lessons and dance with in the night-clubs where, in their own element, they can get on equal terms with the gods. Here, 'On the beach at Waikiki', they were just like those other elites all over the world, getting by on those years of practising some modest expertise, carefree and apparently far removed from the stresses and strains of the common herd, and all, perhaps, with that sad ambition to marry a rich tourist.

These were sour thoughts from the envious mind of a duffer. After watching, for the hundredth time, men pick up girls on their shoulders and carry them effortlessly towards the shore while others pirouetted on their boards and others whizzed in balancing on one leg, I made several attempts to emulate the novice's art of just covering a hundred yards on the stomach. But, after suffering many bruises and being several times half-drowned, I paddled back ignominiously towards the shore and just had enough strength left to heave the thirty-five pounds of balsa wood up the golden sand to its garage.

The world had shaken gently to herald my arrival in Japan and now, to greet me in the West, it erupted with equal gentility. Kilauea, on Hawaii Island, is the most active volcano in the world. That morning it erupted violently, firing a flaming column of lava a thousand feet into the sky – the highest lava-toss it has ever achieved. It maintained this fiery fountain throughout my visit, having previously remained semi-dormant since 1868. At lunch-time that day, over a 'Paradise Slenderama Salad', an eye-witness urged me to fight my way on to one of the many planes of Aloha Airlines that were taking tourists to see the sight. 'It makes the Fourth of July look like a lighted match,' said my informant. 'You'd better go quick.' I said of course I would. I didn't. I was tired of aeroplanes, and this terrestrial blow-off seemed to me an aspect of the private life of the globe into which it would be 'bad joss' to pry.

Instead, as a holiday from the sight of my fellow creatures in muumuus and aloha shirts, and rejecting the Sheraton Hotel's invitation to complimentary hula and cha-cha lessons, a flower-arrangement class, and an open duplicate bridge tournament, I went to the Honolulu Zoo. I like zoos and I think this is the prettiest I have ever seen. It wanders all over the Kapiolani Park below Diamond Head and is surrounded by a thick, twelve-foot-high hedge of syringa in bloom – an excellent deodorizer of zoos. Here there were cassowaries, emus, a fine Gibbon ape hurtling round its cage as if desperately trying to run away from its shadow, an angelic Diana monkey sitting on its hands, a young black leopard with soft and beautiful golden eyes, brown and white pandas no bigger than large cats, formidable Great Black Cockatoos and a unique cageful of Birds of Paradise. All these were a rest to the eyes, not excluding the Great Green Iguana, and I stayed there till dusk. Outside the gates, the evening paper posters were saying: 'Oahu Barmaid Claims Rape.' I was back in the world again!

My hotel had been invaded by six hundred prize-winning staff members of the General Electric Company.

They wore leis and sat attentively at long tables under the giant banyan tree in the patio of the Moana, listening enraptured to a Hawaiian guitar 'combo' accompanying a Hawaiian songbird in a grass skirt. In my youth, to the exasperation of my family, I had had a weakness for the Hawaiian guitar and I played records of the Royal Hawaiian Serenaders when I should have been out of doors killing something. I even went so far as to have lessons with the instrument from an Italian woman in Chelsea. Listening now to the boinging and moaning, I appreciated my family's exasperation. Now the plaintive music sounded like the sort of background stuff that accompanies 'The Teenage Monster from Outer Space' or the dream sequences in films about lunatics and drunkards, and I would have howled like a dog between gulps of my Old-Fashioned had it not been for the earthy voice of the Sheraton Hotel coming at frequent intervals over the loud-speaker system: 'On the beach at Waikiki – when you belonged to me.' 'Mr Fratinelli, please. Telephone call for Mr Fratinelli.' 'I have a call for Mrs Finkleberg. Mrs Finkleberg, please.' The guitars whoinged and zinged like a badly sprung mattress. I slunk to my room.

From a long list of local restaurants, readers of my books will understand that I immediately settled on 'M's Smoke House'. M, if I may be allowed the digression, is my fictional head of the Secret Service. How like the cunning old rascal, I thought! Here he is, quietly salting away Secret Service funds to build up a nice hard-currency nest-egg to supplement his pension. I took a taxi down town and asked the driver about the place. 'Real good eats,' he said appreciatively. 'You want to go to the mezzanine – place they call the Cheerio Room. Best steak and lobster in town.'

'But who is this chap, M?' The driver shook his head doubtfully. 'Don't rightly know. Never seen him.'

It fitted perfectly! Sly old devil! There was probably some American cut-out who acted as the front. But, alas, it was the weekend, and M's place, cunningly situated between the Chamber of Commerce and the Bank of Hawaii, was closed. Regretfully I retired to the Sorrento Spaghetti House (in America, when in doubt, I always go to an Italian restaurant) and consumed spaghetti Bolognese with garlic, and a bottle of 'domestic' Chianti.

Back in my hotel bedroom, I looked out at the sea which lay like gunmetal under a crescent moon. One or two night surfriders were still at it on the darkened creaming waves. Far below me, on the moon-burnt beach, an elderly woman, probably a General Electric cashier, was holding up her muumuu while the small waves washed her feet. She looked forlorn and unloved in this place of the eternal honeymoon. The next day, probably, she would be back in Seattle, Iowa, New Orleans. Now, in the path of the moon and with the gay flambeaux and the crooning guitars behind her, she was having her last paddle. She seemed to represent the tragedy of all ended holidays. I drew the jalousies and went to bed.

Going round the world too quickly is like attending

a series of dinner parties and leaving with the soup. Beneath the surface, Hawaii is ruled by the five great sugar and pineapple families (Hawaii produces seventy-five per cent of all the world's pineapple), and queen of this benevolent syndicate is one powerful old lady. I had a letter of introduction to this lady and I would dearly have liked to explore where-power-resides in this very prosperous fiftieth State of America. Instead, I drove to the other side of the island and had lunch with the informative British Consul and his family, and then had to catch my plane for Los Angeles. Without many regrets. The Hawaiian Islands are, as I have said, of great beauty and, since Captain Cook discovered them, we should have clung on to them as the 'Sandwich Islands', which Captain Cook named after the Earl of Sandwich. But we had presumably not enough people for these small and distant territories and America (shame on her!) annexed Hawaii some sixty years ago. Now Henry Kaiser (he of the Liberty Ships) is in the process of re-annexing them from America for tourist development. The result is that while the outer islands are still comparatively unspoilt, the main island of Oahu, containing Honolulu and Pearl Harbor, is just another reservation for the pensioners and the 'alimoners'.

These factors made it all the more reassuring to get back into the gracious arms of Japan Air Lines, whom I had once again (who will blame an airline for one burned-out bearing?) chosen to carry me farther and who, after a good night's rest (but I do urge J.A.L. not to give one an omelette stuffed with mushrooms and chopped onions for breakfast), deposited me shortly after dawn at the thunderous airport of 'The Angels'.

And now for the full solar-plexus blow of the West!

## INCIDENTAL INTELLIGENCE

Hawaiian legends say that clever MENEHUNES inhabited these islands before the Polynesians arrived, about 900 years ago, and that these wise 'little folk', or pixies, still live in isolated valleys and hidden forests. They came out to work when needed. We have chosen MOKI the MENEHUNE to be your guide in Hawaii, for who could better qualify?

There are a few ancient grass huts here and there which old Islanders cling to, along with old legends and traditions – but for modern humans, here are a few elegant substitutes for the old grass shack:

The Royal Hawaiian Hotel, Moana, Surfrider, Biltmore, Edge-water, Princess Kaiulani, Reef, Breakers, Hawaiiana, Hawaiian Village, Halekulani, The Palms.

All these hotels are at Waikiki, all of them are either right on the beach or so near that a few steps take you to those articles you came for – sand for lolling and the sea for swimming! Their prices range from $6 to $16 for single rates, and from $7.50 to $28 for a double, European plan. The Royal Hawaiian's rates are on the American plan, so they are between $32 and $50 a day, double.

Smaller hotels? Certainly! Here are a few around the Waikiki area: Coconut Grove, Aina-Luana, Coco Palms,

Hale Kai, The Islander, King's Surf, Hotel Kaimana, The Kahili, Leialoha Hotel, Lewers Apartment-Hotel, Pau Lani, Royal Grove, Waikiki Studio Apartments, Comstock, Hotel Pacific Polynesia, with rates from $4.50 to $12.50 per day, double, or weekly rates from $30 to $50.

Of course hotels are not limited to Waikiki. You can stay at the Alexander Young Hotel in down-town Honolulu, or the Thailiana Hotel near the town of Kailua across the Pali. There is Cullen's Ranch at Hauula, too, if you want a view of lush open spaces.

*To Dine Wondrously*
What sort of food do you like? Chinese, Korean, sea food? Japanese, American, broiled? Hawaiian, Italian, French-fried? Natural fruit-of-the-land such as mene-hune eat?

Name your gastronomical delight – we'll show you where to find it! All the Waikiki Hotels have panoramic dining-rooms, panoramic from up-above looking down, or from the beachfront looking out. If you notice the food at all with all this soul-filling nectar around you, you'll find it delicious.

Then, we'd give you a gentle shove in the direction of Fisherman's Wharf for delicacies of the sea; Canlis's Broiler where you throw your glasses to the winds, so you can't read the prices but can see enough to relish the juice-oozing thick broiled steaks; The Gourmet with its Parisian atmosphere and fancy menu.

Then to Trader Vic's for that South Seas dash; Queen's

Surf for dining on wave-washed moonlit nights – if there's a dram of romance in your soul; The Tropics, both at Waikiki and off the Ala Moana, for melting broiled meats; Waikiki Sands for the most reasonable and varied salad bar in town; Wagon Wheel for fair-priced American fare; Waikiki Lau Yee Chai and Wo Fat's down town for the acme in Oriental dishes; the Korean Kitchen for you-know-what.

There's M's Ranch House in Aina Haina and M's Smoke House down town for charcoal specialities; Rocco's Farmhouse for Italian food; Ciro's and Alexander Young Hotel's Hob Nob in downtown for American food, and Chez Michel's near Wahiawa give you ragout and crepes suzette – *très magnifique!*

In default of a private eye such as Dick Hughes for the Orient, and despite the painful quaintness of the style, I can do no better than to quote these brief extracts from the comprehensive *Hawaiian Guidebook for Visitors* by Scotty Guletz (South Sea Scotty).

It accepts no advertising, which is a recommendation, and can be bought anywhere in Hawaii for one dollar.

# 5

# Los Angeles and Las Vegas

The yellow cab driver was smoking a big cigar at eight o'clock that morning. He didn't want to talk. Neither did I. I sat and glumly watched the procession of gas stations and hot-dog stands on the hour's drive to the Beverly Hills Hotel which is still, despite the modern attractions of the Beverly Hilton, the friendliest hotel in Hollywood. I noted the 'Squeeze Inn. Steaks!' the 'Golf ! Stop and Sock!!!', a driving range, and the 'Sunset Pest Control' hard by the famous Sunset Boulevard. Also, via a detour, I renewed my acquaintance with America's Waugh Memorial, the cemetery immortalized in *The Loved One* – and then to yet one more hotel bedroom, the basket of fruit in cellophane from the manager, and the din of the telephone.

As all foreign authors know, Hollywood likes to have first bite at anyone who is 'new' and even moderately successful, and at twelve-thirty I was having lunch in the Brown Derby with a producer who wanted to make a fortune out of me in exchange for a glass of water and a crust of bread. I was treated to the whole smart rag-bag of show-biz pressure-talk in between Eggs

Benedict and those eighty per cent proof dry martinis that anaesthetize the uvula. 'We gotta see which way the cookie crumbles, Iarn.' (There are only first names in Hollywood.) 'Now don't get me wrong, you got a good property there. Don't throw it away for peanuts. As we say, "If you want to throw snow on a stove, don't bellyache if it melts."' 'Let's play this by ear, Iarn.' 'Of course you want to make money. Who doesn't? But they say around here: "A Jew worries how much money he's going to lose, an Englishman how much he'll make, and the American how much *you'll* make." Now, at our studios, we want everybody to make money. How would it be if . . .' And so it went on, a mixture of hollow bonhomie combined with ultra sharp horse-trading.

In due course, I fought my way out of the place and went far down town to visit my old friend, Captain James Hamilton, Head of Intelligence of the Los Angeles Police Department. Since I was last there five years ago, the Police Department has been torn down and rebuilt in marble, but Captain Hamilton has constructed for himself a replica of his former office, a grey box with no ornament but a heroin pedlar's pair of scales and a new acquisition – a map of Sicily. This seemed a curious decoration for a police chief's office and I asked him about it. He produced a large plan which looked rather like those charts of an atom being split. The interconnected circles contained Italian surnames. 'I'm really going after the Mafia,' explained Hamilton. 'We keep on having trouble from them. A man, an Italian, gets bumped off for no reason at all. Two years later, it appears he was one of the killers of another Italian in Chicago and, in the mobese for murder, he "had to be hit" for some reason of Mafia politics. Things like that keep on cropping up. I'm going to go on plotting these Mafia families and then, after somebody's uncle has somebody's cousin bumped off, I'll have something to start a case on.'

I had always thought that the power of the Mafia in America had been ridiculously exaggerated by writers and reporters, but when, a year or so before this, the New York police had rounded up the big Mafia conference at Apalachin, I had been inclined to change my views, and Captain Hamilton's serious approach to the problem made me think once again.

This solid bit of police intelligence work in progress is typical of Hamilton. He is a powerfully built, good-looking man of Scottish ancestry, aged about fifty-five, and he has held his post in the second biggest Police Department in America for some ten years. He has often been used by Erle Stanley Gardner as a source of police material and also by the late Raymond Chandler. *Dragnet* was written around the Los Angeles Police force, and Hamilton provided much of the material and vetted all the scripts. When I had last visited him, five years before, he was finishing an operation to rid Los Angeles of big out-of-town gangsters who were trying to muscle in on the territory. He had told me that the Los Angeles police were capable of looking after local crime, but what they feared were hook-ups with Chicago and New York mobs which would make his task infinitely more difficult. So he put his territory out of bounds to the rest of the American crime syndicates. The way he did it was to have one or two innocent-looking plain-clothes men posted at the airport and the railroad station. (No self-respecting gangster would travel across America by motor car.) These detectives were armed with concealed cameras in a book, an overnight bag, or some such innocent object. On the arrival of a plane or train, they watched the passengers and took photographs of any suspected or known crim-inal. Once identified, the man would be followed to his hotel or apartment building. From then on he would be 'leaned upon'. The process of 'leaning on' an unde-sirable is extraordinarily effective. Whenever Mr X left his room, he would find two plain-clothes detectives walking at either side of him at his elbow. If he went into a drugstore for breakfast, the men would sit on either side of him and order the same breakfast as he did. If he took a cab, the detectives would follow and, when he got out, range themselves again alongside him. The same thing would happen at lunch and dinner. Not a word would be spoken and the man would not be molested. After as little as twenty-four hours of this treatment, added to the certainty that his telephone was being tapped, the gangster would have had enough of it and leave town.

But now, Hamilton explained to me, things were not so easy. The mob was back in Los Angeles, but this time in the labour protection racket. He opened the drawer in front of him and passed over a hundred-dollar bill. 'That was stuffed in one of my men's pockets yesterday by this guy.' He had the police card on his desk. Attached to it was the usual harsh police photograph. It showed a glowering man with an Italian name. He had a string of convictions for carrying arms, violence and manslaughter, but his latest description was 'labour organizer'. 'It's the same old story all over the country, but without the sub-machine guns,' explained Hamilton. 'Protection, extortion, sabotaged machinery, a fire in your factory. All under the cloak of the labour unions. And, of course, the dues are collected by men like that' – he pointed to the photograph – 'and after they've had their cut the rest goes to the big union bosses who send their kids to Columbia and Vassar. They've put away the pineapples and choppers. Nowadays, crime's gone respectable.'

'Los Angeles has become a Mecca for the dregs of civilization.' Who said that? Not Mr Khrushchev, who was given a most unfriendly welcome by the town. Those are the words of the Chief of Los Angeles Police, W. H. Parker, faced with an annual increase in crime which is positively staggering, with burglary, grand larceny and rape, for instance, over one hundred and fifty per cent up over the 1950 rate. Crime, says the Chief of Police, has increased six times as fast as the total population of Los Angeles city and twice as fast as all business activity in Southern California. But the worst of it, said Hamilton, was narcotics, and the increase in juvenile crime by around fifty per cent. Of the latter, the forthright Chief of Police has written:

Crime among youth is encouraged and nurtured by:

1. The decline and fall of mid-Victorian values in Anglo-American civilization, leaving the individual to mature in a society that fails to establish a clear moral definition of right and wrong.

2. The direct influence of adult criminality or, in other cases, by a passive contempt by a large section of our adult population for law and order.

3. The increasing emphasis of our society upon not only materialism, but upon *materialism without effort*.

4. A cultural imbalance between Man's advancement in technology and a commensurate level of conduct. Thus we are attempting to substitute scientific proficiency for social responsibility.

These are strong words. I dare say we in Britain would second them.

But to return to narcotics. Captain Hamilton said that the FBI had estimated that in Los Angeles County alone there were six thousand confirmed dope-addicts and that the number was now increasing at the rate of one thousand a month. These staggering figures (there are four hundred and forty-two registered drug-addicts in the whole of the United Kingdom) are due to the almost wide-open supply of narcotics over the Mexican border, only some hundred and fifty miles away. There was no way of controlling this traffic, said Captain Hamilton. Every weekend, ten or twenty thousand motor cars cross the frontier for the Mexican horse-races. To search this vast number of cars was an impossibility. The Mexican Government refused to do anything about their poppy-growing industry, which was the source of the opium and heroin. 'What the hell do they want all those poppies for in Mexico?' said Captain Hamilton angrily. 'Table decoration? It's time the State Department did something about it.' His only hope, he said, was to make drug-peddling so hazardous that the market would dry up.

'But how the hell are you going to do that?' he asked. 'My department has to look after four hundred and sixty square miles of territory with a police force that has increased seven times less than the increase in crime. We've 1.88 police officers to every thousand population. Add to that the biggest traffic-policing job in the world and you can guess how many men we've got to spare for the narcotics business. Last year the number of narcotic arrests was five thousand seven hundred. We seized hundreds of pounds of marijuana, cocaine, heroin, opium, peyote and the rest. But that's a drop in the ocean. With this spread down to the teenagers (we arrested around two thousand of them for narcotic violations in 1958), what the heck do the citizens expect us to do? Nobody likes arresting juveniles – it's a last resort. But somebody's got to keep an eye on these kids and save them from themselves. Their parents won't do it.'

Hamilton explained: 'You see how it is. You have a couple with children. The father goes out to his business and comes home whacked in the evening. The mother wants to earn a bit of extra money, so she takes some light work in a near-by factory. There she's got plenty of company and new friends and some simple manual task that's a million times easier than looking after a bunch of squawking kids – you know what hell they can raise. So the kids are looked after by neighbours and baby-sitters and, when they are around ten years old, they just go out on the streets. Then they get caught up in the local teenage gangs, start smoking cigarettes and drinking liquor. Then one of the older boys says, "Why not try a puff of this? It really sends you." Then, a bit later, the older boy says, "You can make good money peddling these around your school." And there you are! The circuit's complete.'

It all made very clear sense to me, and I said so. So what was he doing about it?

Well, said Captain Hamilton, he had tried the obvious course – penetrating the rings by stool-pigeons. He had taken young trainees straight from the Police Academy and had them taught all the tricks and lingo of the narcotic traffic, fixed them up with dirty lodgings and off-beat clothes and had sent them into the Los Angeles underworld like ferrets after rabbits. In due course these lads moved from one pedlar to the next until Hamilton had organized a big swoop and had got one hundred and twenty-six drug-pedlars under arrest. Then had come the pay-off. Thanks to a famous case, *The People* v. *McShann*, of October 1958, in America the prosecution must disclose the identity of an individual when he is a material witness. The judge ruled accordingly in this instance. To save the lives of his stool-pigeons, Hamilton had had to withdraw the charges against ninety out of the one hundred and twenty-six traffickers. This McShann decision effectively prevents the police from using undercover agents to ferret out crime. Other recent court decisions restrict the police in searching a suspect before he is arrested, wire-tapping, or installing dictographs. Suspects may now make one private telephone call from jail, as opposed to the usual police call to the arrested man's attorney, employer or relative. This allows one member of a crime ring, in the course of a seemingly innocent conversation, to alert all the rest of his gang.

Hamilton had, of course, known the McShann decision before he brought his case and, to dodge the decision, he had arranged that, after a stool-pigeon had obtained the address of a trafficker, he would pass the address back to headquarters and the actual purchase of narcotics would be carried out by an ordinary plain-clothes detective. Even this had not succeeded. The judge had still ruled that the original informant, the stool-pigeon, should be produced in court.

Hamilton quoted two typical cases of over-humanized law from an address given by Virgil Peterson, Director of the Chicago Crime Commission, to the American Bar Association. (The Commission is the heir to the famous 'Secret Six' formed by Chicago businessmen to combat Al Capone and his rivals.) In the first case, an officer testified that he was on his regular beat as a motorcycle cop when he received a radio call reporting a burglary in process in an apartment building. He immediately went to that address. Upon finding nothing suspicious on the first floor, he went to the second floor where he saw two suspicious-looking men coming towards the stairway leading through the hall. He questioned them and observed that the pockets of one of them were bulging. Upon searching the two men the officer found a bracelet, camera and cigarette case engraved with the initials of the victim whose apartment had just been burgled. All the property recovered had been stolen from that apartment. When the men were taken to court, it was ruled that the police officer did not observe the men in the hall committing any crime, nor did he know that, in fact, a crime had been committed. Therefore, arrest and search were 'unreasonable'. The police evidence was suppressed and the two burglars were turned loose. One of them had a record going back twenty years with a total of thirty-nine arrests, a number of which were for burglary and possession of burglary tools.

On that very same day, June 4th, 1958, two officers who were on routine patrol saw a black Ford coming out of an alley running parallel to a bowling establishment. The officers did not then know that the bowling alley had been burgled, but the black Ford made a sharp turn at a high rate of speed and their suspicions were aroused. They gave chase and succeeded in forcing the Ford to stop. One of the men in the Ford tried to run for it while his confederate remained crouched on the floor of the car. On searching the Ford, the officers found 2,455 dollars and some cheques, as well as a sledge-hammer, crowbar and two guns. Again the court, applying the Federal exclusionary rule of evidence, held that when the officers stopped the Ford they did not then know, in fact, that a crime had been committed and, since they did not observe the defendants violate the law, the arrest, search and seizure were unreasonable. The police evidence was suppressed and the two burglars were turned loose. Both had previous criminal records.

These two extraordinary cases rest on Justice Frankfurter's famous Mallory decision when a convicted rapist appealed to the Supreme Court. This opinion states that: 'The police may not arrest upon "mere suspicion", but only upon "probable cause" . . . The arrested person may, of course, be "booked" by the police but he is not to be taken to police headquarters in order to carry out a process of inquiry that lends itself, even though not so designed, to elicit damaging statements to support the arrest and ultimately his guilt.' On this decision, Mallory, a confessed and convicted rapist, was turned loose – as were the burglars mentioned above.

Hamilton said there were countless similar cases of this nature where a known criminal was protected by an overall humanizing of legal procedure which, while entirely desirable in the protection of the innocent from wrongful arrest, search, etc., was, in effect, giving criminals almost limitless sanctuary. 'If the courts go on leaning too far backwards to maintain theoretical individual rights,' said Hamilton, 'we shall end up by tying the hands of law enforcement so tightly that we shall destroy the first law of the individual – the right of self-preservation.'

'Here in America,' he said, 'we have got these problems – a vast narcotics industry that's ruining our youth, teenage gangs, the Mafia, the big crime syndicates, graft of every kind and description – what amounts to a soaring crime wave – and the police are being told to do something about it. And what happens? A good officer makes an arrest of a criminal with a record as long as your arm and next thing he's pounding a beat for the rest of his life because of some crazy court decision. Everybody's in favour of the rights of the citizen, but that doesn't mean that the drug trafficker should have super-rights. It don't make sense.'

I said we also had our troubles in England. There had recently been the case of a man called Podola who had shot a policeman and, because he had got a black eye in the course of his arrest, had almost been made into a public hero. It seemed to me there were periods when the liberal spirit got a little bit out of hand. On this diplomatic note we parted company and Captain Hamilton sent me back to the Beverly Hills Hotel in a prowl car on whose radio I listened to a pair of police helicopters regulating the traffic on the famous Los Angeles Freeway over which, with its connecting roads, 630,000 vehicles would have travelled during this twenty-four hours. It seemed to me that Captain Hamilton and the rest of his department had one hell of a problem fighting crime and the legislature at the same time. As the movie mogul had remarked earthily to me at lunch regarding some similar dichotomy: 'You can't sit on two chairs with one bottom.'

At night, from an aeroplane, the great gambling resort of Las Vegas looks like a twinkling golden river in the black vastness of the Mojave Desert across the high Sierra from Los Angeles. Alongside the ranks of slot machines in the small airport is an automatic machine that, in exchange for a dime, gives you a quick shot of pure oxygen if you apply your face to a rubber mouthpiece. This, according to the machine, stimulates, calms the nerves, and gives you encouragement. You need all of that if you are going to take on the casinos, who pay taxes on a declared profit of $80 million a year but are believed to bring in a further $450 million that somehow don't get included in the accounts. I duly indulged with no perceptible result and proceeded to the Tropicana (happily placed on the corner of Bond Road and the Strip), the latest of the million-dollar hotels that has sprung up on the famous Strip.

It was ten o'clock at night and the casino, so arranged in all the Strip hotels that you cannot move in any direction without passing through it, was crowded.

It was nearly midnight and I was exhausted after my two high-pressure days in Hollywood, but I was determined to test out my luck. I changed two five-dollar bills into the single silver dollar cartwheels that are the common currency of Las Vegas and walked boldly up to a dollar machine. There is every shape and size of slot machine in Las Vegas, and the different models swallow anything from a dollar down to a copper cent. This one had a particularly intimidating expression. Heat radiated from its brilliant coloured lights and from its disgusting machinery, but I thought it looked a worthy opponent for my strong right arm. It offered a series of odds ranging up to a jackpot of $150, and this small fortune suggested that it had been set for a formidable percentage in favour of the House. A House can set these machines to pay any percentage it wishes and they can be adjusted daily. Normally the percentage is around ten per cent to the House but, if a particular establishment is doing badly, a row of machines can be adjusted to pay a small percentage in favour of the customer. The news of this bonanza row gets round Las Vegas like lightning and the slot-machine addicts pour in and fill the establishment up until, at dead of night, the mechanics come and readjust the odds and the House gets back into the money again.

I squared up to my monster and fed it ten single dollars. With each pull of the handle lights blinked and the stars, oranges, plums and those three rosy cherries whirred merrily. Then would come the heavy clonk as my dollar fell into the damnable iron belly and that deep, metallic sigh that meant a nil return. In this way I disbursed very quickly all my ten dollars and said to myself: 'I told you so. This machine has an evil face. It's an evil machine. Try and get your money back on a quarter dollar machine.' I duly changed a further ten dollars into quarters and warily examined the ranks of quarter machines. Two of them had rather pretty, friendly faces, and, sure enough, the first of these started to dribble coins back at me. (In view of what is to come, I record the fact that the machine is the Star Chief, number 306/301 in the Tropicana Hotel and it announces in large letters 'Joker Wild with all winning combinations. Seventeen ways to a jackpot.') I scrabbled these out of the iron mouth and suddenly, remembering some bowdlerized Nannie's dictum of childhood, it crossed my mind that it would be lucky not to scrabble them all out but to leave one behind 'for the pot'. At once there came more and healthier dribbles and my righthand trouser pocket began to get heavy.

Suddenly the handle stuck. A stony-eyed deputy sheriff with a pistol hanging from a belt lined with brass cartridges came up. He gave one glance at the machine and said, 'You forgot to put a quarter in. Funny. Our machines don't work until you put money in them.' I swallowed the sneer with good grace, and, now inspired, began playing both the two friendly looking machines, one with each hand. Now they both started sicking up coins for me. By some miracle I had obviously struck a couple of one-armed bandits that were really 'hot', and then, in quick succession, came not one, but two $25 jackpots and coins fairly vomited out of the machines and even spilt over and rolled on the floor. My right leg was almost anchored to the floor by its burden of silver, and people at neighbouring machines were beginning to stare at me – the man with the golden arm. But now the machines were going cold and only an occasional triple cherry came to cheer me. Wisely, and fearing for the seams of my trouser pocket, I went back to the old grannie at the *caisse* (no doubt the old girl had lost her pension at the machines and 'Gamblers Anonymous' had converted her from felon into wardress) and unloaded my hundredweight of silver in front of her. She poured the coins into a perforated aluminium soup plate, pressed a button and the coins whirled and disappeared down a hole. Numbers appeared on the machine and she paid me seventy dollars.

I was so encouraged by my good fortune that I asked for ten dollar cartwheels to have a last crack at the great iron stomach of my original enemy, the dollar machine.

One by one they boinged down into the monster's bowels with only two cherries, plus one orange, to slacken the brute's appetite. But I now felt confident. I somehow knew that, by leaving one coin in its iron mouth, I was going to hammer this hideous robot. And then, suddenly, there they were! The three silver stars on a green background eyed me with their three sparkling eyes. There was a great healthy rattle into the cup, but not the glorious flushing I had expected. Uncertainly I put my hand into the awkward shark's mouth. There couldn't be more than fifteen dollars there. Had the beast defeated me after all by cheating?

But suddenly the same deputy sheriff with the big

gun was at my elbow. 'Hold it, mister,' he said sharply, 'don't move.' I almost expected the crash of a gun butt against my skull for having tried to beat the syndicate, but he merely grunted, 'It's O.K., you hit it. Now leave it alone.' I respectfully stood back and, feeling pregnant with luck, attacked the next-door machine. It swallowed six dollars indifferently. Then there was my hard-eyed acquaintance back again. He handed me a parcel of notes. I counted them. They came to a hundred and thirty-five dollars. 'But it says a hundred and fifty dollars,' I complained. The man produced his sharklike sneer. He gestured towards the iron mouth. 'You've got the rest in there, mister.' 'Oh yes, sure,' I said, glad that the colloquialism had come out pat. I clawed out the rest of the money, changed the cartwheels with grannie and I went off jubilant to bed.

I had had three jackpots. I had positively hammered the syndicate. I spread the money on the bed and counted it. Two hundred and ten dollars. Whoever said the Las Vegas machines were crooked? The whole place was a mechanical Christmas tree! The telephone suddenly jangled. It was 2 a.m. Was the syndicate after their cut? I lifted the receiver. A drunken, plaintive voice said, 'Is that you, Mamie?' I said sharply, 'No, it isn't, it's her husband,' banged down the receiver and, pleased with my all-round brilliance and *savoirfaire,* went to bed after washing the filth of the United States currency off my hands. I had taken on the one-armed bandits and, by golly, I'd licked them!

Some of the hotels and casinos of Las Vegas are

owned in a considerable proportion by gangster money. These syndicates, as they are politely named, are four – Texas, Cleveland, Detroit and Chicago. The equally powerful Miami gang has no money to spare from the equally lucrative hotel and gambling investments to be found in Florida. Much conspiracy is involved in the whole operation and the operations of each hotel, plus gaming house, are shrouded in secrecy. Unobtrusive security arrangements are everywhere, from the numerous house detectives and deputy sheriffs to the handling of the million or two dollars that flow into the Strip every day of the year. From time to time, while play is at its height in a casino, if you are observant, you will notice a quiet flurry of movement in and around the tables and slot machines. The collection of the 'boxes' is going on and the management is very much on the alert. The 'boxes' are the treasure chests beneath each table and inside each machine that collect the money and, from time to time during the day (play goes on all through the twenty-four hours), these 'boxes' are whisked away behind the bars of the cashier's department and thence to the accountancy rooms in some remote corner of the building. In a well-protected room in this department, the money is then counted in the presence of a representative of each of the major stockholders in the hotel and then, at carefully changed and staggered hours, an armoured car drives off from the back of the hotel to deposit the money, or at any rate a proportion of it, in the bank. This well-oiled piece of

## HOW TO GAMBLE SENSIBLY

First you must get a strong grip on yourself and defeat the inner voice. You can't beat Aristotle, but you might – just might – trick the old boy. *You can control the psychology that is working against you.*

Decide the maximum amount you will lose and stick to it! If you violate this rule, nothing can help you except Fort Knox. It's better to divide your amount by days so that you can't lose your maximum for the whole visit the first day and have to wrestle psychology for the rest of your visit.

Now, here's the hard part: decide the maximum you will win and stick to it; this prevents your becoming a jazzy chass [a term of contempt describing a winner who is trying to get rich]. If you follow these two rules, you're well on the way to having fun without pain.

When you're ready to play, watch the game for a while. Games run hot and cold – that is, for short stretches the house will win or lose fairly steadily (naturally winning more than they lose) – try to sit in a game on a 'cold' dealer or croupier; when he turns 'hot' go to another table.

Your wins and losses will follow unpredictable cycles. Do not double when you lose – double when you win. Your possibility of winning twice in a row is greater than winning after a loss. [I doubt this. The table has no memory. F.]

Set a maximum you will lose on each table.

When you lose it, go to another table. If you get ahead, put aside some pre-decided portion of your winnings, and if you get down to that, quit the table and go to another. This process will limit your loss on each table and, if you hit a streak of luck, will let you get away from the table ahead of the game (maybe, perhaps, could be, could not be).

Above all else, if you catch yourself making a bet and thinking of the things you could buy with the amount of the bet, QUIT! Never let the amount you are betting become large enough to be important to you! Nothing or no one can give you a system for winning; but if you follow these simple rules you can control your losses and enjoy your visit.

I spent the rest of the next day doing a slow crawl of the fabulous hotels and enjoying every fabulous sight, from the garage that offered 'free aspirin' to the Wee Kirk o' the Heather with its wishing seat, and the neighbouring Hitching Post with its wishing well, where you can get a quick Nevada divorce. I also noticed the 'Cambridge Institute of Sleep Education. "Learn While You Sleep".' (On the corner of Maine and Fremont, in case I have any students among my readers!) I won my lunch at the Golden Nugget, my favourite down-town casino, which, in addition to every kind of gambling game and device, has a Dow Jones ticker and a score-board giving the result of all major sports throughout the States. There the sheriffs have flatter stomachs and the atmosphere is Western and gas-lit. It is a real pro place and the customers are pros – crew-cut desperadoes with Western hats and incipient stomachs, Cubans and Mexicans with sharp clothes and toothpicks rolling along their teeth, and the usual mob of blue-rinsed women tugging away at the machines, their sharp, greedy eyes watching the whirring plums and cherries as if they hated them. These caricatures of humanity carry their coins in children's buckets and it is them, and not the big gambler, the syndicates love. Inevitably, so long as they play, they will leave their ten per cent behind, whereas the big gambler at the crap table might get hot and take the syndicate to the cleaners, as did one young G.I. who achieved fifteen straight passes at craps – a momentarily bitter experience for the House, but one that has turned out to be the finest bit of promotion work Las Vegas has ever achieved. (Incidentally, if you can master the game, craps is by far the fairest game to play in an American casino. The House's edge is only 1.41 per cent, whereas in American roulette, with two zeros, the House's edge is 5.26 per cent for even-money bets, compared with the European single zero wheel where the odds are only 1–35 per cent against.)

For those who seek further and more expert information on gambling odds, I commend an article in the *Saturday Evening Post* of November 21st, 1959, by Professor Philip Fox of the University of Wisconsin, who has really taken the subject apart. Two interesting quotations from the Professor's article which I noted down are: 'People lose the ability to discriminate when they are confronted by vast numbers. They have no concept of what 1,000,000 really means. Maybe I can dramatize the difficulty by pointing out that 1,000,000 days since the birth of Christ will not have been recorded until A.D. 2738.' The next is: 'When I see a "student of form" poring over a dope sheet, I recall a remark made by the late Colonel Edward Bradley who bred four Kentucky Derby winners: "There are fifty-four different ways the best horse in a race can lose honestly."'

That evening I had an excellent dinner at the Thunderbird and then a crack at the black-jack at the Desert Inn, by far the nicest hotel in Las Vegas and full of action. Black-jack is our old vingt-et-un of childhood days, but here it is played for large stakes by the grown-ups with a seven per cent take for the House. The green baize cloth is sternly inscribed 'Banker must draw on 16 and stand on 17'. I lost twenty dollars quickly and happily. Happily because the table was a happy one and the dealer, crew-cut and horn-rimmed, was rather charmingly cynical about the game and his customers. I then moved on to another table where the dealer looked tougher but stupider. I doubled up, had a whisky 'on the house' from a pretty girl with very little on, and made fifty dollars. On that, I wisely closed my gambling season, and after a short night's sleep at the Tropicana, left by United Air Lines for Chicago.

After paying all overheads, I had hammered the syndicates for one hundred dollars and three stolen ash-trays!

## INCIDENTAL INTELLIGENCE

LOS ANGELES – or correctly, El Pueblo de Nuestra Senora La Reina de Los Angeles de Portucula – is blessed with first-rate hotels, apartment-hotels and motels.

Good restaurants abound, from the expensive to medium-priced, from gourmet class and expense-account category to the family trade.

Among the top hotels are the *Statler-Hilton* in downtown Los Angeles; the *Hotel Ambassador* with its two-acre lawn fronting one of the world's busiest thoroughfares, Wilshire Boulevard, running east to west, sixteen miles, from Pershing Square to the Pacific Ocean (in the *Ambassador* is the *Coconut Grove,* one of the best night-clubs in L.A., and three good restaurants); and the *Town House.*

The *Beverley Hills Hotel,* on Sunset Boulevard, has the atmosphere of a luxurious country club; excellent service and run by Mr Stuart Hathaway, who visits London and the Continent every year – 'to see hotels and improve our own'.

The *Beverly Hilton,* gay, smart, smooth, is the newest in Los Angeles County and is a show-place. The restaurants, *L'Escoffier* on the roof with a superb view of the city and the ocean and the mountains, the *Rathskeller,* and the *Traders,* are first class.

Next to the *Rathskeller* is the *Red Lion,* a Beverly Hills version of a pub, with tartan-covered walls, a fireplace, and a very good lunch in comfort and quiet. No women are permitted in the *Red Lion* until after 3.30 p.m.

The *Beverly Wilshire Hotel,* also on Wilshire Boulevard, has been refurbished by the proprietress, Mrs Evelyn Sharp, and has a magnificent coffee-shop, with drugstore attached.

Along Sunset Boulevard, towards the Ocean, is the *Hotel Bel Air,* in the form of a long hacienda with bungalows attached, set with gardens and patios. It is one of the most charming hotels in the Southern California area – and expensive. Royalty and ex-royalty, like Princess Soraya, like it. It is secluded, private, and tranquil, has an excellent restaurant and very good service, and a good bar with three knowledgeable bartenders. The Sunset Strip, a section of Sunset Boulevard between Hollywood and Beverly Hills, is the night-spot and cabaret and coffee-house area. At the night-spots, it is wise to inquire as to the couvert and minimum, otherwise the bill may be smashing.

Los Angeles is not a night town, although tourists can find whatever they want, from girls to grog, even on the Strip which is policed by the Sheriff's Department as it is in the Los Angeles County area.

The top entertainers and the revues are in Las Vegas, where the money is and where the hotel casinos can afford the investment because the people gamble as well as gambol.

Disneyland and Marineland should be included in the grand tour, and at both places there are good restaurants.

One spot, the *Malibu Sports Club* restaurant, on the Pacific Coast Highway, is fascinating – it is on a fishing pier and you dine right over the ocean. At sunset, it is superb; by moonlight, romantic; and the cuisine is de luxe. It is run by a bon vivant and gourmet, Henry Guttman, also an actor-singer of parts.

LAS VEGAS, world's gambling capital – and the sky's the limit, from a dime in the one-armed bandits up and up – is a fantastic caravanserai.

Smack in the middle of the desert, on a plateau, with a superb backdrop of mountain peaks, Las Vegas offers tourist, visitor and gambler an incomparable variety of motels and hotels. The hotels are super gambling casinos. As you enter and walk through the foyer, batteries of slot-machines beckon. Twentyfour hours a day there is the click of chips, the clink of silver dollars, the cacophony of the machines and the overtone of piped-in music.

In the vicinity of hotel or motel, there is never tranquillity or silence. Silence in Las Vegas scares folks.

But in the air-conditioned luxury suites of the *Tropicana*, the *Desert Inn*, the *Dunes*, the *Sands*, the gaudy *Flamingo*, the sprawling *Sahara* (Marlene Deitrich's pied-à-terre in Nevada), the *Riviera* and the *Thunderbird*, the music can be muted, and from a colossal chaise-longue you can watch British and French show-girls sunning and frolicking in antiseptic sunshine in the late afternoon, around vast Roman swimming-pools, or revel in superb sunsets painting the peaks in purples and crimsons and ochres.

Each hotel has an identity and atmosphere.

The *Sands*, noted for summit meetings of the Group,

formerly the Clan, headed by Mr Frank Sinatra, a director, often aided by Messrs Dean Martin, Peter Lawford, Sammy Davis Jr, Joey Bishop and composer Jimmy Van Heusen – well, the *Sands* is always jumping.

Noted for a fine cuisine, the *Copa Room* is a surprisingly spacious cabaret, with week in, week out, a top show.

The *Tropicana's Theatre Restaurant*, as well equipped as a West End theatre, and currently sports the Folies Bergère Revue, 'direct from Paris'.

The *Dunes* boasts of Minsky's Follies of 1961 starring the renowned ecdysiast, Lili St Cyr, a charming, stately blonde who reads Proust while taking a bubble bath in public.

At the *New Frontier* there's a revue, 'Oriental Holiday', with scores of nude Nipponese, and the Imperial Japanese Dancers, in costumes ceremonial and abbreviated.

Girls, the long-stemmed type, are very popular in Las Vegas; a show is considered incomplete without at least a score of them. 'The cash customers like 'em,' says Mr Ben Goffstein, the *Tropicana's* boniface, a former Manhattan newspaperman who, after a quarter of a century on the Las Vegas plateau, knows what the customers like.

The Strip, a short stretch of the highway which ribbons through the desert and cleaves Las Vegas, gleams and glitters at night with the neoned hostelries and gambling casinos. During the day it is dusty and pallid.

The night is beneficent to Las Vegas. Against the vast

black velvet of the heavens, star-gleaming, there is a carnival quality about this incredible oasis, incongruously named after the swamps which once were nearby.

Recommended and expensive is the *Aku-Aku Restaurant* in the grounds of the *Stardust Hotel*. Dinners Oriental and Polynesian a la carte, from 6 p.m. to 6 a.m.

Recommended anywhere in Las Vegas are steaks, provided you will be specific to your waiter or chef, like 'charred both sides' or 'just rare' or 'medium'. Without exception, the restaurants provide charcoal-broiled steaks, and without exception, a steak and a salad, cheese and coffee is enough.

The California varietal wines are pleasant. The blazing heat of summer seems to affect imported wines and in any case, Nevada is a hard-liquor drinking state.

Recommended too, the fishing on near-by Lake Meade, and water-skiing if you have the energy.

N.B. For the shallow pocket, down town is more rewarding than up town.

# 6

# Chicago

The early papers were saying 'Great Lakes Freeze as Cold Snap Hits'. It had been summer all the way from Hong Kong, but now I was travelling back into winter and the prospect was depressing. The United Air Lines plane levelled out over the Hoover Dam and we made for the Great Divide and the Middle West across Utah and Colorado, Nebraska and Missouri and into Illinois, white with snow, while I consumed Old Forrester on the rocks and an early Nabokov, just published in the States, *Invitation to a Beheading,* which reminds me that, on my entire trip round the world, I never saw a single other passenger reading a book in any of the many planes in which I travelled. Everyone read magazines or studied business correspondence, or just sat and looked out of the window at nothing. One further small literary aside: on no airport bookstall after Zurich did I see a single British magazine or newspaper of any kind, though everywhere there was *Time, Life* and *Newsweek.* Come to think of it, we have no publication in England that could stand up to the remarkable technical job these publications do in covering world affairs from the American viewpoint. They are a splendid show-case for the American way of life – whatever that hackneyed slogan means – entertaining, splendidly illus-trated, and remarkably frank about the dark side of America. Musing on the subject, it seemed to me that only a revamped version of the *Illustrated London News* could possibly provide comparable reading matter with an English and Commonwealth slant for the foreign traveller.

Chicago Midway Airport is one of the most congested in the world and one of the most dangerous. (A four-engined freight plane crashed into a neighbouring housing estate two days after my own landing and, when I came to leave, planes were queuing nose to tail and taking off at minute intervals.)

I should have taken the helicopter (chopper or whirly-bird in the vernacular) to Meigs Airfield on Chicago's lake front, but I did not know about the service, and it took me an hour, through some of the grimmest suburbs in the world, to get to my hotel, where, for the second time in succession – the same thing had happened at Las Vegas – I was shown at first attempt into an already occupied room. The much-vaunted American efficiency should look to its vaunt. When I had got to the correct room, I picked up the telephone and asked what the time difference was with New York, which I wanted to call (in fact, it is one hour ahead). The girl said she didn't know but would ask the supervisor. The supervisor also didn't know and connected me with long distance. Believe it or not, the long distance operator also didn't know and offered to put me on to the Weather Bureau! I finally gave up and called New York anyway.

In Chicago, I had put myself in the hands of *Playboy*, the new magazine sensation that has already passed *Esquire* in sales. *Playboy* is a highly sophisticated cross between *Esquire* and *Cosmopolitan*, with a pinch of *New Yorker* and *Confidential* added. It is housed in the smartest modern newspaper building I have ever seen and peopled entirely by the prettiest girls in America and some of the brightest young men. My photograph shows the bearded editor, Ray Russell; Charles Beaumont, one of America's newest novelists and a passionate writer on motor racing; and the back of the head of the prettiest private secretary in the world. She is just taking a note of what I wanted to do during my brief stay – learn about crime in Chicago today, pay a sentimental visit to some of the geographical high spots of the Capone era, and – no doubt to the reader's surprise – spend one whole afternoon in the Chicago Art Institute.

My next visit was to Ray Brennan, the famous crime reporter of the Chicago *Sun-Times*, who was to instruct me on item one. Ray Brennan, for thirty years one of the toughest men on America's crime beat, knew all the answers. Yes, of course Chicago was still riddled with crime, he said. But, as with Los Angeles, nowadays the gangster preferred to operate without guns. The labour rackets were just as effective and, on the face of it, law-abiding. The Mr Big of Chicago was now a certain Tony Accardo. Marshal Caifano was another big shot.

Paul 'The Waiter' Ricca had temporarily left the stage to serve three years for income-tax evasion at Terre Haute, the country club of American prisons. Number four was Joey Glimco who was Hoffa's local representative and head of the taxi-cab union. All these men had acted 'The Great Stone Face', i.e. pleaded the fifth amendment, before the Federal Grand Jury investigating organized crime in Chicago.

Tony Accardo, openly described in the newspapers as 'Crime Syndicate Kingpin', is a typical example of the new-fashioned mobster. He is handsome, well-dressed, well-educated and an excellent golfer. He lives in a large mansion in the smartest section of River Forest, the fashionable suburb of Chicago. He gives generously to charities and takes his wife and children regularly to Mass on Sundays. His famous Fourth of July parties are attended by leading citizens including high-up politicians, and he had just completed a European tour to London, Venice, Rome and the Riviera with his wife, giving interviews to the local press as if they had been Chicago's mayor and mayoress. An interesting feature of this semi-royal tour was that his companion throughout the tour was a Lieutenant Anthony Degrazio of the Chicago Police Department, who, not long before my arrival in Chicago, had been charged by his furious Department with 'conduct unbecoming an officer and disobedience – consorting with a known criminal'. Civil service proceedings against him were then under way.

Marshal Caifano, 'convicted auto thief and bank

robber', has an equally respectable front: in his case, the famous Tam o' Shanter Golf and Country Club, whose election committee were perhaps ignorant of the fact that Caifano was arraigned as a suspect in the Chicago gangland-style killing of Francis 'The Immune' Maritote and Charles 'Cherry Nose' Gioe in 1958. When FBI agents were working a close tail on Caifano during the recent Chicago crime hearings, one of them joked: 'We were sticking so close to golfer Caifano that we were worried one of us might get killed by his back swing.'

Paul 'The Waiter' Ricca, having chosen jail in preference to deportation to Italy where he has been under sentence for two murders ever since he fled to America, also has a fine mansion on Bonny Brae Road, River Forest, and some idea of his financial standing can be gained from the government claim for nearly $250,000 unpaid taxes.

These were the sort of men, said Ray Brennan, who now ruled Chicago gangland. I asked if he could give me a typical example of the sort of operation from which nowadays the mobsters made their millions. The steady income, said Brennan, came, of course, from drugs, prostitution, and gambling, all of which were rife in the town and particularly in the neighbouring territory of Cicero, a great battlefield in the old Capone days. But, like everywhere else in America, it was labour and similar rackets that were most popular. 'Give you an example,' said Brennan. 'An operation we call "The Sweetheart Arrangement". So you open a new bar, Fleming's Bar, down on Blank Street. So a union comes along and you've got two or three help, so you have to buy union cards at five dollars a month to cover those three help. They don't pay anything and they don't get any benefits. The money just goes back to the mob. Then another branch of the mob comes along, the caterers or the wine merchants, all owned by the mob. So you have to buy your wine and your steak, even your olives, from one of these suppliers. You say you won't do it? I'll tell you what happens. The mob owns the police captain of your district, pays him perhaps $100, $200 a month, and every bar is covered by hundreds of by-laws – lighting, heating, fire-escape regulations and so forth. Well, there are dozens of ways you can break any of those without knowing it and the captain will have your joint closed down. Even better, you're serving at your bar and a fellow with a beard comes in and asks for a Scotch. You give him the Scotch and he drinks half of it. In comes a cop who has been waiting for just that. The guy with the beard is sixteen years old, a minor, and you'll be in real trouble for serving liquor to a minor. The gang has got plenty of these bearded teenagers available and they just planted one on you to teach you not to be troublesome. And so it goes on. You're just little people. The bigger ones have fires and sabotage and strikes if they don't pay up or deal through the merchants they are told to deal through. Quite simple really. If you manage to dodge these troubles and you're going ahead and doing good business, the mob comes along and says they'd like to invest – just twenty-five per cent maybe. But of course they don't actually put up any money. They just get the twenty-five per cent. So there you are, ending up as an employee of the gangs, a front man for a mob enterprise.'

Brennan agreed that of course plenty of violence still went on. 'Give you an example. Only last month a man called Richard Hauff who's got a golf club around here and is a bit of a mystery man about town, was pistol-whipped one evening while he was out on a midnight date with a hoodlum's ex-wife. A few minutes later the police picked up for questioning a certain Cosmo Orlando who used to own the Melody Casino – a local honky-tonk. Orlando's an ex-convict. The police found him hiding in bushes a block from the beating up. You know what his alibi was? He said, "I was out for a walk." Not so long before that, a man called Carlo "Bananas" Urbaniti got five years for the possession and sale of heroin. He and two F.B.I. agents called Love and Ripa were all wounded in a gun battle when the G-men raided a River Grove tavern. Around about that time a certain Joseph Broge, a so-called beer distributor, was ambushed and shot down. Turned out he had been distributing pornographic gramophone records for a company belonging to a certain Sam Giancana who was once Capone's chief gunman. We get something like that from time to time, but it's nothing like the old days when there were pitched gun battles going on all over the town.'

Brennan had just written the life story of Roger 'The Terrible' Touhy of the famous Touhy Gang that had brewed beer in Prohibition days and had stood up to all the other gangs, including Capone's. Touhy had been mixed up with Jake 'The Barber' Factor, now a real-estate operator in California and at one time wanted for extradition to England for a two-million-pound stock swindle. Touhy was arrested, falsely he says, for the 'kidnapping' of Factor and he had just cleared himself of that charge and of the remainder of his ninety-nine years' sentence. He came out of jail the day after I left Chicago. Brennan's book, *The Stolen Years,* brings back all the gun-smoke scent of the blood-stained 'thirties in Chicago.

The next day, with two friends from *Playboy,* I took a car and we revisited some of the famous gangster black spots of the era. The first on our list was the Cathedral of the Holy Name on the steps of which a gangster in search of sanctuary had been shot down in broad daylight. Opposite the cathedral was the site of O'Bannion's famous flowershop on the corner of State and Superior.

O'Bannion was the victim of a famous handshake murder. He was clipping the stems of a bunch of chrysanthemums in the florist's which was the cover for his bootlegging and hijacking operations, when a blue sedan stopped outside the entrance and three men came in.

'Hallo, boys, are you from Mike's for the wreath?' O'Bannion held out his hand.

'Yes,' replied the leading man, firmly grasping the hand. 'We are.'

The negro porter who related this then heard six deliberate shots and, after a pause, the finishing shot through the head.

O'Bannion's funeral was the greatest gangster funeral ever seen. The body was borne through the town in a solid silver coffin resting on a bed of roses; twenty-two bearers carried floral tributes, and they were followed by a famous jazz band which played hymns during the procession. Ten thousand mourners attended the funeral, at which the finest wreath, costing a thousand dollars, came from the man who had ordered the killing, Al Capone.

The property has not flourished since O'Bannion's day. Now it is half a deserted parking-lot and half a grimy rooming-house whose ground floor is devoted to the Cappa Club for Young Christian workers.

We proceeded to Wabash Avenue, between State and Michigan, where Big Jim Colossimo had the warehouses where the hijacked whisky was taken. Now the warehouses have gone, and instead there is the Three Minit Car Wash, the Thompson Electric Company (truck parts), Madam Eden, Phrenologist, and the Sun-Kist Lanes Bowling Alley, together with a small shop advertising 'Live Bait, Nite Crawlers'. But behind this block, the El still crashes by on its way to the famous Loop in central Chicago, and the police sirens distantly wail. It is an area full of ghosts.

Then to the site of the famous garage where the St Valentine's Day Massacre took place at 2108 Clark Street, another grimy neighbourhood, with the garage area replaced by the Belle Vue Hand Laundry and Balaton's Barber Shop. After killing off the O'Bannion gang, Al Capone went for Bugs Moran and his mob, and seven of them were the victims of the famous St Valentine 's Day Massacre: they were machine-gunned in a garage by three mobsters dressed in police uniforms, though Bugs Moran himself was not among the dead.

Opposite, the grimy lace curtains in the windows were drawn as they must have been when the gunmen, disguised as police, peered from behind them, their tommy-guns at the ready, as they watched for Bugs Moran's gang to come to their last rendezvous.

The Biograph on Lincoln Avenue, where John Dillinger was shot down, is unchanged, with dusty naked lights in the roof and round the small central box office where Dillinger bought the tickets for himself and the famous Girl in Red who had informed on him to the police and knew that he would die as soon as the film was over. While the film was going on, police surrounded the cinema with orders to shoot to kill and, when Dillinger and the Girl in Red came out, she dropped her bag, stopped to pick it up, and Dillinger walked into the flaming guns. He shot back and got into the little alley next door. He was finally killed in the mouth of the alley and the second telephone post in the alley still has the bullet holes of the killing. The girl got a $30,000 award 'for information' and Dillinger's gang never caught up with her.

Today it is still a meagre, depressed area with its 'Biograph Barber Shop', 'Schneider's Tuxedos' and 'Valentine Pest Control' staring from across the road at the fateful cinema, outside which the crowd had fought for a scrap of the great killer's clothing or a lock of his hair. Two hundred dollars was bid for his silk shirt, and for days afterwards scraps of paper 'stained with his blood' were sold outside the Biograph for a dollar apiece. Today the old Biograph, dingy in its black and red paint, clamours for you to 'See our laff and thrill show'. This place, too, is haunted. It was time for a drink.

That afternoon, to wash the smut of ancient crime out of my mind, I repaired to the Chicago Art Institute. I had been there once before when it firmly established itself as my favourite picture gallery in the world. Here, if you like the French Impressionists, there is everything – rooms full of Degas, Pissarro, Renoir, Monet, with at least twenty superb examples of each. The Toulouse-Lautrecs are as fine as any in the world and the Cezannes and Gauguins, let alone the Picassos, are of a quality not to be seen at the Jeu de Paume, and possibly not even in Russia. It was a Saturday afternoon, but the spacious, beautifully lit gallery was almost empty, though the Christmas-card shop on the ground floor was crowded. This was the first really peaceful time I had had to myself for three weeks, and I made good use of it before getting back to my accustomed beat – dinner with my newly found friends in the famous Pump Room of the Ambassador Hotel and a visit to the hottest strip-tease in town at the Silver Frolics, a display in a large ballroom, full of commercial travellers and other businessmen, of positively exquisite boredom and lack of finesse.

And so, my brains boiling with a fine confusion of impressions, to bed.

(Ten days later, in London, editing these notes on Chicago, I read in the evening paper that, while I was editing them, Roger 'The Terrible' Touhy was ambushed and killed by two gunmen dressed as policemen in West Side, Chicago. He and a retired police sergeant, with whom he had spent the night discussing Brennan's book, were mown down from behind by five sawn-off shotgun blasts. Touhy had been released from prison on November 24th after serving twenty-six years. Somebody from the blood-stained Capone era has a very long memory indeed!)

## INCIDENTAL INTELLIGENCE

*Hotels*
Reservations should be made in advance, for ever since the days of Abraham Lincoln, Chicago has been inundated with conventions and conferences.

If the aim is somewhere central, the big hotels in the area of the Loop – like the *Palmer House,* the *Sheraton,* the *Pick-Congress,* the *Sherman,* the *Sheraton-Blackstone* – would be the obvious choice. To give an idea of price range, a single room at another of these Loop hotels, the *Conrad Hilton,* can be had for $7 to $17 a day.

Rush Street, on the Near North Side, is the centre of Chicago night life, and the *Ambassador Hotels* (the *Ambassador East* and the *Ambassador West*) are within easy range of it. Expect to pay about $15 for a single room in these quietly expensive five-star hostelries.

*Executive House,* where prices for a single room start

at $12, overlooks the Chicago River, which flows backwards through the city; it has attractive modern furniture and a generally new look. In the same bracket is the *Drake Hotel* (starting price $9).

Newspapermen favour the *St Clair*, which is not extravagantly priced and houses what is probably the most handsomely appointed Press Club in the United States. This is one block off elegant Michigan Avenue, and near it is the *Eastgate*, another comfortable place to stay.

People who bring their cars would be well advised to put up at a motel. The *Lake Tower Motel* is conveniently placed in the middle of town, while a good one on the north side is the *Sands*. To the south, there is the *50th on the Lake Motel*. Advantages of staying in a motel include the absence of a tipping line.

## Restaurants

Chicagoans boast that their restaurants of many and varied nationalities enable a visitor to 'eat around the world' without leaving the city. This is true, and Chicago's Chinese and Japanese restaurants are probably the best in America outside San Francisco.

At the *Azuma House* one can sit on cushions, having removed one's shoes, round a table where excellent sukiyaki is prepared sur place. The *Shangri-La* offers a lavish Cantonese menu.

At the *Epicurean*, chicken paprika and other Hungarian dishes attract many musicians and artists: the host calls himself the Strudel King. In most American cities you can find a moderately priced Italian restaurant where that vast wheel, the pizza pie, is consumed by a single customer with ease and relish; the Chicago specialists are at the *Pizzerias Uno* and *Due.* You can have cocktails outdoors at *Riccardo's* sidewalk cafe and restaurant, which has Neapolitan food and singing waiters. Also recommended is *El Bianco,* featuring a cheese and antipasti trolley.

The *Red Star Inn* is German, with a long and not expensive menu which includes stuffed young goose. A modest place where you bring your own wine is the *Cafe Azteca,* where, as one would expect, the food is Mexican. Don't miss *Jacques' French Restaurant,* where you dine outdoors in summer.

Among the deluxe restaurants, the most fabulous is the *Pump Room* at the *Hotel Ambassador East,* which is supposed to recall Beau Nash and eighteenth-century Bath, but throws in waiters bearing flaming food on swords and Gertrude Lawrence ice-cream, flambé at your table.

Also extremely expensive but smaller and more intimate is the *Red Carpet,* whose cuisine is mostly French with a Haitian accent.

If among-the-tables musicians are no objection, try *Sasha's,* a small place with a daily 'gourmet's choice'. This is fairly new, and so is *Maison Lafite,* which also offers exotic dishes, mostly French.

Just one whiff of that vast butchery, the Chicago stockyards, is enough to make a sensitive person abjure meat for ever. Yet the *Sirloin Room* at the *Stock Yard Inn* is listed among the thirty best restaurants in America.

You mount the 'steak throne', pick the piece you want, and put your brand on it. The raw meat is then cooked the way you like it, and if this is *bleu*, better specify very, very rare. Not surprisingly, there are many other Chicago restaurants which specialize in steak.

With its splendid waterfront, Chicago also has first-class 'seafood' restaurants, and one of the best is the *Cape Cod Room* at the *Drake Hotel*.

The three best-known resorts for dinner, dancing and cabaret are the *Empire Room* in the *Palmer House Hotel*, the *Chez Paris*, where you can hear such celebrities as Nat 'King' Cole, Sammy Davis Jr and that lugubrious girl Keely Smith, and the *Boulevard Room* at the *Conrad Hilton*, where there is usually an ice show.

Among the smaller clubs are *Orchid*, where Frances Faye may be singing about her strange friends; and *Mister Kelly's* or the *Cloister*, where you can savour the gibes of Mike and Elaine or Mort Sahl. Another choice spot is the *Junior Room* at the *Black Orchid*, which, like the others, is on the Near North Side.

Something special, requiring a member's key to get in, is the *Gaslight Club*, where nude portraits enliven the Victorian decor and you can enjoy, if such is your taste, the society of advertising executives on lavish expense accounts.

Jazz buffs make for the *Blue Note* and the bands of such leaders as Basie and Duke Ellington. For Dixieland music, go to *Jazz, Ltd*. There are many others, Chicago being a well-known centre of the art.

Late-late-late snacks are served until six in the morning at the *Tradewinds,* where stage, sporting and other notables meet in the small hours.

Chicago's major sightseeing targets are detailed in the guide-books, but do not overlook the Chicago Historical Society in Lincoln Park, which not only specializes in local lore but also dramatizes American history in an interesting series of period rooms. Above all, don't miss the Chicago Art Institute. It has the finest French Impressionists outside Russia.

A leisurely drive along the twenty-five miles of magnificent lake front is an absolute must. Those who go night-clubbing should stay up long enough to see the sun rise over Lake Michigan.

# 7

# New York

I enjoyed myself least of all in New York. It was my last lap and perhaps I was getting tired, but each time I come back (and I have revisited the city every year since the war) I feel that it has lost more of its heart. Steel and concrete, aluminium and copper sheathing for the new buildings, have smothered the brownstone streets that had so much warmth in the old days. The whole of the beautiful Washington Square area has disappeared, and up town the new resettlement areas – vast blocks of tiny apartments for the negroes and the Puerto Ricans – have now overwhelmed the old happy sprawl of Harlem.

There are still thrilling moments – when your taxi goes over the hump on Park Avenue at 69th Street and the lights turn to red and you pause and watch them all go green the whole way down to 46th, your heart turns over for New York. But this is an architectural, a physical, thrill. Go into the first drugstore, ask your way from a passer-by, and the indifference and harshness of the New Yorker cuts the old affection for the city out of your body as sharply as a surgeon's knife. It is partly the hysterical pursuit of money, the fast buck, that chills, but it is also the disdain of the New Yorker for the guy who doesn't know his way about, who isn't on the inside.

In New York you don't get politeness unless you pay for it. Here, the tipping system has gone mad. You are ruled by the head waiter, the bell captain, the reservation clerk, the credit manager and the black-market theatre-ticket operator. They are the Establishment, and you must be 'in' with these people or you will sink without trace. And, of course, in New York the expense-account aristocracy have increasingly ruined one's old haunts, deflating the quality of the food and inflating the prices.

(At Christmas-time and New Year, for instance, fifty-dollar bills are slipped into head waiters' hands all over America so that they will 'look after you' in the following year.) The latest expense-account joke is that two businessmen are having luncheon together. When the check comes, one man says, 'Give me that, I'm on an expense account, it's deductible.' The other man quickly snatches the check from him, 'No you don't. I'm on cost-plus. I can make a profit on it.'

My attitude was perhaps soured by the fact that there were only three days to go before Thanksgiving, when all America eats turkey with cranberry sauce, and my name was mud throughout the country because Mr Arthur S. Flemming, U.S. Secretary of Health, had announced the week before an almost nationwide ban on the sale of cranberries. This fantastically unpopular pronouncement by the Food and Drug Administration

had been due to the fact that two shipments of cranberries from the Pacific North-West crop were found
to contain a residue of a chemical weed-killer, aminotri-
ozole, which can cause cancer in rats. Hundreds and
thousands of pounds of cranberries and cranberry products were seized, and no cranberries could be sold unless
they had been cleared by laboratory tests. So this
certainly wasn't a good time for any Fleming to be
around in the United States.

In addition, New York, and indeed the whole of
America, was traversing yet another of those troughs
of moral depression and self-chastisement they have
suffered so frequently since the war, starting with the
McCarthy scandals, then the revelations about Murder
Inc., the Little Rock affair, the ghastly wave of juvenile
crime, Mr Sherman Adams of the White House and the
Affair of the Vicuna Coat, the Teamster Union hearings
with their appalling revelation of rackets all through
the labour world, the smashing success of Russia's sput-
niks, and now, finally and worst of all because it struck
at practically every home in America, the television
scandals and the confessions of Charles van Doren, a
national hero. These confessions and the wholesale revelations of dishonesty in other branches and amongst
other local heroes in the television business hit America
in her conscience as hard as when the Chicago White
Sox were accused of taking bribes to lose the 1919
baseball World Series. Then, it is said, a small boy went
up to his hero, an outfielder, 'Shoeless Joe' Jackson, and
pleaded, 'Say it ain't so, Joe.' Now the whole nation

was making the same plea to its current idol; but it was so, a thousand times so, and America was beating its collective breast so dismally that one felt it only needed a scandal at the heart of the White House or in the hierarchy of the Roman Catholic Church for the whole nation to commit hara-kiri. No nation likes to be held up before the world as a pack of fools and crooks, and everyone I met seemed to have a load of guilt and foreboding on his shoulders already sore from self-flagellation.

'There's worse to come yet,' they were moaning on Madison Avenue, the home of the television and advertising moguls. 'They're investigating the ratings systems now. After that they're going to get after the local station heads. If you give a disc jockey a hundred bucks a week payola to plug just one record, how much do you think the station head pulls in for closing his eyes to it? And think of all the other programmes that are subject to plugging. I can tell you, Iarn, if you want to get any programme, a detective series say or a variety show, on to these local stations all over America, you've got to square the station head first or he'll take your rival's programme and get squared by him. Payola accounts for upward of twenty-five per cent of the network's overheads.' The same psychology showed itself in occasional bitter, self-defensive cracks at England. 'Glad to hear your country's getting back on its feet, Iarn. But I hate to say this, and don't misunderstand me. That paying-off of your debt to the International Monetary Fund, you know, that last £360 million. Well now, don't misunderstand me, but running this country costs around $81 billion every year and that £360 million you turned in would be just about enough to run the United States for one day.'

But what was riling New York particularly when I went through was a lengthy indictment, 'The Shame of New York', for which America's reputable liberal weekly the *Nation* had cleared one whole issue. 'The Shame of New York' was an investigation by two journalists of repute, Fred Cook and Gene Gleason, into the rackets behind New York municipal government. Written with vitriol and apparent authenticity, the authors had taken New York apart, from the Mayor down to the cop on the beat, starting with the interesting statistics that there are an estimated nine million rats in New York compared with the eight million population (two citizens were actually gnawed to death by rats in 1959), and that the city's police force of twenty-four thousand men is an army larger than the military forces of many Latin American countries. There is not room here to give more than a specimen quote of the eighty-page indictment, but this, from the introduction, is typical:

## CITY WITHOUT A SOUL

The illnesses of New York are many and they run deep. The ruthlessness of large-scale redevelopment, cloaked under the laudable aim of slum clearance, is only one of many cankers. Wherever you turn, there is crime. Some sections of the city are veritable jungles, the streets unsafe at night, the more remote sections of beautiful parks unsafe even in the day-time. Periodically, youthful gangs explode in violence that makes sickening, sensational headlines. There are gang fights, muggings, rapes in the schools, murders. It is commonplace for a horrified Press to blame these excesses upon the especial 'depravity' of the new, rising and degenerate generation.

But it is perhaps even more reasonable to view them as the expressions of a sick society – as the kind of outbursts that are inevitable in a city that, in many respects, has lost its very soul.

And this, a few lines later on, from a Tammany Hall veteran who talked to the authors:

Every town has its Tammany Hall. I'm no lily, but this is the limit. I've never seen it so bad in a lifetime of politics. You ask me what's wrong with Tammany Hall? The Mafia. The underworld and the leaders they control – and a Press agentry that makes a fool of Lincoln's statement that you can't fool all of the people all of the time.

If it is not Frank Costello today, it is whoever can make it pay for the privilege of making book, numbers, pimping, selling junk [dope] or anything else that is illegal. Today, if a political boss arrived at his office and found that in his absence the Mayor, the Governor and Genovese [Vito Genovese, often called the kingmaker of gangdom], had phoned, he would call Genovese back first.

Like anywhere, the little guy in the street wants a ticket fixed. Or maybe he wants to get on or off a jury. But he's paying one helluva price for it in the long run. Can't they see the fantastic and open connections of politics with the mob? It doesn't make any difference what the party is. I can name you one election in this town some years ago where all the top candidates were controlled by the mob. One was owned by Thomas (Three-Finger Brown) Luchese; one by Costello; one by Genovese. The mob couldn't lose. They had it sewed up.

Well, there it is – New York as seen by two New Yorkers. Perhaps my instinct that the town was rapidly losing its heart hadn't been so wrong.

The truth of the matter is that the East sharpens one's mind about the West and, by comparison with the Orient, I had learnt and sensed in Los Angeles, Chicago and New York that America is temporarily in poor health and she is very conscious of the fact. Her scientific know-how has been shown up by the Russians, her industrial know-how by the six months' steel strike and by the Teamsters and other union investigations, and now her private morals have suffered under the microscope of the television investigations. What is the matter? I suppose, and many intelligent American writers support my suspicion, that she has four basic troubles – first, the collapse of the family unit which today hardly exists in American towns; secondly, Momism and the vast economic power (via alimony, inheritance and other factors) held by women in America; thirdly, self-hypnotism about the 'American way of life ', a concept which needs drastic reexamination by those who invented the slogan; and, fourthly, escapism and flight from reality, whether this takes the shape of the tele-vision myth and the enchanted world of the ad. man which seek to show people as better than they know perfectly well they are, or of such escapist drugs as the tranquillizer pill, the fat blue sleeping-pill, and the psycho-analyst's couch.

On this latter point, the abdication of free will to the chemical companies, Mr Dan Jacobson had an inter-esting comment on drugs in a recent issue of the *Spectator*. He wrote:

> Surely, it is clear that what the totalitarian state tries to do to its citizens is something very similar to what the drug-taker is doing to himself. He is denying his self the right to its own misery, its own happiness, its own unpredictability; he invades himself with a weapon from outside, and destroys what is most spontaneously alive and sentient within him.
>
> Perhaps the inviolability of the individual is a nineteenth-century superstition, and we are all going to end up, as Aldous Huxley has prophesied, drug-addicts of a kind; perhaps the totalitarian State of the future will realize how much more

easily it can bring about its aims through the judicious use of tranquillizers and stimulants, rather than through mass-rallies and death-camps.

Whatever is going on in American society, those who love America and have many American friends can only mourn the way the world's stripling 'most likely to succeed in the class of 1900' and heir to world supremacy is growing up. Fortunately the country has a strongly beating heart and, once you have that, the marginal frailties, if taken in time, can be quickly subordinated. If taken in time! But the watching grandparents are worried and the body-snatchers sharpen their knives.

These are depressing reflections, but they are widely shared in America where, as I have said, they create an atmosphere of deep malaise from which I was glad to escape; and, anyway, I was longing to be off on the last lap. Rather sadly I repaired to the oyster bar in Grand Central Station and consumed with relish perhaps the only dish that has maintained its integrity in the New York of my experience – creamed oyster stew with crackers, and Miller's High Life beer – and then I was off to Idlewild. It was time for home.

## INCIDENTAL INTELLIGENCE

*Hotels*
(*Out-of-date and uninspired, I fear – as would be a year-old guide to any capital city.*)
   We all know about the *Waldorf-Astoria,* roosting-place

150

of kings, queens, presidents and press lords; and the *Pierre*, where Barbara Hutton is to be found when in New York; and the now overrated *St Regis*, where Edith Sitwell and her brothers stay; and the *Plaza*, whose wedding-cake style (*circa* 1907) did not deter the late Frank Lloyd Wright from living there.

The *Stanhope*, opposite the Metropolitan Museum, is a less obvious choice, although it is also a five-star hotel, where a single room costs something in the area of $16 a night. Mrs Jesse Sharp, who owns it, aims to give the kind of service you expect in London but seldom get in New York, and guests who indicate the time of their arrival are even met at the pier or airport. A quiet, immensely dignified place where you get individual, tender, loving care.

The *Carlyle*, also up-town on the East Side, and also five-star, is another hotel of character; it has preserved its decorum in spite of the unaccustomed publicity which hits it during the occasional visits of the President and his entourage.

In the same general area is the *Volney*; as this hotel has been for years the home of Dorothy Parker, it must be beyond criticism. Five-star, of course.

Mention of Dorothy Parker recalls the days of the celebrated Round Table and Alexander Woollcott at the *Algonquin*. This is a good place to stay if you wish to be within strolling distance of Broadway theatres. Sir Laurence Olivier lives at the *Algonquin* when he is in New York, and so does Terence Rattigan.

This is not quite so outrageously expensive as some,

and neither is the *Warwick*, which is also convenient for the theatre. Remember, in telling taxi-drivers to go to the *Warwick Hotel*, that although the second W is silent in English, it is pronounced in American, otherwise utter confusion will result – say 'Worwick'.

A modest-looking hotel down town on East 39th Street is one of the most expensive: this is the *Tuscany*, which is considered more chic than the huge places that resemble Grand Central Station at the rush-hour, and pay you about as much attention. Rates here are from about $17 to $22 a night for a single room, but that includes a colour TV set and a refrigerator.

The *New Weston* is less expensive and more conveniently situated for the Fifth Avenue shops, but it is infested with English people.

Really cheap hotels are generally unappetizing, but a pleasant one, with single rooms (with bath or shower) ranging from $5 to $10 a night, is the *George Washington*, on the fringe of Greenwich Village near Gramercy Park. Right in the Village, the *Van Rensselaer* is another good choice among less expensive places.

*Restaurants*
There are so many restaurants in New York that probably the best way to choose is to walk slowly until you see one you like. One of the most expensive, where the French food is superb, is the *Chambord*, unpretentiously situated on Third Avenue. The bill for dinner for two, with aperitifs and wine, will probably run from about $30 to $60. Serious eaters also frequent *L'Armorique*

on Second Avenue. For sumptuous decor, magnificently embossed menus, big-name clients and grandly expensive dishes with resounding classical names, try the *Forum of the Twelve Caesars.*

This is very, very expensive, and so is the *Four Seasons,* launched by the same company, with opulent settings (changed four times yearly) to match the impressive bronze Seagram Building where it is situated. Here, too, is the *Brasserie,* more moderately priced, and open for twenty-four hours daily. Another experience not to be missed is luncheon or late dinner at the '21' *Club.* Fashionable and also madly expensive places where one goes to see and be seen are the *Colony* (not to be confused with the *Colony Club*) and *Le Pavilion,* where the celebrated Henri Soule provides exquisite food.

On the moderate side, a good place for lunch is *Le Chanteclair,* where you will find Stirling Moss and other racing motorists when they are in New York. For tremendous portions of Italian food, try *Leone's:* it is not far from Madison Square Garden, and boxers and other sporting characters frequent it. Two very pleasant French places are *Le Moal* on Third Avenue (Normandy and Provencal cuisine) and *La Toque Blanche,* near United Nations. A really cheap French place is the *Champlain,* on the West Side not far from Rockefeller Center; it is packed full and terribly noisy, however.

If you are looking for a not too expensive place for after-theatre supper, think of *Sardi's:* although familiar Broadway faces are on exhibit and most of the menu is not cheap, there are reasonably priced choices among the snacks.

Every visitor should try a delicatessen at least once, to sample the American way of life. The *Stage Delicatessen* is full of Broadway characters and also of the exuberant talk of the owner, Max Asna. When broke, there is always the automat of *Horn and Hardnut,* and *Glorifried Ham 'n' Eggs.*

Outside of *El Morocco* and the *Stork Club* (both for dancing) and the *Copacabana* (where there is cabaret), and the rest of the well-trodden night-spot trail, one might try Julius Monk's *Upstairs at the Downstairs* and the *Downstairs at the Upstairs.* Both these whimsically-named joints are under the same roof on West 56th Street: go to the *Downstairs* for sophisticated songs at the piano, and to the *Upstairs* for a full-length revue. No dancing, but drinks and/or supper.

For jazz, there is the famous *Birdland* on Broadway, and the equally celebrated *Jimmy Ryan's* on West 52nd Street, among many others. For the rest, it depends on who is currently performing. There may be somebody interesting at the *Blue Angel* or the *Embers.* In Greenwich Village, I would pick the *Bon Soir,* especially when Mae Barnes is singing there, or the *Village Vanguard,* which was the jumping-off place for Harry Belafonte, and, more recently, Miriam Makeba from South Africa.

In the small hours, one of the noted bars on Third Avenue is in order. Say *Costello's* near 44th Street, or *P. J. Clarke's,* where a hamburger tastes good at about 3.30 a.m.

If you make the mistake of omitting the trip to the top of the Empire State Building as being too banal for your notice, look down on the city from a helicopter, price five dollars. Poets read every night at 2 a.m. at the *Seven Arts Coffee Gallery*, a 'beat' haunt near Times Square. And don't miss Staten Island, which has a shabby, run-down charm and is reached by New York's best bargain, a five-cent ferry from the Battery.

So that was that. I had gone round the world in thirty days, and all I had to show for the journey was a handful of pretty light-weight impressions and some superficial and occasionally disrespectful comment. Had I then, have I today, no more serious message for Britain from the great world outside?

Well, I have, but it is only a brief and rather dull exhortation to our young to 'Go East, young man!' See the Pacific Ocean and die!

It was a source of constant depression to observe how little of our own influence was left in that great half of the world where we did so much of the pioneering. I cannot remember meeting a single Briton all the way from Hong Kong to New York, with the exception of the British Consul in Hawaii. Of course, Japan was conquered and occupied by the Americans, and American culture, communications and trade have almost a monopoly of the Pacific. They are even penetrating Australia, our last and, because of the miracle of her athletic prowess, most glamorous bastion. But it is a measure of our surrender that there are, I think, only three staff correspondents, excluding Reuter, covering the entire Orient for the British press, and our trading posts are everywhere in retreat.

So a trip round the world, however hasty, brings home all too vividly the fantastically rapid contraction of our influence, commercial and cultural, over half the globe, and our apparent lack of interest in what can broadly be described as the Orient.

Can this contraction be halted or even reversed? Only, I think, if the spirit of adventure which opened the Orient to us can be rekindled and our youth can heave itself off its featherbed and stream out and off across the world again. One way for a young man to do this, if he hasn't got the *Sunday Times* behind him, is to take a job as a steward or deckhand in a ship, any ship, and go and see the other side of the world for himself. Travel broadens the mind and it is broad minds we need in a world that is so very much broader than the posters of travel agents suggest.

After this trite little homily, back to the *Sunday Times*. My series, as I have said, entertained readers of the paper and, since it is in the nature of good editors to flog a successful formula until it is well and truly dead, in the spring of 1960 I was cajoled into taking to the road again, but this time round a narrower circuit – round the thrilling cities of Europe.

# 8
# Hamburg

She was big girl with a good figure. She wore nothing but a frilly white bathing-cap and short black bathing-trunks. During the fight in the pool of peat mud she had become streaked with the stuff, and one wondered how she would ever get clean again. With a ferocious shout of 'Huzza!!' she put her head down and charged the smaller girl with ferocity. The smaller girl gave a realistic 'Ouch!' as the bathing-cap hit her square in the stomach, she then described an elegant cartwheel over the larger girl's head and fell with a dull squelch into the black morass. There was clapping and cat-calling from the predominantly male audience. The referee, a girl in gold lamé, began to count.

It was two o'clock in the morning in Hamburg. I was in the inner heart of the notorious St Pauli night-club district. This heart is appropriately called 'Die Grosse Freiheit' – the Great Freedom – and in this small area survives the last bastion in Europe of 'anything goes'.

I had come here by way of Ostend, Antwerp, Rotterdam, Haarlem, Wilhelmshaven and Bremen on the first leg of what was to be a six-thousand-mile tour of the thrilling cities of Europe.

Appropriately enough, as I thought, Europe had greeted me with flowers – so many flowers that in the end one was almost sickened by the profusion of graceful stalks bowing to the northern, Simenon weather and by the eternally smiling faces.

Rotterdam was in the grip of the spring *Floriade* and then, from Leiden well past Haarlem, the thousands of acres of tulip and hyacinth fields spread their patchwork quilt over the dull landscape. Even the rubbish heaps in the fields were composed entirely of flower petals, and the Belgian cars driving back after the weekend were decked in huge garlands of red, yellow and 'black' tulips. It is the predominance of these harsh colours in the fields – the acres upon acres of red, yellow and deep purple – that tire the eye and the senses. The occasional fields of cream and slate-blue hyacinths are a relief, and in individual nurseries there are, of course, all the rarer varieties down to the tiny striped and spike-leaved tulips, but the great masses of colour in these strong tones are exhausting.

From there on (why do Dutch cows wear overcoats?*), northwards over the wonderful sixteen-mile dyke across the Zuider Zee, one enters the beautiful lost worlds of Friesia and Lower Saxony, and I kept always as close as possible to the coast to savour the forlorn, riddle-of-the-sands atmosphere and to get a glimpse of the chain

---

* A correspondent suggested it is to identify and protect a cow in calf.

of West and East Friesian Islands – signposts towards that group of names – Wilhelmshaven, Bremen, Bremerhaven, Cuxhaven, the Kiel Canal – which possess that authentic ring of ill omen for anyone who has served, however briefly, in the Royal Navy.

The last time I had paid serious attention to these island names – Wangerooge, Spiekeroog, Norderney, Borkum – was when, as a young lieutenant RNVR in the Naval Intelligence Division in 1939, I had studied them endlessly on Admiralty charts and put up a succession of plans whereby I and an equally intrepid wireless operator should be transported to the group by submarine and there dig ourselves in, to report the sailings of U-boats and the movements of the German fleet. Everything in those foolhardy minutes on Admiralty dockets was thought out, everything provided for. There would be a pedal generator for the wireless set, we would live on shellfish, my excellent (as I claimed) knowledge of German would be enough to bluff our way out of trouble in case some inquisitive fisherman turned up. What nonsense they were, those romantic Red Indian day-dreams so many of us indulged in at the beginning of the war – to blow up the Iron Gates on the Danube, to parachute into Berlin and assassinate Hitler, and all the rest! When I ordered a drink amongst the gaunt, endless ruins of Wilhelmshaven on my way to Hamburg, the contrast between the waiter's Low German and my own Bavarian-Tyrolean mixture told me just how long I would have survived on Wangerooge!

These war-time memories, that one had thought

banished forever in 1946, come back in a town like Wilhelmshaven where the giant V-boat pens still clutter up the harbour front, and where vast chunks of blasted concrete lie among tangles of rusted metal. One seems still to hear the ghostly strains of 'Wir fahren gegen Engel-land' whispering of the days before the bombs, the days of Iron Crosses, of daggers of honour and of secret weapons that would win the war for Germany. And then one hears the giant whistle of the bombs that shattered the dream. It was good to escape these ghosts for the warmth and life of Hamburg.

When the referee had counted to nine, and the taller woman was standing facing the audience with her hands clasped victoriously above her head, silently the smaller one got up from the mud, took two large handfuls of the stuff, crept up behind her adversary and crammed them down the seat of her bathing pants. With a howl of delight from the audience, the fight went on until, appropriately, the smaller girl tripped the larger, who measured her length with a terrific explosion of mud fragments which caused the front row of spectators to pull over their heads the sheets with which the thoughtful management had provided them. The bout was awarded to the small girl, a stage was slid over the huge bath of mud and we proceeded to the bucolic pleasures of 'They also sin in the Alps', described aptly as a 'Sex Nacht revue'.

All this and much more, until four o'clock in the morning, takes place in the Bikini, but the hardy night-hawk has still got a choice of some twenty other haunts from the Galopp, where semi-nude women ride horses round and round a small ring, through Casanova with its 'Strip-tease Explosiv', and an indeterminate Lokal advertising in English, 'You get here the strongest beer of the world', the Aladin where guitars twang softly all the night, to the Erotic, and on beyond.

The Erotic (*Sinnlich! Schamlos! Sundig!* – Sensual, Shameless, Sinful) concentrates on giving value for money, and four shows are displayed more or less at the same time. First, on a small stage, there is conventional strip-tease backed up by a semi-transparent panel in the wall through which the performers may be seen clothing themselves before their appearance. At each interval there is a serial semi-blue film depicting pretty girls with nothing on cavorting on a rocky seascape which might be somewhere in the south of France, but is more probably in the Baltic. And, for good measure, an assortment of full-size colour photographs of nudes are shown on an adjoining panel in the wall. All these you can see for about five shillings while an agreeable half-hour passes.

Now all this may sound pretty devilish in cold print on a Sunday morning in England, but in fact, except to the exceedingly chaste, it is all good clean German fun. People are cheerful. They laugh and applaud and whistle at a kind of erotic dumb crambo which is yet totally unlascivious. Everybody wandering up and down the garish, brightly lit alleys seems engaged in a light-hearted conspiracy to *pretend* that 'anything goes'. When you have been into one nightclub you have got the tone of all of them, and the tone is a homely and harmless 'good time' to be topped off perhaps by a visit to the Zillertal, a gigantic Bavarian beer hall with a brass band that blows and beats to crack the windows, where everyone's eyes are glazed with beer and where the waitresses scream dramatically as they get pinched.

For those who are not finished off by these pleasures there is the Blauer Peter, which does not open until four o'clock in the morning and closes, roughly, at midday. Here you can enjoy really hot jazz by small combination bands, as you also will at the New Orleans which specializes in Dixieland jazz.

If you are in search of sin more solid than these naiveties, you walk across the broad street of the Reeperbahn (Ropemakers' Walk) and up Davidstrasse, past the bogus-Dutch block of the police station that cuts into the pretty facade of the St Pauli theatre. Fifty yards up this street on your right you will find a tiny alley protected from prying eyes by a tall wooden barrier bearing the words 'Adolescents forbidden'. When you go through this, you are greeted by a most astonishing sight – the brilliantly lit alley, blocked also at the other end, is thronged, like a long stage or narrow piazza, with strolling men. At first sight, the neat, three-storied houses on both sides of the alley are like any others except that they are all brightly lit as if for a gala occasion, but when you stroll down the alley you find that the bottom floors have been turned into wide show-cases elegantly furnished and decorated to resemble small parlours or drawing rooms, and, in each show-case, sitting in comfortable chairs or lounging on chaises-longues, are girls of varying ages and charms, all scantily, though not immodestly, dressed. These girls are, to put it bluntly, 'for sale' at a price, I am reliably informed, of twenty Reichsmarks.

This street is no guilty hole-in-the-corner business such as we know in England, but a brightly lit, colourful, gay place of pleasure and laughter. During my visit (purely in the interests of sociological research!) there was not a drunken man to be seen, and if there had been I gather he would have been thrown out of the street by the two policemen who stand nonchalantly by the entrance. Some of the girls in the show-cases looked pretty bored with the whole procedure, but most of them smiled and chatted away or got on with their knitting or petit point with studied nonchalance. The street, I gather, operates throughout the twenty-four hours, with a population of some three hundred girls who do six-hour shifts. The street and the houses are spotlessly clean and medical supervision is very strict.

Prostitution is not legal in the rest of Germany, but Hamburg, after brief enslavement under Hitler, is once again a 'Free City' and a law unto itself. Far from being shy about St Pauli and the Davidstrasse, it is extremely proud of its liberal attitude towards the weaknesses of mankind. It is not in the least impressed that France and, more recently, Italy have outlawed prostitution and driven it underground with the inevitable results – protection rackets, disease and squalor – which we know so well in England. The Hamburg patriarchs, with a tradition of enlightened municipal government dating from Charlemagne who founded the city in A.D. 811, cannot understand that two great nations such as France and Italy, so proud of their social and cultural freedoms, should have allowed two blue-stocking women, Marthe Richard, Minister of the Interior under the first post-war French government, and Signora Merlin, an Italian Senator, to dictate the morals of two such 'passionate' peoples. In Hamburg, normal heterosexual 'vice' is permitted to exist in appropriate 'reservations' and on condition that it remains open and light-hearted. How very different from the prudish and hypocritical manner in which we so disgracefully mismanage these things in England!

I was altogether immensely impressed by Hamburg, which is now one of my favourite cities in the world. Perhaps I was favourably conditioned through staying at one of the few remaining really great hotels in Europe. This is the Vier Jahreszeiten (no connection with Herr Walterspiel's excellent establishment in Munich) on the Inner Alster, one of the two fine artificial lakes that add so much to the beauty of the heart of the city. It was built, or at any rate modernized, around 1910 – the golden age for hotel design – and the rooms and bathrooms are solid, comfortable and elegant, with good period furniture which spreads lavishly down the corridors and into the public rooms. The cooking in the grill room – there are also a restaurant and a basement *Keller* – is first-class German, which at its best is as good as there is, and the wine list has everything. The chef even makes his own smoked salmon, but this is of course the region for sea fish and eel (eel soup is the speciality of Hamburg). I can particularly recommend the crayfish tails with dill sauce and buttered rice, and the saddle of venison with smitane sauce and cranberries. But what makes the Vier Jahreszeiten outstanding is, as in all great hotels, the quality of the service. Here and in other good out-of-the-way hotels as yet unsullied by the tourist smear, 'service' is not yet a dirty word, and in these days to be surrounded by helpful, friendly faces is a luxury without price. Hamburg is particularly blessed in this respect because the Hamburger is a most excellent person, solid, friendly and cheerful, and apparently with a soft spot (Hamburg has been the most important harbour in the Continent of Europe for several hundred years) for the foreigner.

Traditionally democratic, there is yet a powerful aristocracy, or more properly elite, of reserved and ancient families in Hamburg. Without titles or other marks of nobility, they are generally accepted as being the 'City Fathers', with a patriarchal concern for Hamburg more powerful and effective than the municipal government. And how pleasing it is to be in a city which is really proud of itself, proud of its flag, which until a hundred years ago was better known overseas than the flag of Germany, proud of its dislike of the Prussians and its mistrust of Hitler, proud of its shipyards and of the way it has rebuilt itself after the war! And how well its town-planners are working, and what a contrast with some of the modern hideosity of the new Berlin! Here they are still rebuilding individual homes and modest apartment houses close to the earth, and not giant steel and glass structures that would ruin the character of the city.

Hamburg suffered terribly during the war. It was a comparatively easy target from England. Because of its naval importance, it always had a high priority from the Admiralty, and it was, to the delight of the scientists who advised on 'bombability', terribly combustible. Nearly fifty per cent of its dwellings – a quarter of a million of them – were annihilated, fifty-five thousand people were killed and hundreds of thousands wounded.

Over a period of nine days, from July 24th to August 3rd, 1942, occurred the great incendiary attacks called the *Katastrophe*. In these nine days, forty-eight thousand people were killed. People escaped from their burning houses and crumbling cellars into the streets only to stick immovable in the softened asphalt until this also caught fire, so that thousands of people out in the open were burnt to death in rivers of flame. For a whole week after the *Katastrophe* the sun was unable to penetrate the smoke. After this, three-quarters of a million people left the city and lived for months in the surrounding fields and woods. Learning these grisly facts I remembered how, in those days, studying the blown-up photographs from the Photographic Reconnaissance Unit and reading the estimates of damage, we in the Admiralty used to rub our hands with delight. Ah me!

At the end of the war Hamburg was saved by its

patriarchs. On Hitler's orders the town was to be defended to the last brick and demolition charges to implement the Fuhrer's scorched-earth policy were installed on a huge scale. Bremen did the same and was almost totally razed to the ground, but at the last moment the Hamburg patriarchs overrode the local Gauleiter and his henchmen and engineered the surrender of the town.

In 1946 the Allies completed the work of the bombs by destroying the slips in the great harbour and blowing up the yards and floating docks. Destruction was only halted when the town council pleaded that further explosions would breach the Elbe tunnel. Long arguments ensued and were only brought to a close by a sporting gesture from the British Consul, who took a chair to the centre of the Elbe tunnel and sat on it smoking his pipe at the moment when the final explosion was due. But, for reasons which I could not discover, the demolition was again postponed and finally cancelled, though the British Consul remains a local hero to this day.

A tour of the harbour, where the names of Blohm and Voss, Howaldt and Deutscher Werft, the great ship-yards where the U-boats were repaired and refitted, and where the *Bismarck* was built, brought back the war-time ghosts. But now the thirty-one miles of piers (the harbour is sixty-two miles up the Elbe from the sea) and the giant floating docks are ninety per cent effective again after the clearance of some three thousand wrecks, and the great shipscape is full of drama.

The weather prevented a day trip to Heligoland to visit the bird sanctuary, or to Sylt, half of which is still an R.A.F. establishment and the other half the largest nudist colony in the world (an intriguing combination!). Here on Sylt, at a certain point on the beaches, is a notice saying 'Nature Colony' and from there on it is an offence to wear clothes. A Hamburg friend who occasionally visits the place gave me a delightful picture of well-bred Hamburg citizens with no clothes on greeting friends with painful clicks of the heels and gracious 'Küss die Hand gnädige Fraus'.

Half-way down the Elbe there is an establishment which is apt to cause confusion and embarrassment to visiting ships and particularly to units of foreign navies. Here some enterprising innkeeper has set up 'Welcome Point Schulau' with a large coffee house and tea gardens. The Hamburgers come here to watch the ships sailing in and out of the river and the innkeeper has devised a private welcome system. As soon as an arriving ship comes within range, huge loudspeakers blare out three or four bars of the *Flying Dutchman,* followed by further bars of 'Stadt Hamburg', a local folksong. The ship is then greeted in German, followed by her native language, and the welcome is closed by the national anthem of the ship's country of origin, followed by a few more bars of the *Flying Dutchman.* At the beginning of the national anthem the Hamburg flag on top of the coffee house is dipped. Much the same rigmarole is followed for departing ships. Ships' captains who have been through this before now merely wave a cheerful hand, if that, but units of the Royal Navy have been known to go through frenzied counter-gallantries with hastily mustered hands standing to attention and every kind of ceremonial refinement – all much to the delight of the paying customers ashore.

Other pleasures of the city are Hagenbecks Zoo – built in 1884 and the first zoo without fences – a feature of which is the circus-animal training school, where you can judge whether this science involves cruelty or not; the *'Planten un Blomen'* (Hamburg dialect) Park, which is an enchantment; the Church of England, appropriately situated in the middle of St Pauli, where a resident English chaplain has officiated since 1612; the Hamburg History Museum, where there is the longest model railway, scale $\frac{1}{32}$, in Europe; the Modern Art Gallery, outstandingly well designed and containing an exciting collection of Impressionists and modern pictures (I just missed a much-lauded Hans Arp exhibition); excellent theatres (they gave the premiere of Lawrence Durrell's *Sappho* here); the Hansa Theater, the premier variety house in Germany, where drinks and snacks can be served during the show at all of the four hundred and eighty seats; several excellent restaurants headed, for me, by Ehmke, and, lower down the list, Onkel Hugo's in St Pauli, which is a good starting-point for the night life.

There is much literary and artistic activity in the town, which is the headquarters of the great post-war publishing empire of Springer; and Hamburg is the centre of the modern German film industry, at whose extensive studios Paul Rotha is now filming the life of Hitler with, surprisingly enough, the full collaboration of the Soviet Government, who have made available to him all their rich documentation on the subject.

One small point for the gastronome: you will be unable to find a hamburger in Hamburg – chopped steak is known there as Deutscher steak, and you would be considered eccentric if you were to slice open a roll and stuff your Deutscher steak inside it in the fashion of American hamburgers.

A last word of reassurance on the night life of Hamburg on which I may be thought to have dwelt immodestly and too long. The local guide-book says, 'The greatest charm St Pauli offers is that here you can watch people of all nations amusing themselves as they do at home.'

Ahem!

## INCIDENTAL INTELLIGENCE

*Hotels*
Five-star: Undoubtedly the best is the world-famous and dignified *Vierjahreszeiten,* the *Four Seasons,* in the Neuer Jungfemstieg. Hamburg's patrician families also swear by its cuisine, its grill and its snack bar, the *Condi.* The other main five-star hotel in Hamburg is the *Atlantic,* over-looking the Alster at its wateriest; it is more pretentious, but has superb service. The British Control Commission used it as a transit hotel after the

war, but that has not affected its quality today. I recommend also the *Baseler Hospiz,* on the Esplanade, comfortable, quiet, small and reasonably unpretentious. Its one hundred and ninety-eight rooms mostly have baths or showers. Rebuilt since the war-time bombing. Food is good North-German style, no frills, but wholesome and appetizing. Medium priced.

One-star: The *Park Hotel Beyer,* on the Blumenstrasse, a quarter of an hour from the centre of Hamburg, quiet, comfortable and small. Room prices range from 13 Marks, (£1 1s. 0d.) for single room without bath to 40 Marks (£3 4s. 0d.) for double room with bath, both without breakfast. Cheaper but brasher and noisier is the newly built Hotel *Im Parkhochhaus am Dammtor,* Drehbahn 15, in the centre of the city.

## Restaurants

Five-star: *Lembcke,* on the Holzdamm 49, near the *Atlantic Hotel.* Famous for the quality of its meat; popular with the local theatrical community, a sort of Hamburg Cafe Royal as it used to be, with a touch of neo-Victorian or neo-Wilhelmian about it. As an alternative the *Kleine Führhaus,* Harvestehuder Fährdamm on the Alster. One of Hamburg's fashionable restaurants, patronized by all the visiting *Prominenz.* Another old-fashioned and excellent restaurant on the Gansemarkt in the town centre is *Ehmke.* Speciality: oysters.

One-star: I can recommend the *Fischereihafen-Restaurant,* on the Neuen Fischereihafen in Altona, right on the fish harbour itself. Small, popular with food-lovers, fairly inexpensive. Speciality: Hamburg crayfish and eel soups, and a sort of Hamburg *bouillabaisse*.

## Night-clubs

Five-star: For dancing, used by the jeunesse dorée of the patrician families: the *Riverside*, Alster Arkaden. Usually a first-class band. Owned by an Italian. Excellent food, no floor show but usually frequented by lots of pretty girls.

One-star: The Reeperbahn has everything to offer, from the big, breezy strip-tease girl-shows at the *Trichter* and the *Allotria* to quieter dance-hall places like the *Café Lauser*, where the dancing partners are the prettiest in Hamburg but only dance with the customers if invited to. It is different at the *Café Keese* where ladies can make the running and male guests have to take the floor when asked.

Out-of-the-Way: The *Glocken-Kate*, Eichholz 15, an unusual but popular night-spot visited mainly by Hamburg people. The owner, an ex-ship's cook, puts on nightly performances on a remarkable one-man band, a sort of Madame Tussaud orchestra of dummy figures playing different instruments and all done by means of strings, ropes and pulleys. Absolutely no deception! A sort of Dali-ish nonsense which appeals to the Hamburgers.

# 9

# Berlin

Every capital city has its own smell. London smells of fried fish and Player's, Paris of coffee, onions and Caporals, Moscow of cheap eau-de-Cologne and sweat. Berlin smells of cigars and boiled cabbage, and B.E.A. dropped me into the middle of the smell on the kind of day I associate with this lugubrious city. The sky was asphalt-colour above the asphalt-coloured town, and the Prussian wind, as sharp as a knife, blew the rubble dust into one's eyes and mouth.

Berlin was fifty per cent destroyed during the war as part of the great *Strafe,* the great corporal punishment meted out to the people who have caused more pain and grief in the world than any other nation in this century. Around eight million Germans were killed in the last war and, in West Germany alone, there survive nearly three and a half million victims, maimed, widowed and orphaned, drawing war pensions amounting to over four billion D-marks annually, and the reverberations of the tremendous thrashing Berlin received still hang on the air.

As I walked and drove through the West Sector and

the East, noting the smattering of new buildings and the rather meagre and sham-looking new streets and housing projects, I was accompanied by the echo of vast and shattering explosions, and expected at any moment to see the town crumble away again in smoke and flames.

The tidying up goes on apace, but there are still acres and acres that will have to be knocked down before there can be any real impression of a new city rising from the ruins of the old.

This is very much more so, of course, in the Eastern Sector, where remembered death and chaos and, worst of all, present drabness hang most heavily on the air, and where there is no speck of colour or glitter in the cleaning up that has already, with typical Russian bad taste and skimped workmanship, been achieved. This contrast with the West is underlined by comparison between the two great Berlin streets, Kurfürstendamm in the West and Under den Linden in the East.

The former, though only a shadow of its old self, is brightly lit and thronged and busy. Its rather uninteresting shops are wide open to business and the cafes are crowded. But Unter den Linden now contains only a handful of drab, makeshift shops against a great backdrop of ruins, and the new lime trees are skimpy and stark. Few people are about and few cars and, as in all the Eastern Sector, one wonders where in heaven everybody is.

The seventy million cubic metres of rubble in Berlin are gradually being made into mountains, which then will be turfed and have trees planted on them. These mountains are known as *Monte Klamotten* – Rubbish Mountains – and the total operation is known as 'Hitler's Collected Works'.

There are also the flattened plains, from which the new buildings are gradually rising to give living-space and workroom to the two and a quarter million West Berliners, and I spent some time visiting the more publicized of these new erections, notably the Hansa Settlement and the Corbusier 'living unit' built more or less on his 'Modulor' system, and vaunted as the 'new face' of Berlin.

This 'new face' is the 'new face' we are all coming to know – the 'up-ended-packet-of-fags' design for the maximum number of people to live in the minimum amount of space.

This system treats the human being as a six-foot cube of flesh and breathing-space and fits him with exquisite economy into steel and concrete cells. He is allotted about three times the size of his cube as his 'bed-sitter', once his cube for his bathroom and once for his kitchen. So that he won't hate this cellular existence too much, he is well warmed and lighted, and he is provided with a chute in the wall through which he can dispose of the muck of his life – cartons, newspapers, love-letters and gin bottles – the last chaotic remains of his architecturally undesirable 'non-cube' life. These untidy bits of him are consumed by some great iron stomach in the basement.

Having taken a quick and shuddering look at

Corbusier's flattened human ants' nest in Marseilles some years ago, and having visited his recent architectural exhibition in England, I had already decided that he and I did not see eye to eye in architectural matters, and I am glad to learn that the Berliners, however anxious to clamber out of their ruins into a new home, are inclined to agree with me. When they heard of his plan and were later sharply lectured by him on the life beautiful, they christened him the 'Devil with Thick Spectacles', and his two-thousand-person apartment house – if it can be so called – is still ungratefully known as the 'Living Machine'. Much to his rage, their chaotic wishes partially triumphed over the symmetrical bee-ant mathematical principles on which his mumbo-jumbological Modular system is based. This system lays down, in part, that the correct height of a room shall be a six-foot man with his arm raised straight above his head (try it!). Corbusier complained that the increase in height from 2.26 metres to 2.50 metres that the Berliners forced upon him had painfully upset what he describes as his 'architectonic masterpiece', and he was even more bitter when the authorities decided that his 'living units' were, in fact, not the 'paradise for children and mothers' which he claimed they were, and turned them into apartments for bachelors and childless couples. The shop centre which he wished to place in the middle of his sixteen storeys was put down on the ground floor, which spoilt 'the grandeur of the entrance hall'.

The argument was a wonderful example of the eternal struggle between the designer-planner and the awkward

'Our Man in Germany', Antony Terry, sometimes in company with his wife, Sarah Gainham, the noted thriller-writer and correspondent for the *Spectator*. Between them, they know most of Germany, and certainly every inch of Berlin, and in Terry's Volkswagen we proceeded on a series of splendid zigzags between pleasures and duties which, for the sake of brevity, I will cannibalize into a rather haphazard catalogue.

Queen Nefertiti, for instance, rescued from the coal-mine at Eisenach, where she and most of the German art treasures spent the war, is now back in the Dahlem museum, her proud, smiling lips looking as kissable as ever. Hitler's bunker in the Eastern Zone finally resisted all attempts by the Russians to blow it up, so it has now been converted into a hillock of rubble and will soon be a pretty green mound in the middle of a children's playground. The ruins of the Gedächtnis-Kirche rise, and will apparently for ever rise, like a huge ugly thumb at the top of the Kurfürstendamm – gloomy memorial to yet another war. The church's aesthetic shape could be greatly improved by a few more artistically sited explosions. The grim ruin will be somewhat cheered by a carillon of six new bells, for which Prince Louis Ferdinand, the last of the Hohenzollerns and grandson of Kaiser Wilhelm, has composed a melody. The Stauffenberg memorial, a naked youth in bronze, commemorating the July 1944 attempt to assassinate Hitler, stands in the gloomy, cavernous courtyard of Hitler's Army and Navy Communications Centre, against a background of massive chunks of reinforced concrete that will for ever resist the demolition experts. The porter, Knoeller, who was there at the time of Stauffenberg's execution, showed us the spot where he had stood facing the firing squad. 'No,' he said, 'there were no bullet holes in the walls; all such executions were carried out against a background of broken rubble, so that the masonry should not show evidence of the shooting.' This is a particularly haunted area of Berlin, hard by the Landwehr canal, into which the body of Rosa Luxemburg was thrown after she and Karl Liebknecht were captured and shot, 'while trying to escape', by the Brigade Ehrhard during the Spartakus rising of 1919.

The Hotel Adlon, where I had revelled before the war, is in the Eastern Sector and is now only Number 70A, Wilhelmstrasse. Nothing remains of the former glory, about which a whole book has been written, and you enter the surviving bullet-marked three storeys through the old servants' entrance. We had cups of thickly grained coffee in the 'restaurant', a kind of tatty 'good-pull-up-for-carmen' with the beige wallpaper and dusty potted cacti that are the hallmark of Russian restaurant decor. The only other guests were a peaky, taut-skinned little man with a compulsive, hysterical face, obviously an informer or a blackmarketeer, whispering to a prosperous-looking businessman while his tow-haired mistress (we assumed) sipped her Caucasian Burgundy.

The Pergamon Museum is perhaps the only real 'must' in the Russian Sector. Here, in great majesty, have been reassembled the famed classical treasures of Germany, recently handed back by Russia. Here, in particular, is the Pergamon Altar Frieze, assembled in one vast hall against an architectural background of great splendour. As the Michelin guide would say, it is definitely 'worth the detour'.

Incidentally, this splendid museum is noteworthy for one particular piece of Communist nonsense. Throughout, the exhibits are not dated 'B.C.' but 'V.U.Z.' (before our times), and 'A.D.' is not given at all.

From these grandeurs to the Alexanderplatz for a nervous glance at the East German Secret Police Headquarters, hard by Gunther Podola's old private school and the grimy house where he spent much of his youth. On the other side of the square are the remains of Hitler's notorious Secret Police Headquarters. The whole area, for me, was full of past and present screams, and we scurried off across the frontier to the friendly lights and busy turmoil of West Berlin and a *Molle und Korn* (boiler-maker and his assistant) of beer and schnapps.

Over this 'traveller's joy', beneath the infra-red heaters of the Cafe Marquardt, we watched our neighbours consuming the economic 'one cup of coffee and seven glasses of water' of the old-time cafe squatters, and, outside, the dangerous traffic hurtling up and down the Kurfürstendamm. Antony Terry said that Germany has the highest traffic-accident rate in the world – more than double the English figures. The Germans, anyway a hysterical race, are now almost

maddened by overwork – particularly in the management class. They spend their days in their offices and
then roar off down the autobahns. They fall asleep at
eighty miles an hour, and their cars tear across the
middle section, head-on into cars in the opposite lane,
or dive off the shoulders of the roads into the trees.
To prevent this, the drivers munch Pervitin or Preludin
to keep themselves awake, thus submerging their
exhaustion and heightening their tension. Heart disease,
accelerated by over-eating food cooked in the universal
cheap frying-fat, carries them off in their early fifties,
and the newspapers are every day full of those black-
bordered memorial notices saying that Herr Direktor
So-and-so has passed away 'at the height of his powers'.

Antony Terry drives ten thousand miles a year on
the autobahns and, referring to our M1 and our hunger
for more super highways, he doubted whether such
panaceas would reduce our accident rate. These huge
roads, he said, create their own type of accident and,
by building them, you only replace one kind of accident
with another kind. People get semi-hypnotized and doze
off at the wheel.

After a couple more 'boiler-makers' we went on to
the Ritz, one of the half-dozen first-class restaurants
in Berlin, with a menu in eight languages. There, over
a wonderful dinner, Terry passed on the gossip of the
day – how the famous publishing house of Ullstein
had just been bought by Springers, the great post-war
publishing phenomenon; of the *Reptilienfonds*, the
reptile or slush fund of the West German ministries

for what is comprehensively known as 'Middle Eastern good relations' – the providing of suitable feminine entertainment for visiting heads of minor states; of the fact that there was no beatnik movement in Germany because there were now no traditions to revolt against; of the small importance of the *Halbstarke, Zazous,* or teddy boys in Germany; of the complete standstill in all literary and artistic progress of any kind since Hitler because of the absence of Jews, the former leaven in the heavy German bread, and of the greatly exaggerated hullabaloo recently created, largely by newspapers wanting 'a story', about the resurgence of Nazism and anti-Semitism.

And so for a brief tour, which ended at four o'clock in the morning, of Berlin night life.

It is certainly not what it used to be in Berlin, though there is still the emphasis on transvestism – men dressing up as women, and vice versa – which used to be such a feature of pre-war Berlin. Now, at the Eldorado, for instance, and the Eden (where a home-made bomb went off, wounding three guests, ten minutes after we had left) some of the 'women' are most bizarre. The one I particularly took to, a middle-aged flower-seller such as you might see sitting beside her basket of roses in Piccadilly Circus, is known as the '*Blumenfeldwebel*'. 'She' had been a corporal in a Panzer division and has an astonishing range of Berlin/Cockney repartee. Some time ago, when a famous English film producer was working in Berlin, she attached herself so closely to him that she was finally given a walk-on part in the film, and all she was interested in now was to try and get over to England to get another job from him. Another startlingly beautiful 'woman' had been an under-officer in charge of a military clothing store; but the most startling was 'Ricky Renee', an American aged twenty-five who was born in Miami, had only a modest success as a male tap-dancer and decided to turn 'woman'. He has been so sensational in his new role that he even appeared as a woman in a strip-tease act in the Italian film *Il Mondo di Notte*.

The 'waitresses' were most ingenious at serving one while somehow keeping their huge hands and feet out of sight and modulating the deep tones of their voices when they took your order, but otherwise they were buttressed, bewigged and made-up as extremely handsome and decorous 'ladies'.

Two of the other night-clubs were also splendidly Germanic – the famous *Resi,* a vast hall where nothing happens except that there are dial telephones on the tables so that you can communicate with any girl who takes your fancy round the room, and a 'cabaret' which consists, uniquely, of a giant waterworks which shoots dancing jets of coloured water into the air to the accompaniment of the 'Dance of the Bumblebee'.

The other night-club, even less inspiring, consisted of a smallish area with a sawdust ring in the centre containing two plump and docile horses. In between drinks, one was permitted to mount a horse and trot it a dozen times round the ring – a remarkable way to pass an evening.

Espionage is one of the main industries of Berlin – East and West – and I spent most of one day exploring the fringes – the centre is far too well protected – of the great spy battle of which Berlin has been the battle-field since the end of the war. I concentrated on one great independent operator – a notorious middle-man who sells his 'informations' for whatever sum whichever of the Western secret services will pay. I will call him O. He lives in the leafy suburbs in a monstrous Hansel and Gretel villa whose innocence is only belied by the spy-hole in the front door. He is a small, plump, amused man (all such agents have a humorous, ironical attitude towards what they describe as 'the game') with the perfect command of languages that comes probably from a Slav origin. He chain-smoked Muratti filter cigarettes with the first gold tips I have seen for years. He was as apparently open-handed and ready to gossip as any civilized man who has plenty of small 'informa-tions' which sound secret but are not, and he correctly assumed that I would be tactful and not probe too deeply behind the gossip.

'You must understand that it is all getting so much more difficult, Mr Fleming. My friends [spy-talk for his Western employers] are more selective and the opposi-tion's security is now very good. There have been fifteen years to indoctrinate the Eastern Sector in security and now anything which is important, any secret, is cut up into slices – the tactics, location, technique, finance, personnel behind, let us say, a chain of missile bases – and possession of one slice of knowledge in each of those departments of knowledge is confined to a small cell of people – only those who *have* to be in the know. This makes for confusion and bad liaison on the project, since there is bound to be over-lapping between these realms of knowledge, but it also makes for very tight security. Then if there is a leak, that leak can be traced to one cell of about five people. After that there are the investigations – background, friends, bank account, the usual things, and then there is the execution. So penetration is most difficult and dangerous. And then there is the question of the payment for informations. In the good old days one could offer refuge in the West and money and good living and the "democratic way of life" – freedom and all that. Today it is not so easy, and everyone is surprised that Soviet and East German officials and officers and so on are not bringing over informations in exchange for these things. Such a misunderstanding is foolish. The answer is that in the East people no longer want these things. Life is very much better now in the Soviet bloc. To the intelligent people, the people we would like to come over, the future with Communism looks just as good, if not better, than life in Europe and America. Such people are not attracted to democratic chaos. They think we over here are making a hash of things in the name of Democracy. They greatly prefer the symmetry of Communism and the planned economy – particularly when the plans seem to be successful. And – the sputnik and so on have helped here – they are quite sure they are on the winning side, that Russia is stronger than the West. These people are realistic. Why should they exchange these solid things for the trashy "comforts" of the West where they would have to start all over again, suffer from the homesickness which they have so strongly, and perhaps be traced and shot for treachery into the bargain? No, Mr Fleming, we must admit that the millions of dollars spent on propaganda – the huge transmitters, those ridiculous leaflet balloons and so on – are wasted money and effort at this moment. Successful propaganda only comes from strength. To offer people better shoes and clothes, and jazz, is not enough. And, of course, you must remember that the youth in the East, the German youth, is now almost fully educated in Communism. He is sixteen years old and Communism is all he knows. If his parents tell him otherwise, they are being as old-fashioned as children all over the world consider their parents.'

All this suggested to me that O. would soon be out of a job, but he explained that in espionage Parkinson's Law operates with particular zest. There were some ten thousand Communist agents now in Western Germany, he said. They were concentrated in many hundred organizations, divided again into cells. Against this army, a huge counter-intelligence army had to be arrayed. Then, with the increased difficulty in penetrating the East, a larger force of specialists had to be employed by the West. Thus, to gain a smaller bulk of Eastern 'informations', many more Western spies were required. But on both sides the whole business had become far more professional. There was not the old free-for-all of the happy ten years after the war, when a huge game of grown-up cops and robbers was being played across the frontiers, and kidnappings, murders and 'traitors' were the order of the day. Had I, for instance, ever heard the true story of the 'Great Tunnel'? That had been a lark, all right.

I said I had read some scraps about it in the papers at the time – in 1956 – but the story had been played down, I had supposed, for security reasons.

O. laughed. 'More probably embarrassment,' he said. 'You can't be insecure about a story the Russians published in all their papers, with pictures of the tunnel and the English equipment. The Russians even took all the Western correspondents out in buses and took them down the damned thing to see for themselves. It was really a marvellous affair. This is how it all happened.

'Some time in 1955 your intelligence people were looking at the town plan map for Greater Berlin when some bright communications man spotted that the main trunk telephone cables between East Berlin and Leipzig at one point passed underground only about three hundred yards from a bulge in the American sector. Others of your people worked out that these cables would be carrying the traffic between the headquarters of the East German Army at Aldershorst and Zossen, East Germany's Aldershot, so to speak. There was even more excitement when it was proved that a Russian official teleprinter cable was another of the lines. So your people got together with the Americans and plans were made to tap these cables by digging a tunnel under the fields from a near-by American radar station as far as the Schonefelder Chaussee, under which the cables ran. Obviously it was a terrific technical job, and a very tricky one because all the time Russian patrols were passing along the road, and the security aspect in the American sector was another problem. I believe there was a bad moment when the peasant who owned the field began cutting his corn and the watchers in the American sector saw that the roof of their tunnel had made a ramp right across his field that was even more obvious when he put the land under the plough again. However, he didn't seem to mind then, although it's amusing that after the whole thing blew up, so to speak, the peasant sued the Americans and the innocent Russians for ruining the subsoil of his field, and trespass and Heaven knows what all. Anyway, the tunnel was finished and the line tapped and hundreds of batteries of tape-recorders were plugged in to the lines and operated for months all through the twenty-four hours, and hundreds of British and Americans were employed translating all the wonderful stuff they must have got out of the tunnel.

'Then, of course, the inevitable happened. The stretch of road where the tunnel met the cables was always kept under watch, and one day the watchers saw one of those usual telephone repair gangs arrive in a lorry and start lazily digging up the vital few yards of road. There was nothing to do but evacuate as quickly as possible, and no time to dismantle the rooms full of machinery underground. Two or three of the personnel were left to listen behind the door of a compartment and they heard the amazed comments of the workmen, who had apparently just chosen that particular spot to look for a fault in one of the cables caused by a rainwater leak. Then the game was up, and lorry loads of Russian experts and troops with tommy-guns arrived and blocked off the area and started their investigations. The whole story was given to the press and worked up into a big scandal, involving the Americans, of course, and also the British, because all the technical machinery was marked "Property of the G.P.O."! All the Americans could do to save their faces was to put up a notice in the tunnel directly under the frontier line saying, "Beware. You are now entering the American Sector." They even forgot to turn off the electric light in the tunnel!

'Anyway,' concluded O., 'those were the great days. Now, both sides are more *"korrekt"* – and of course no one wants any untidy scandals in the spy war while Summits are the order of the day. But that doesn't mean,' he laughed, 'that in Greater Berlin today there isn't one whole division of Allied spies on one side of the frontier and one whole division of Communist spies on the other. It is still a very big and important business.'

O. then handed me a copy of a hush-hush East German intelligence document giving the complete 'family tree' of the secret service organization in the Ministry for State Security in East Berlin, from which I note the existence of two interesting departments,

*Abteilung* 4, 'For military espionage and deception in the NATO forces in West Germany and in NATO headquarters in Paris', and *Abteilung* 8, 'Diversion and sabotage, preparations for "X" Day', and over this parting gift we said goodbye.

I left Berlin without regret. From this grim capital went forth the orders that in 1917 killed my father and in 1940 my youngest brother. In contra-distinction to Hamburg and to so many other German towns, it is only in Berlin and in the smoking cities of the Ruhr that I think I see, against my will, the sinister side of the German nation. In these two regions I smell the tension and hysteria that breed the things we have suffered from Germany in two great wars and that, twice in my lifetime, have got my country to her knees. In these places I have a recurrent waking nightmare: it is ten, twenty, fifty years later in the Harz Mountains, or in the depths of the Black Forest. The whole of a green and smiling field slides silently back to reveal the dark mouth of a great subterranean redoubt. With a whine of thousands of horsepower, behind a mass of brilliant machinery (brain-children of Krupp, Siemens, Zeiss and all the others) the tip of a gigantic rocket emerges above the surrounding young green trees. England has rejected the ultimatum. First there is a thin trickle of steam from the rocket exhausts and then a great belch of flame, and slowly, very slowly, the rocket climbs off its underground launching pad. And then it is on its way.

Yes, it was obviously time for me to leave Berlin.

## INCIDENTAL INTELLIGENCE

*Hotels*

Five-star: For comfort and a bit of the solid, efficient, old-style atmosphere and service one remembers from pre-war, though in modern streamlined form: *Kempinski,* Kurfürstendamm (West Berlin's Piccadilly), corner of Fasanenstrasse and the centre of what night life there still is in the Western sectors. Plushier, even more five-star, ultra-modern and with *square* beds (you can sleep any way round you like) is the *Hilton.* Its rooms look out over a wonderful all-round view of the grey bomb-battered city. Those sleeping on the lower floors are awakened early by strange birds squawking in the city's zoo just below.

One-star: For those seeking to recapture the Berlin atmosphere of 1945 amid the ruins I suggest one of the small, reasonably priced one-star hotels just by the former Anhalter Station. This is in the waste-land of rubble that was once Berlin's business centre and was flattened in the final battle for the city. It is a few yards from the Russian sector – though still firmly in the West and a quarter of a mile from the Potsdamer Platz, the East–West sector border trouble spot. One of these 'atmosphere' hotels on the Soviet sector border is the *Alemannia.* The Volkspolizei here is within shooting distance but doesn't. One-star but clean. One can eat there too, simple Berlin kitchen. Less exciting: the *Astoria Hotel* near the Zoo in the British Sector (Fasanenstrasse) is small but efficient.

## Restaurants

Five-star: Renowned for Oriental chi-chi of every kind and for its famous customers, the *Ritz* in the Rankestrasse (centre of town). For good, clean, appetizing, reasonably-priced food of the Berlin type: the *Aben,* at the Halensee end of the Kurf-Grstendamm, much patronized by the gourmets among the British regiments stationed in Berlin, or the *Berliner Kindl,* where Berliners of all classes go for a good meal in the evening, with beer. Chinese food, for those who like it, in at least five excellent restaurants of this type, the best undoubtedly the *Lingnan,* Kurfürstendamm, the *Canton,* Stuttgarter Platz, and the *Hongkong,* next to the *Maison de France,* Kurfürstendamm. For Swabian cooking (richer and more seasoned than Berlin food) in an old-fashioned, restful background with a zither-player who specializes in the *Third Man* theme and Viennese 'Schrammel', there is *Kottler's* in the Motzstrasse, and Berlin gourmets swear by *Schlichte* in the Martin Luther Strasse. Despite its austere furnishings and rather-too-bright lights, *Schlichte* undoubtedly has wonderful cuisine.

For 'British, Americans and French only' (still respect-fully 'messieurs les alliés' in four-power Berlin), the *Maison de France,* a reasonably priced official French restaurant where the food is not over-good but there is dancing and a pleasant enough atmosphere, and a good bar with an excellent barman who knows his stuff. Anything from Amer Picon ('pour les fievres nevralge-uses des colonisateurs') to Scotch. Cheapest possible French-owned student-type restaurant with excellent

freshly cooked food, though atmosphere ever so slightly
Frenchily grubby: the *Paris* in the Kantstrasse, across
the road from the West Berlin opera house and near
the university and zoo.

## Night-clubs

West Berlin's night spots are not what they were in the
gay, spendthrift post-war years, but they do offer some
interesting sidelines such as transvestism. One of the
two main night-clubs of this type is the Eldorado, Martin
Luther Strasse (U.S. sector), which presents transvestism
as a sort of joke, with the floor show taking the mickey
out of itself. The *Eldorado* is definitely one or two-star
in its prices, but fairly respectable; one could almost
take the family there and not know the 'girls' are not
what they seem unless one knew it beforehand. Prices:
entrance charge 1s. 8d., Scotch (nip) 5s. 6d., French
brandy 4s. 2d., beer 3s. 4d. Turkish coffee (pot) 3s. 4d.,
wine about £1 a bottle.

Five-star (but not expensive): the *Old-Fashioned*,
admission only after knocking three times and asking
for Franz Schubert (the owner, no relation of the other
Franz Schubert); dancing, excellent Italian band, quite
a lot of pretty girls among the customers. Patronized
by whatever society is left in the Four-Power City. The
*Cherchez la Femme*: little *boîte* in the Fasanenstrasse,
semi-nude dancing of a strictly respectable type and
occasionally neo-strip-tease act. *Charly's*, Wittenberg-
platz, plushy; *boîte* for dancing only, to juke-box
(latest Berlin craze); fashionable with Berlin's moneyed

jeunesse dorée at the moment, but not expensive. *Badewanne* (the Bath Tub), Nurnberger Strasse, jive cellar, good to look at for a few moments, popular with visiting theatrical personalities, cheap and loud but bursting with Berlin vitality. *Resi*, in the Hasenheide in one of West Berlin's toughest, most working-class districts; recent statistics show that seventy per cent of its customers are foreigners. Most popular of all Berlin mass entertainments. A vast palais de danse with telephones and pneumatic-tube postal service connecting the hundreds of tables, so that strangers can make dates or pass anonymous compliments. *Remde St Pauli,* near the zoo, centre of town in British sector; noisy, raucous, slap-and-tickle sort of show, based on Hamburg's Reeperbahn, with 'underwear displays' (ladies *and* gents), and girls, girls, girls (on the stage, no hostesses). Like the *Resi*, it has reasonable prices.

*Out-of-the-way*
*Rififi,* open twenty-four hours a day for the younger generation of Berliners to spend their spare time with juke-box and jive. The dancing is not for visitors unless they are expert too, but it is worth seeing once, on a visit. The customers (and the busty proprietress) could have come out of the film *Rififi,* but visitors are treated kindly and otherwise ignored.

of us islanders, from the first cobbled kilometres at Calais, Boulogne, Ostend, to the sad day when you re-embark as the lucky ones' cars are being unloaded, Continental touring is one of the most delightful experiences in our lives.

I drive a Thunderbird. I make no apologies. I bought my first, the lovely two-seater, four years ago and it did 50,000 fast miles without so much as a bulb fusing. So I bought another, the four-seater, and it had only done 1,000 miles when I started from Ostend. Blithely I had ordered all the gimmicks – automatic gears, power steering, power brakes – and at first I hated and feared these devices which seemed to give the car power over the driver instead of the other way round. But by now I was already used to them, and I had regained authority over the fifty-horse-power, seven-litre engine, and could almost – you never quite can with these damnable 'aids' – make the car do what I wanted. Of course it is a marvellous car for fast touring – very comfortable, roomy, and as quick as hell. Ninety miles an hour with a reserve of thirty was a comfortable touring speed on the autobahns, and the kilometres clicked by like the leaves of a book until one could gratefully drift off into the winding side roads of the countryside chosen for luncheon or the night. For that is the way to treat the autobahn – as the quickest way between beautiful places off the beaten track. That day I did Hamburg to Kassel for luncheon and then slipped off on to the 'romantic' road from Bad Herzfeld to Würzburg, Rothenburg,

Dinkelsbtihl and Augsburg, staying the night in the heart of this beautiful region.

It was here, after leaving the autobahn, that one met with the things dear to the lover of Germany and Austria – the vast dandelion meadows, the delicious smell of dung and sound of sawmills in the little villages, and the dreaming spires of small churches. The spring had been wonderful at home, but how fortunate to be able to pursue it northwards and catch all the fruit trees in bright bloom again! It crossed my mind that one day one should start with the spring in southern Spain and drive slowly northwards, perhaps even as far as Moscow, living with it all the way.

But then the next day one was on the autobahn again, flying on to Munich and Salzburg, engaged simply in covering the kilometres in order to be in Vienna by the evening.

Driving six hundred miles in a couple of days, which my programme demanded, one gets to think a good deal about the actual business of driving a motor-car. The Germans are the most dangerous motorists in the world. The year before, 13,500 Germans had been killed on the road and just under half a million injured. These are terrible figures among a population of fifty-two million, and nobody knows what to do about it. It is no good building 100 m.p.h. roads and putting a 50 m.p.h. speed limit on them, and anyway the German statistics showed that the majority of accidents were caused at speeds between 30 and 50 m.p.h. Germanic tension and hysteria, plus that basic inferiority complex which makes every German insist that only *he* has the right of way, lie somewhere behind these tragic statistics, but here, and along the autobahns of Italy, I had some autobahn thoughts which may be worth passing on.

First of all, your driving mirror (surely not 'looking-glass' in this context, Miss Mitford!) is almost as important as your windscreen, and the slower your car the more you must watch what is coming up behind you. Flashing headlights, which I hope British manu-facturers will soon fit, with a button on the tip of the indicator arm, are far more effective than horn-blowing, for so many small cars on the autobahns drive with the windows nearly closed to keep out the windhowl. Above all, it is wise to assume that people will behave oddly at the *Ausfahrts* and *Einfahrts* where there are joining roads. Personally, among the Herrenvolk – the Herren in their Mercedes or Opels, the Volk in their Wagens – I found road-discipline excellent, and I only saw one accident, a Volkswagen crumpled like a paper bag being craned out of a hedge-row by the rescue service; but everywhere on the cement surface there are those terrible graffiti of the skid-marks, where, on a perfectly straight stretch of road, something has gone terribly wrong for someone.

As one drives along, one muses about automobile design and one wonders why certain minor refinements are not universally adopted. If America, for instance, fits all her cars with double headlights side by side, are they perhaps better than English and Continental single headlights? Is France right to insist on yellow headlights? If not, why do they do it? Does a hanging chain behind really help car sickness? If the chain, for reasons of insulation, is compulsory on petrol lorries in Austria, why not in other countries? Why in England do we have bend and corner signs with 'bend' and 'corner' written underneath, when the rest of the world seems to manage without these childish explanations? Why do we not adopt the international sign for a skidding road? Why do the A.A. routes remain so stuffy and old-fashioned, and confine their comments to 'fast, undulating road', 'well-wooded countryside', and interminable lists of churches? Fortunately nowadays every motorist abroad picks up, from Shell, B.P. or Esso, the excellent free maps and regional guides whenever he fills up with petrol, but it is surely time for the A.A. to apply some of their overflowing revenue to hiring a small team of first-class travel writers to improve the content and style of their touring routes!

By far the most impressive car on the autobahns was the Volkswagen. These miracle cars seem to thrive on speed, and they hammer along at a steady 80 m.p.h. with, according to all accounts, astonishingly little driver fatigue. It is extraordinary to think that England was offered the Volkswagen business as part of reparations. A delegation (one can see them!) was sent out by the British motor industry, lavishly entertained, and, after a cursory glance over the main factory, agreed that cars with engines at the back had, in the eyes of Coventry, no future, and went home. Out of pity for this ugly duckling, and to provide employment, the British occupation authorities placed an order for 20,000 cars to put the business on its feet again. Today (1959) they are turning out nearly 4,000 vehicles every twenty-four hours, and last year they exported 404 thousand. The business has just been turned into a public company with a capital of £50 million, and the break-up value of the concern and its assets are estimated by the Deutsche Industrie Kreditinstitut at £125 million. Credit for the basic design belongs to Dr Porsche, father of the present head of the Porsche sports-car business. To eliminate any 'bugs' in his design he had the original prototypes tested to destruction in the Austrian Alps by relays of S.S. men. He was, incidentally, like the inventor of the first automobile, an Austrian. I wonder what the British motorcar delegation think of his invention today!

Whenever possible I follow great rivers on the wrong side. I keep, for instance, to the west of the Rhône and off the fast, murderous N7. So, with the Danube, I crossed over at Linz and, after a short patch of attractive though dangerously narrow minor road, got on, at Grein, to the beautiful 'wine road' that hugs the north shore of the Danube more or less all the way into Vienna.

I had not been to Vienna, seriously, for thirty years. It is not one of my favourite cities. I learned German in the Tyrol from Mr Ernan Forbes Denis, husband of the famous novelist Phyllis Bottome, and then honorary Vice-Consul for the Tyrol, based on Kitzbühel. They were both ardent students of the great psychologist

Alfred Adler – Phyllis Bottome wrote Adler's life – and I learned far more about life from Ernan than from all my schooling put together. But living in the Tyrol for so long made me such a devoted lover of the Tyrolese that I took against the brittle and, it seemed to me, artificial gaiety of the Viennese and their much vaunted *Gemütlichkeit* which I translated, and still translate, into a mixture of shallowness, cynicism and untidiness. (I have been back to the Tyrol countless times since those early days and I am confirmed in the opinion that they are my favourite people in the world.)

Returning to Vienna after so many years' absence, I found two great changes for the worse: the appalling congestion and noise that have hit all the capital cities (they have a good name for the motor-scooter – *Schlurfrakete* – Spivrocket), and the collapse of the pulsating intellectual life that was one of the great delights of Vienna before Hitler marched in.

I remember, in those days before the war, reading, thanks to the encouragement of the Forbes Denises, the works of Kafka, Musil, the Zweigs, Arthur Schnitzler, Werfel, Rilke, von Hofmannstal, and of those bizarre psychologists Weininger and Groddeck – let alone the writings of Adler and Freud – and buying first editions (I used to collect them) illustrated by Kokoschka and Kubin. As I remember it, all these and many others made of Vienna a kind of Central-European Left Bank into whose fringes it was delightful to penetrate. In those days there seemed to be count-less small satirical cabarets frequented by these people where, for a few Shillings, one could boast of having rubbed shoulders with genius. All this has utterly gone (though the Simplizissimus cabaret still has some of the sharp, destructive Austrian wit); and what has come musically out of Vienna, the city of Haydn, Mozart, Beethoven, Bruckner, Schubert, Strauss and Lehar, in the last twenty years?

The intellectual demise of Vienna must, as must that of Munich and Berlin, be put down to the wholesale departure of 200,000 Jews who, whatever else their failings – and the race is generally considered to have shown itself in poor colours at this confluence of Slav and Central-European Jewry – create an atmosphere in which the intellect appears to flourish astonishingly.

I doubt if Vienna will ever regain her Bohemian atmosphere. With the total absence of an aristocracy or of any other elite (except for the ski champions), the Austrian bureaucrat, who is essentially a small man waiting for his pension, has complete control of the country. There is not a single Austrian millionaire, and not even a *nouveau riche* clique to provide artistic patronage. Moreover, neutrality does not create a stimulating atmosphere, and there are no tax benefits in Austria as there are in Switzerland to attract the modern intellectual exile. Nor does Vienna seem to regret her abdication from the world of the spirit. Although she has produced two Nobel Peace Prize winners and twelve Nobel Prize winners in medicine, physics and chemistry, how many of these people worked or received encouragement within their own national frontiers? It was an

Austrian who constructed the first typewriter, another who invented the sewing-machine, another who constructed the first automobile, and another the first incandescent gas-mantle, to say nothing of the Kaplan turbine and the slow-motion camera. But who *developed* these things? Certainly not the Austrians. The truth is that the Austrian of the cities is a wonderful shrugger of shoulders, a witty denigrator, a man who really means it when he says, 'What does it matter?' 'Who cares?' And basically he hates all modern inventions and 'progress' for the simple reason that Franz Joseph hated them.

It is of course in this splendidly frivolous attitude to life that lies the real 'charm' of Austria for the visitor, and the despair of governments. By comparison with Italy, France and Switzerland, for instance, how wonderful it is to be in a beautiful country whose inhabitants are so incompetent at extracting money from tourists, who make it a matter of personal pride not to cross the streets by the zebra crossings, and who mock at every effort by the government to make Austria into a great nation again!

I had an interesting talk with the Chancellor and Leader of the People's Party, Dr Julius Raab, on this point. He was justifiably proud that Austria had now overhauled Switzerland and was third after France and Italy in the European tourist stakes. At the same time he and the Foreign Minister, Dr Kreisky, who also kindly received me, were inclined to be portentous about Austria's place in the world and the seriousness of her 'mission'. I suggested that, apart from the low cost of living, it was the beauty and frivolity of Austria that visitors enjoyed, and that perhaps the pursuit of a higher political and strategic status for Austria might be of less importance to the well-being of her people than more hotel bedrooms and the completion of the Vienna–Salzburg autobahn, then being lethargically stitched together like some Irish road project. My unstatesmanlike suggestions were greeted with polite but noncommittal nods and, in the case of Dr Kreisky, a man of great intelligence and with an outstanding record of resistance to National Socialism, with a switch of the conversation to the possibility of the Atomic Control Commission making its headquarters in Vienna alongside the International Atomic Energy Agency, which is now housed there. Fortunately, in a country where the state subsidy for the Opera House is rather more than the entire budget for the Foreign Service, we tourists have not much to fear from the consequences of such leaden prospects.

Most of the delightful myths about Vienna are just myths. The town is not built on the Danube, the Danube is not blue (on inquiry, Chancellor Raab said that once in his life, under a bright blue sky, he had in fact seen it blue), and Viennese girls are not a tenth as beautiful as English girls. It is most unlikely that they would be. Vienna is a fantastic *macédoine* of races, with a basic stock of Poles, Czechs, Hungarians and Rumanians and a strong Jewish strain. This, with the possible exception of the Hungarians, is not a promising stud from which to breed beautiful women. They have been made to sound beautiful by Viennese music and song and by the faulty memories of our grandfathers. In fact, they are attractive, amusing, forthcoming and fairly chic. They also fall deeply, slavishly, in love and have a powerful weakness for young Englishmen, as Austrians have for young English girls – a very happy state of affairs between friendly nations.

Viennese night life is not, and never has been, what it is cracked up to be. With the exception of the Heurigen wine gardens and Stuben, it is as dull and stereotyped as most night life. I have never particularly liked gipsy music being played in my ear, but you can still find a few virtuosos in Vienna, notably at the Monseigneur Bar. Anton Karas, surely one of the luckiest men in the world, continues to make a fortune out of his 'Zum Dritten Mann', where he 'ziths' energetically at his zither every night for the benefit of American tourists who often insist on having their photographs taken seated behind his instrument. At the Heurigen, life on the outskirts of Vienna amongst the vineyards continues to delight, and in May when I was there, with the lilac and fruit trees in bloom, it was as easy to drink pints of the young and dangerously acid wine under the moon, with an accordion being played in the background, as it must have been for generations. Here, in Grinzing, with the accordion or violin sobbing and the local Tauber tearing at your heart-strings with those 'moon' and 'June' themes which work so magically when they are in foreign languages, with a *Paprikaschnitzel* inside you and your twentieth Viertel waiting to be drunk, the dream sequence continues to unroll with a smoothness and a temporary truth that remain proof against cynicism and worldliness.

Other material pleasures are the Hotel Sacher (now sold out of the Sacher family), which remains one of the best hotels in Europe, and Demels, the high temple of Viennese pastry-making. Demels recently won a court case against Sachers to allow them to manufacture the famous Sacher Torte, originally invented by a Sacher chef for Metternich. Here 'all Vienna' come for their 'elevenses', and the place is loud with 'Küss die Hand's in the best Viennese tradition.

No doubt I should have visited the Opera and the picture galleries in Vienna, but I did not do so; I prefer Nature to Art, and I concentrated on the Vienna Boys' Choir and the Spanish Riding School after a day spent visiting the Iron Curtain on the far side of the Neusiedler See, the home of strange migratory birds from all over Europe. I last visited the Iron Curtain in Macao on the other side of the world, and this section is no more inspiring – the great, empty, marshy plain of the Hungarian puszta and, across it, striding away to distant horizons, the twelve-foot, bulky, barbed-wire fence punctuated by watch towers. It all seems out of date, melancholy and rather silly-silly until one hears of the occasional Hungarian who is still found at dawn, hanging, riddled with bullets, in these wires where the searchlights have caught him, and when one remembers the 180,000-strong herd of men, women and children who came stumbling across this empty plain a few years ago. Then it becomes vastly depressing, and we scurried away to the nearby village of Bruck, where there is a stork's nest on every chimney and a wonderful wine restaurant; and we drowned our depression to the phrenetic sobbing of one of those eternal gipsy bands.

The Vienna Boys' Choir – there are, in fact, three of them, but one is generally travelling abroad – sings every Sunday in the Hofkapelle. Here, after battling up the narrow stairs, clutching your tickets, and being shown to a seat from which you can see neither any part of the choir nor the Mass that is being held far down in the body of the small church, you must just sit and forget the tourists around you, close your eyes and listen to the piercingly beautiful voices against the full orchestra and organ. You must close your eyes to appreciate the mysterious poignancy of these boys' voices, because the mixture of church service and tourist attraction, though it has to be, is an unfortunate one. When people have paid for a ticket for any kind of performance, they seem to think they have also bought the right to behave as they please. Even during a church service, the loud whispering, particularly in a language I will not designate, the standing up to see better, and even, in the case of a man in front of me, the chewing of gum, is part of the tourist smear that is rapidly desecrating the remaining beautiful places and occasions in the world. And there is absolutely nothing to be done about it. If you want to hear the Vienna Boys' Choir, you have to hear it with around two hundred other people who have also paid to get in. Since quite a few of these people are only collecting the occasion, like a postage stamp, to stick in their albums when they get home, you cannot expect them to pay more than cursory attention to what is going on. At the end of, for them, an exhausting hour during which they are longing for a cigarette, you must patiently submit to being swept up with them and pushed off back down the narrow stone stairs so that they may be just in time to 'do' the Spanish Riding School next door – the second 'must' for a well packaged Sunday in Vienna.

As for my own visit to the Spanish Riding School, I was more fortunate. There was to be a special night performance on Monday evening for which I was lucky enough to get a ticket.

I am not greatly interested in horses. Our brief friendship terminated when, at the age of about twelve, I was allotted a hireling with a large, red, chocolate-box ribbon on its tail to denote a kicker, and was sent off complaining, with my elder brother, Peter, to a near-by meet in Oxfordshire. I stood well away from the meet and was given a wide berth by the rest of the hunt. Unfortunately, when the Master and the hounds set off, they passed close to my beast, who immediately waded in backwards with hooves flying. My diminutive heels and light switch had no effect, and the furious bellows of the Master and whippers-in – 'Get control of your animal, damn it!' – only made me rein the monster in and accelerate its backward progress. We scythed our way through the hunt, kicking the Master's mount and

208

one or two hounds on the way, and were only brought up by a clump of gorse. We waited, I pale and trembling, and my monster sated – a dreadful Bateman cartoon – until ordered home, 'until you can learn to ride'. Since that day, and after equally horrible experiences in the Cavalry School at Sandhurst, I have profoundly agreed with whoever said that horses are dangerous at both ends and uncomfortable in the middle.

But the Spanish Riding School is something different. It is the most graceful exhibition of sheer style in beautiful surroundings to be seen anywhere in the world. And on this occasion I took trouble, in the stables and from the writings of the present commandant, Colonel Podharsky, to find out more about it.

The Lipizzans date from 'Caesar's snow-white steed which Hispania did him send'. Further developed from the original Arab strains during the occupation of Spain by the Moors, the breed was introduced into Austria in the sixteenth century by Maximilian II. The basis of the present stud was established about that time in the village of Lipizza, near Trieste, whence the stud influenced horse-breeding throughout the Danubian monarchy. At the peace treaty after the First World War, this Lipizza stud was divided up between Austria and Italy as part of reparations, the one hundred and nine horses allotted to Italy returning to Lipizza, and the eighty-nine horses for Austria going to Piber in Styria. Today, the Lipizza breed has six dynasties of stallions dating back to the following sires: Pluto, Conversano, Neapolitano, Favoury, Maestoso and Siglavy; and, though extensive breeding of Lipizzans still goes on in Hungary, Rumania, Yugoslavia and Poland, the paramount Austrian stud remains at Piber.

The fate of the stud during the last war was fraught with drama. In 1942 the stud was ordered from Piber to Hostau in Czecho-Slovakia, and there they were joined by the stud from Lipizza to form, for the first time since 1919, a united Lipizzan stud with about three hundred and fifty horses. But, as the war went worse for Hitler and the Russian front approached Czecho-Slovakia, it looked as if the end had come. At the last moment, in March 1945, occurred what must have been a romantic and moving sight. The whole stud, together with its baggage train of original uniforms and equipment, trekked hundreds of miles between the armies to St Martin in Upper Austria. The sight of these beautiful white stallions wending their way towards the west must have lifted the hearts of many. In the midst of shot and shell, the Riding School at St Martin awaited the arrival of the American forces, fortunately in this sector commanded by General Patton, who was himself a great horseman and had been a member of the United States riding team at the Olympic Games in 1912. He took the stud under his protection and, in due course, its homeward trek continued back to Piber.

The height of a Lipizzan is between 14 and 15.2 hands. At birth the horses are black, but their colour changes through grey until they are white at the age of about four years, by which time they have completed their basic training in the three essential paces, walk, trot and canter. Only the stallions are used for performances in the Riding School, and then only for about a quarter of an hour's performance by each horse, with a maximum of forty-five minutes' daily training, to avoid taxing their powers of concentration and restraint.

The Riding Hall itself, seen at its most wonderful at night when the two vast chandeliers each blaze with a hundred lights, was built in 1735 by the younger of the Fischer von Erlachs, masters of the baroque period. The only touch of colour in the hundred-yard-long white hall is the wine-red plush on the balustrades, and I am not being irreverent when I say that the classical virginity of the interior reminds me of my favourite church in the world, the white baroque interior of the Frauenkirche in Munich.

This beautiful Riding Hall, fortunately undamaged in the last war, was also used, under Maria Theresa, for tournaments, carousels, great balls and fancy-dress carnivals of fantastic splendour. In 1814, Beethoven conducted here his monster concert of over a thousand musicians, and this was the scene of the first assembly of the Austrian parliament in 1848. (History does *not* relate that, with the advent of the Nazis, this graceful virginal hall was used as a temporary prison for many thousands of Jews, men, women and children, who were crammed in here for days without food or sanitation during the 'cleaning-up' of Vienna.)

But now these beautiful and hideous memories are gone, it is eight o'clock in the evening and the lights along the walls and in the giant chandeliers are blazing.

The far double-doors under the portrait of Charles VI on a Lipizzan stallion are thrown open and eight of the beautiful horses, their riders ramrod-straight (their motto is 'Ride your horse forward and keep it straight'), pace majestically in and line up facing the royal box. The brown tricorns are raised and replaced over the serious, dedicated faces with one straight-arm sweep, and then, as the hidden orchestra strikes up Reidinger's 'Festive Entrance', horses and riders proceed to the first number – 'All the Paces and Movements of the High School'. The riders in their chocolate-brown redingotes, white breeches and tall black boots to the knees, double rows of brass buttons flashing, and themselves wooden and expressionless, are toy soldiers, and the horses have all the soft, silken, plump appearance of other nursery toys. You notice that, for the first easy exercises, the control on a snaffle is light as the limping trots and sideways chassés gradually smudge the neatly raked field of sawdust and tan bark. Then come the more difficult 'Levades' and the 'Piaffe at the Wall', and, while you are still watching these, in a far corner, one stallion does a sensational 'Capriole'. Now you notice that the curb is being used. The horses are reined in tautly so that the proud curve of the neck is still further arched, there is a fleck of foam on the jaws, and here and there a brown eye shows white with concentration and nerves. But immediately after something difficult, the rider relaxes his horse and allows him to float gracefully the full length of the hall in the beautiful prancing trot that I find the most effective pace of all.

And so act follows act, with 'Work in Hand', 'Pas de Trois', and 'Work on the Rein', until the grand finale of the 'School Quadrille', when the eight horses perform solemn and rather slow arabesques to Chopin and Bizet.

By this time, impressed and delighted though one may be by the discipline and authority of the whole performance, one does rather long for a vulgar touch of the Aldershot Tattoo when perhaps the horses might be allowed one single splendid gallop. But that only shows what a Philistine one is in these matters. Exuberance is not permitted in this dedicated world, and in due course, to the rousing strains of the 'Austrian Grenadiers', the team once again line up, the tricorns are gracefully held out and replaced, and silently, almost funereally, the beautiful horses file out again under the clock until the last clink of spur and bit has disappeared.

After these various elegant pleasures I had one last rendezvous in Vienna – an incongruous one – with the International Atomic Energy Agency installed here in 1956 by the United Nations.

I am allergic to almost every form of international agency, conference or committee. Having worked briefly in the League of Nations around 1932, I believe that all international bodies waste a great deal of money, turn out far too much expensively printed paper, and achieve very little indeed. So it was with a jaundiced mind that I made an appointment to visit the *Atom Kommission*, as the Viennese call it, with the secret intention of making sharp fun of it. Unfortunately I fell into the hands of Dr Seligman, formerly head of the

Isotope Division at Harwell, and U.K. representative at the I.A.E.A. since its foundation, who completely took the wind out of my sails. Dr Seligman is one of those intelligent, humorous, liberal-minded scientists (he reminded me of Sir Solly Zuckerman) who makes science understandable to the layman, and, with a nice mixture of irony and enthusiasm, he completely convinced me that the Agency, which has a modest budget and staff, was doing something really important very well.

I personally leave it to others to worry about the Atomic Age. It seems to me too late in life for this layman to concern himself with such a vast and inchoate subject, but I accept the fact that atoms are here to stay and I now realize that, while a few years ago every small country simply had to have its own national airline, now every small country has to have its nuclear reactor, allegedly at any rate for peaceful purposes.

It is to control the demand and safe supply of these reactors and to teach the operators to work them without blowing up the world that the Atomic Energy Agency has been set up, and I can now appreciate that the existence of such international security measures is absolutely vital to all of us.

What happens is that an underdeveloped country wishing to develop the peaceful uses of atomic energy (and they all do) needs outside help. This is provided by the Agency in the form of a mission which examines the requirements of each country in respect of nuclear physics, raw materials, reactors, the medical uses of isotopes, and the briefing of nuclear personnel. Such missions, for instance, visited India, Indonesia, Thailand and Ceylon in 1959, and there are other similar missions in various parts of the world at this time. Purchases of nuclear equipment, the training of staff, etc., are then carried out through the Agency, and member governments supply the goods and any necessary personnel, presumably in accordance with their individual economic strategies.

Thus the Agency – in which, by the way, the Soviet Union participates with, to me, a rather suspect enthusiasm – can keep track of all power reactors and nuclear material throughout a large part of the world.

In addition to this police activity, the Agency makes independent studies of health and safety techniques including waste disposal – thankless tasks, but surely vital ones.

To give one rather dramatic example, there is a matter on hand at the moment (1959) in the Agency described as the 'Vinca Dosimetry Project'. On October 15th, 1958, there was a brief uncontrolled run of the Vinca Zero power reactor in Yugoslavia which exposed a number of operators to considerable radiation. The exposed men were flown immediately to the Curie hospital in Paris and there treated by new methods of counteracting radiation injury which apparently aroused keen attention in the scientific and medical worlds. Meanwhile, in the following April, the Yugoslav reactor 'went critical', as they say, again, and unknown elements in the control of such emergencies were revealed. As a result, the Agency in Vienna decided that a full-scale reconstruction of these dangerous circumstances should be undertaken whereby the precise doses and distribution of neutron and gamma rays to the originally injured men could be established in the interests of radiation safety.

Yugoslavia has agreed to this project and many nations are participating, including the United Kingdom, who loaned the heavy water needed to restart the reactor, and the United States, who provided, from Oak Ridge, four plastic phantoms filled with a salt solution which, in the experiment, will suffer various dosages of radiation.

Dr Seligman confirmed what the Foreign Minister adumbrated – that the Atomic Energy Control Commission, for so long a subject of debate at Geneva, would, if and when East and West can agree to its creation, also have its headquarters in Vienna. It is odd to think that such a pretty, frivolous city is becoming the headquarters for such solemn and ultra-modern undertakings.

Musing on these incongruities, I left the city of romantic dreams and took off for the Semmering Pass and the beautiful road through the Alps, for Salzburg, Innsbruck and points west.

## INCIDENTAL INTELLIGENCE

### Hotels
Five-star: Still the best is Sachers, just the same as ever, wonderful service and food, hard to get into unless

you have influence or can book well in advance. Even if you cannot manage to get a room there, *Sacher's Blue Bar* and *Red Bar* are Vienna's meeting-places for a pre-dinner or pre-opera drink. The original chocolate Sachertorte cakes are to be had on the premises, the same recipe as Emperor Franz Joseph liked, although discerning Viennese prefer the Sachertorten you get at the old-fashioned coffee-shop of *Demel*, a few streets away in the Kohlmarkt. Alternative five-star hotel: the *Ambassador* (but known to the Viennese as the 'Kranz') on the Neuer Markt, back of the Kärntnerstrasse. Ask for one of the rooms where the walls are lined with thick red silk. Excellent restaurant.

One-star: *Hotel Allstria*, in the Wolfengasse, off the Fleischmarkt, near the Danube Canal. Comfortable, cosy and old-fashioned but quite efficient in a restrained, never-get-flustered Viennese sort of way. It lies in a narrow alley and is nearly opposite one of Vienna's oldest restaurants, the Griechenbeisl.

*Restaurants*

Five-star: Again, *Sachers* is hard to beat, and its superb cuisine has quite recovered from the days fifteen years ago when it was a British officers' and Control Commission canteen, and the best it could turn out was baked beans and dried-up rashers on toast, with NAAFI tea.

*Am Franziskaner Platz* and the *Drei Husaren* in the Weihburggasse. But the Viennese leave the five-star restaurants to the foreigners and prefer picturesque one-star places like the *Weisser Rauchfangkehrer* (the White Chimney-sweep) in the Rauhensteingassc, where one sits in niches and drinks the eternal white wine from the vineyard slopes of Gumpoldskirchen, just outside Vienna, and listens to sentimental piano music. Its good family cooking is much more like real Vienna than any of the five-star places. Viennese gravitate between this and places like the romantic candle-lit *Kerzenstüberl* in the Habsburger Gasse and the *Lindenkeller* in the Rotenturmstrasse.

## Night-clubs

Five-star: *Maxim,* which has a floor show and girls which remind one of Berlin in the good old naughty days before World War II. It is far and away more sophisticated than anything one can see in the *spiess-bürgerlich* Berlin night life of today. Likewise *Eva,* an even more intimate night-club of the same somewhat exotic type.

One-star: A spot of history is attached to the *Fatty George* in the Peters Platz. It was called the *Oriental* during the war and was much used by the Gestapo to trap unwary German soldiers on leave and recovering from the rigours of the Eastern front into 'careless talk'. Microphones were fitted behind all the seats. In those days the owner was a character named Achmed Bey whose name still brings tiny frissons to the Viennese. Today the *Fatty George,* run by a coloured band-leader, is rather more harmless and is dedicated to the blaringest rock and roll. For those who prefer songs sung in

Viennese dialect as well as to dance, there is *Marietta's*. One of the present-day cabaret stars in *Marietta's* fled to Britain and served in the Pioneer Corps during World War II to avoid being sent to a Nazi concentration camp. Though the foreigners like the night-spots, Viennese prefer to sit in Heurigens and drink wine and sing nostalgically their traditional songs. These places are all pretty cheap. The claim to fame of the *Esterhazy Keller*, apart from the fact that all its wines come from the Esterhazy estates, is that it is in a thirteenth-century cellar so deep in the bowels of the earth that not even the invading Turks nearly four hundred years ago dared to descend into its murky and sinister depths. Another city-centre wine cellar of equal antiquity is the *Urbani Keller* in Am Hof, which has wonderful wine but where the musty smell reminds one nostalgically of the tunnels of the Metropolitan Railway between Baker Street and Finchley Road.

*Out-of-the-way-and-not-to-miss*
In scarcely any guide-book and hardly known about even by life-long Viennese is the quaint Clock Museum in the Neuer Markt, right in the centre of Vienna. Its aged but charming owner, who has presented it to the City Administration and has stayed on to run it as a hobby, is so passionately fond of his collection that he only opens the exhibition on one or two days a week and spends the rest of the time pottering in the deafening all-pervading ticking and chiming that fill the room from the thousands of clocks and watches. The collection

# 11

# Geneva

To include Geneva among the thrilling cities of Europe must seem to most people quixotic. What about Paris, Istanbul, Venice, for instance? Well, Paris is too big, Istanbul is too Asiatic, and Venice is a cliché. It had crossed my mind to write a joke essay on Venice and discuss the town without ever mentioning the canals, the gondolas, the churches or the piazzas. With a straight face, I would concentrate on the artistic purity of the railway station, the workings of the stock exchange, the intricacies of Venetian municipal finance, the history of the municipal waterworks and power station. I might even have found an erudite explanation in Venetian folklore for calling such a very small bridge the 'Bridge of Size'. But apart from perpetrating what, at the best, would have been a pretty damp squib, there is absolutely nothing to say about Venice. It is there, and all that one can tell people is that they should go and see it for themselves. Instead I chose Geneva, clean, tidy and God-fearing, a model city devoted to good causes – the city of Calvin, of the Red Cross, and of the United Nations.

For to me Geneva, and indeed the whole of Switzerland, has a Georges Simenon quality – the quality that makes a thriller-writer want to take a tin-opener and find out what goes on behind the facade, behind the great families who keep the banner of Calvin flying behind the lace curtains in their fortresses in the rue des Granges, the secrets behind the bronze grilles of the great Swiss banking corporations, the hidden turmoil behind the beautiful, bland face of the country.

As soon as you get over the Arlberg Pass and down into the Vorarlberg (which, incidentally, voted to become a Swiss canton in 1919 but was snubbed by Switzerland), everything is changed.

Even the yodelling is different. In Austria and Bavaria, yodelling is light and airy and gay and mixed up with romance. In Switzerland, the yodel has deep undertones of melancholy that sometimes descend into an almost primeval ululation akin to the braying moan of the Alpenhorn – an echoing plaint against the strait-jacket of Swiss morals, respectability and symmetry. For the solidity of Switzerland is based on a giant conspiracy to keep chaos at bay and, where it blows in from neighbouring countries, or pollinates within the frontiers, to sweep it tidily under the carpet.

Switzerland is one great 'Mon Repos' and, to keep this European pension spick and span so that, apart from other considerations, the rates at the lodging-house can remain high, the Swiss Government – which is more of a management than a government – and all the Swiss people labour constantly to keep up a front of cleanliness, order and impeccable financial standing.

This cultivated innocence seems, to the traveller arriving from happy-go-lucky Austria, to verge almost into infantilism in the Swiss-German cantons where the linguistic use of the diminutive rings almost like baby-talk. The diminutive suffix 'li' is everywhere, from the *Bürli, Mädli* and, of course, *Kühli* (boys, girls and cows) to the famous *Müsli,* the nature food with which Dr Bircher-Benner endeavoured to save the life of Sir Stafford Cripps. My favourite is *Kelloerettli,* a derivation of *quelle heure est-il?* which is Berner-Swiss for a watch. With surroundings clean as the whistle of a Swiss train, soothed by the clonking of the cow-bells, besieged by advertisements for dairy products and chocolate, and with cuckoo clocks tick-tocking in every other shop window, the visitor to Switzerland feels almost as if he had arrived in some gigantic nursery.

In many other respects it is a great refreshment to arrive in Switzerland from any other country in Europe. Here at last you do not have to lock your car when you leave it on the street. There are no beggars, pimps or gangsters. Super petrol from the pump really is super. Privacy is respected and there are no gossip-writers. The lavatories are spotless and the waiters and shopkeepers have that desire to please that is only genuine in a really thrifty nation. In exchange for this cleanliness and orderliness, you yourself must, of course, conform by also being clean and orderly. Swiss management and officialdom are extremely managerial and officious, and to slip up chaotically by parking your car in the wrong place, leaving the smallest scrap of litter, or failing to have the right kind of ticket on a train may lead to positively magisterial retribution. For the thwarted or affronted Swiss readily goes, as the psychologists say, 'into paroxysm', as any member of the British Ski Club who has offended the guard on a Swiss train will agree. These states of paroxysm – the reaction of the symmetrist to chaos – are signs of the deep psychosis that results from restraint. They are the lid blowing off the pressure-cooker. Statistically, further symptoms show themselves in the suicide rate, where the Swiss stand fifth in the whole world, with nearly double the suicide rate of the United Kingdom; the divorce rate, which is the fourth highest in Europe; and alcoholism, which, thanks to a partiality for schnapps, is the prime cause of lunacy in the country. In the latter connection, a friend of mine who lives in the old town of Zurich tells me that, on Saturday nights, when the suburbanites and the neighbouring peasants forgather for the weekly lifting of the pressure-cooker lid, the night is made hideous by revellers who do not just fall down when they are drunk but stand outside in the streets and bay at the moon with terrible cries from deep down within their frustrated libidos.

But these tragic manifestations are hushed up (you may not mention suicide as a cause of death in a Swiss newspaper) for the sake of 'Mon Repos', and other human frailties are kept tidy. Extra-marital love, for instance, though it may end in the divorce court, is usually managed with great decorum. It is an understood thing that the Swiss businessman has a mistress, but it is also understood that the mistress shall not be kept in the home town but established in a neighbouring city which the businessman has reason to visit at frequent intervals. And it is typical of Swiss values that Lotte or Lisa shall not be some beautiful odalisque lounging all day on a satin chaise-longue while she dips into a chocolate box and reads the fashion magazines. The Zurich businessman expects his loved one in Berne to earn money in a respectable job, keep their love-nest spick and span and prepare dainty meals for him when he comes over for the night. She must be a good Swiss citizen as well as a good Swiss mistress. Further, to tidy up the whole picture, abortion is legal in most cantons, though here again the process is respectably formalized. The girl, of whatever nationality, must first go to a G.P. who will certify that she is not fit to bear a child because her blood pressure is too high or too low or because she is physically run down in one way or another. The G.P. will then recommend her to a gynaecologist who, in turn, will recommend her to a clinic, thus spreading the risk and the responsibility – and, incidentally, the financial reward which through this triangular co-operative, mounts to between £80 and £100. Similarly with gambling. The Swiss are not great gamblers (though I believe it was a Swiss who invented the football pool system) except on the Stock and Bullion Exchanges, but casinos have recently been permitted to operate in most of the large cities on condition that boule only is played and the maximum stake shall be five Swiss francs – two conditions that effectively neutralize the vice.

Having thus fragrantized most of the common human weaknesses, there remain money crimes, and these the Swiss have not wished to push under the carpet. Instead they have elevated the crime against the holy franc to be the most heinous in their whole society. They have done this because they really mean it. The Swiss franc is the idol at which all Switzerland worships. A friend of mine who has to listen to the Swiss radio at frequent intervals tells me that there is no bulletin in which francs or *Franken* do not feature. Cantonal budgets are given down to the last centime, as is the cost of a local library, a football field, or a new apartment house (such local Swiss news is always given before the foreign news of the day). Since the greatest crime in Switzerland is to do something wrong with money, the smallest burglary is pursued relentlessly by the police, and the value of money is one of the prime pillars of a child's education. If you see a small crowd in the street, it will not be in front of a shop window, but at the window of a bank, all of which give Wall Street prices half an hour after the opening and every hour thereafter.

This mania for money is not new. The Genevese, Henri Dunant, invented the Red Cross, but, in the process of promoting his humanitarian ideas, he let the family business – textile mills in Algeria – go to pot, with the result that he committed the gravest sin that Geneva can conceive of – he squandered capital. Years later, living a pauper's life in the canton of Appenzell, he was awarded the first Nobel Peace Prize. Immediately, though his bankruptcy was thirty years old, his creditors attempted to have the prize seized in settlement of his debt. Dunant managed to stave them off, and when he died in 1910 he left the prize money to charities rather than let a penny go to his family.

The thirst for money is, of course, the chief economic strength of a country that is poor in natural resources and that has, broadly speaking, only services to sell. Originally the Swiss, who had as ferocious a record for fighting as the Scots, hired out their various cantonal armies as mercenaries (the Swiss Guards at the Vatican are the survivors), but in this century they have turned their attention to hotels and sanatoria (with the defeat of tuberculosis they are cannily switching to the modern managerial diseases resulting from stress and tension), and to the creation of the solidest banking system in the world.

The great virtue of Swiss banks is that they are not only solid but secret, and, in the vaults of Zurich, Basle and Geneva lie buried clandestine fortunes worth billions upon billions of pounds. The reason why fugitive money, in its search for safe repose, has poured into Switzerland in such a continuous torrent, particularly since the war, is due to the sympathy of the government for money which is more or less hot (if it was not, it would not be on the run). In a Swiss bank you may have an account or a safe deposit known only by a number, and this number will be known only by you and by one single director of the bank who may not disclose your identity even to his fellow directors. If, for instance, I. Fleming had such an account and a friend were to send £100,000 to my Swiss bank for the credit of I. Fleming, the bank would deny all knowledge of me and return the money. But if the money were sent to account No. 1234, the receipt of the money would be acknowledged in the normal way. Only if criminal proceedings are started against me in the Swiss courts by the Swiss authorities can the director concerned be subpoenaed and made to reveal the contents of my account or safe-deposit box.

To reinforce this device, heavy federal penalties were imposed by the law of November 8th, 1934 (just in time, be it noted, to welcome the flood of Jewish and German funds fleeing from Hitler), on any breach of banking security. I took the trouble to look up the relevant Article 47 B, which lays down:

Whosoever intentionally as organ, official, employee of a bank, as accountant or accountant's assistant, as member of the banking Commission, clerk or employee of its secretariat, violates the duty of absolute silence or the professional secret, whoso-ever seduces or attempts to seduce others to do so, will be punished with a fine of up to 20,000 Swiss francs or with imprisonment up to six months. Both penalties may be inflicted concurrently.

With these safeguards, and amid the silence of the fir trees that climb the innocent Alps and whisper no secrets to the wind, it is no wonder that Switzerland has been universally acclaimed the safe-deposit box for the world.

The hidden riches of Switzerland cannot be estimated in millions or billions, but *Pick's World Currency Report* gave a clue in a recent examination of the average per capita gold holding in all countries. Switzerland easily leads the field with an average holding of 370 dollars of pure gold per head of the population – more than three times the figure for the American citizen, Fort Knox and all. (I do not wish to give the impression that the Swiss are miserly. Not only is the government most generous in charitable donations abroad, but the International Committee of the Red Cross and the League of the Red Cross Societies, as well as the Swiss Red Cross, are heavily subsidized by Switzerland. Moreover, a host of semi-official and private Swiss charitable organizations contribute vast sums annually towards foreign charitable causes.)

It is not surprising that the protection and further accumulation of this national fortune is an obsession with Switzerland, and the emphasis on privacy and security in the country is perhaps as much to attract money, forever on the hunt for 'Mon Repos', as for the peace and protection of the citizens. The atmosphere of a well-guarded bank-vault is strengthened by the continued maintenance of war-time tank traps, camouflaged redoubts, and demolition chambers, not only all along the frontiers but on many bridges and other strategic points throughout the country. (At an intersection on the main road from Nyon to Geneva, for instance, there is a neat villa, window-boxes and all, that reveals itself on closer inspection to be a mighty stressed-concrete pillbox.) Military service is compulsory for all between the ages of twenty and sixty, and every soldier-citizen has to keep his rifle with forty rounds at home so as to be ready to go out and fight in the streets at a moment's notice. Preparations for emergency go to the point where every housewife is required to keep in the larder iron rations, consisting basically of one litre of cooking oil, two kilos of rice and two kilos of sugar per head of the household, and to consume and replace these at regular intervals to keep them fresh. These measures, combined with a powerful, though not very bright, police force, create a glowing picture of law, order and security in a turbulent world. Combined with the honesty, industry and cleanliness of the Swiss, the impression on the foreigner and on foreign capital is little short of paradisal.

Traditionally a haven for refugees from turmoil and persecution, modern Switzerland has gathered to its bosom a new kind of refugee – the fugitive from punitive taxation. The political refugee still exists in the form of fugitive royal families, Italian, Rumanian, Spanish and Egyptian, together with a handful of sheikhs. These sad orphans of the world's storm, evicted from their palaces, have found shelter in the Palace Hotels along the shores of Lac Leman, and there hold strictly mediatized tea and bridge parties and are courted by the local snobs.

There are many cranks attached to this fusty world of ex-kings and queens, including, in Lausanne, one bizarre sect, about thirty strong, that worships our queen. The members believe that Queen Elizabeth is a descendant of the biblical King David, and that she will reign over the world and bring about the millennium. This world rule will have its headquarters in Lausanne where the sect has set up a 'temple' over a garage and decorated it with bright rainbow-coloured draperies and a large red-leather armchair which is to be her throne. A similar but smaller chair awaits Prince Charles. Members of the sect take it in turns to fast for twenty-four hours at a time while awaiting Her Majesty's arrival. The leader, a certain Frederick Bussy, is a bearded gentleman in his late forties who wears white robes embroidered with the British royal coat of arms, and records the prophecies of the sect on a dictaphone for typing and posting to world leaders. Monsieur Bussy is particularly proud that Her Majesty appears to take note of his requests. He told a reporter, 'We suggested Her Majesty should choose King Edward's throne for her coronation and she did so.'

A host of British and American actors and writers are the Voltaires, Rousseaus and Mesdames de Stael of today – Charlie Chaplin, Noel Coward, Ingrid Bergman, Richard Burton, Peter Ustinov, Yul Brynner, William Holden, Georges Simenon, Mel Ferrer and Audrey Hepburn among them. I stayed with Noel Coward near Montreux, and there my wife joined me. Noel Coward is, besides being a friend, one of my heroes, and I was disgusted by the hullabaloo in the press – but not, I think, among his public – when some years ago, instead of allowing him to go slowly bankrupt, his lawyer persuaded him to reside outside England and stay alive. I will not weary my readers with the details of his case, but I have a basic alteration to propose in our tax laws which I will call, so that it looks properly portentous on the statute books, the Quantum of Solace Clause. Briefly, this will allow tax relief to those who, as judged by an independent tribunal, have given the maximum amount of pleasure to their fellow citizens. Most beneficiaries will, of course, come from the creative arts – acting, writing, painting, music, etc. – but they will also come from sport, politics and medicine. Such a clause would, I believe, have the blessing of the general public, it would greatly encourage the arts, and it would serve to keep creative ability within our shores (copy to the Inland Revenue for action!).

Noel Coward arranged a dinner party for us with his neighbour, Charlie Chaplin, and it was a dazzling experience to spend a whole evening with the two people who have made me laugh most of all in my life. Charlie Chaplin lives in a handsome eighteenth-century house in a large, well-treed park above Vevey, with furniture unremarkable but appropriate, both comfortable and 'lived with'. There is no pretension anywhere except perhaps in the glasses at dinner. Charlie Chaplin hates them. They are Venetian and spidery, with gold rims, and Charlie Chaplin described how, on a visit to Venice, for all his efforts to avoid the experience, he and his wife were gondolaed off 'to that damned island where they blow glass'. He blew realistically until he was red in the face. 'And they made me, absolutely made me, spend about a thousand dollars on this junk.' He waved a hand. 'I was absolutely furious at falling into the trap.' Much of the success of the evening was due to Oona, his beautiful young wife, the daughter of Eugene O'Neill. She has borne him seven children in the seventeen years of their marriage. It is wonderful to see two people bask unaffectedly in each other's love, and the relationship lit up the evening.

Charlie Chaplin, in a plum-coloured smoking-jacket which, he said, he wore because it made him feel like a millionaire, exuded vitality tempered with the depreciation and self-mockery one expects from him. After dangerously skirting politics over the matter of Caryl Chessman's execution (though he was disgusted with it, Chaplin said that, by his death, Chessman had achieved more for mankind than any other man since the war), we got on to *Ben Hur,* which Chaplin, who practically never goes to films or theatres and does not own a television set, had not seen. Chaplin immediately became airborne. He was going to make a really great film, it would be a mixture of half a dozen spectaculars – *Ben Hur, Anna Karenina, South Pacific* and others. It would be *Around Romance in 80 Days.* Certainly he would put in the chariot race. The villain with the big knives on his chariot wheels would overhaul the hero, 'a chap called Gulliver or Don Quixote or one of those'. As the villain came alongside, the hero would nonchalantly hold out a side of ham which the knives on the chariot wheels would cut into thin slices which the hero would eat and gain strength so that he would win the race. All this splendid mirage was illustrated with unceasing dumb crambo.

More seriously, he said that he would make one more 'Little Man' film. My wife suggested that the theme should be 'the little man who had never had it so good', and Chaplin seized the idea and tucked it away. He next enlivened us with a graphic account of being invited by the Duke of Westminster to a boar hunt in France, of the clothes he had had to borrow and how his horse had run away with him. And then he was off again, brilliantly 'fed' by Noel Coward, into memories of his early days on the boards in England, of the great actors and actresses he had worshipped, and of his own struggles and first notices.

He is now writing his memoirs. He works every day from eleven to five and has finished nine hundred pages. On that day, there remained only twenty pages to go. He complained of being bedevilled by his Swiss secretary who constantly tried to improve his English. He said he was not surprised, as he had taught himself the language and suspected that his secretary knew it far better than he did, but, even so, he liked his own version and hoped that some of what he had actually written would survive the process of editing by his publishers. We all of course urged him to reject any kind of editorial censorship or correction, but his modesty will, one fears, allow Big Brother's blue pencil to wreak its havoc. (How much better those who 'don't write' write than those who do – Lord Attlee, Lord Moran, Viscount Montgomery and, latterly, Ralph Richardson!) The, evening had to end. It is wonderful when one's heroes in the flesh are even better than in the imagination.

It was the time of the Narcissus Festival, and the fields around Noel Coward's house (which he has not, after all, called 'Shilly Chalet') were thick with the flowers that were to line my route round Europe – tulips in Holland, lilac in Vienna, narcissi in Switzerland and, later, bougainvillaea and hibiscus in Naples. Alas, I had to forsake these innocent Alps (what is the definition of an Alp, by the way, and when does an Alp become a Berg?) and spend my days in Geneva – Voltaire's 'shining city that greets the eye, proud, noble, wealthy, deep and sly'.

Geneva is far, far wealthier than it was in Voltaire's day when, as the Duc de Choiseul, Madame de Pompadour's foreign minister, advised, 'If you see a Genevese jump out of the window, jump right after him. There is fifteen per cent to be gained.' Today, its economy bulging with the wealth of countless international organizations and of big foreign businesses attracted by tax advantages, such as Chrysler and Dupont, with a quarter of its residents foreigners and well over a million tourists every year, the town is bursting at the seams, and the small population of true Genevese – about fifty thousand – have a hard time trying to avoid being overlaid by the giant golden calf for whom, originally with enthusiasm but now with very mixed feelings, they provide pasture.

Parking a car in any city these days is almost impossible. In the centre of Geneva it is totally so. Hunting round and round like a mouse in a trap, it crossed my mind that, for the motorist, 'P' has become the most desirable letter of the alphabet. How blessed it is to be able actually to stop and get out of the car and leave it without the fear of a torrent of abuse when you return to it! So far as Geneva is concerned, the only hope is for them to build vast parking places out over the famous lake.

This beautiful lake, plus the highest fountain in the world and the Rhône that thunders so majestically through the town – all this and Mont Blanc too, do not make Geneva a happy town. The spirit of Calvin, expressed in the ugly and uncompromising cathedral that dominates the city, seems to brood like a thunderous conscience over the inhabitants. In the rue des Granges adjoining the cathedral, the great patrician families, the de Candoles, de Saussures, Pictets, set a frightening tone of respectability and strait-laced behaviour from which the lesser Genevese take their example. The international set – the delegates, staffs of the various organizations and staffs of foreign businesses – do not penetrate even the fringes of Genevese society. They even mix poorly among themselves. The lack of adjustment between the resident Americans, for instance, and Geneva life is such that a booklet – an excellent common-sense one, by the way – has been prepared at the behest of the President of the American Women's Club of Geneva and the Chief of the Mental Health Section of the World Health

Organization, to prepare Americans coming to work in Geneva for what is described as 'Culture Shock' – the impact of the European way of life on an American.

The chief trouble is the language problem, closely followed by the business of bringing up children. In Geneva, as in the rest of Switzerland, Swiss children have butter *or* jam for tea. Swiss children are not allowed to go to most films until they are eighteen, and even the harmless Danny Kaye is forbidden to children until they are sixteen, to be proved by the presentation of identity cards. When a Swiss child comes back from a party, he or she is asked, 'Were you good?' whereas the American parent will ask, 'Did you have a good time?' The Swiss mother finds it difficult to make adult conversation to a foreign mother because only in 1960, and by a very narrow majority, did Swiss women obtain the vote, and then only in a minority of the cantons.

Finally, the general values and moral judgements of the Swiss have hardly developed since 1914, whereas the foreigners' have been turned inside out by two world wars.

But, above all, it is the reserve of the Genevese that chills those many Americans who so much want to be loved (the British don't particularly expect to be liked, or are too obtuse to notice if they aren't). It was this reserve, this holier-than-thou attitude, that Voltaire endeavoured to dynamite in his constant forays against Calvinism. Today it is only the giant scandal that can fracture the smugness. Fortunately, from time to time, the Lord who, I have always believed, has little sympathy for

Calvinism, visits just such a scandal upon Calvin's present-day disciples. The echoes of such a visitation were still
rumbling when I was in Geneva in May 1960 – the case
of Pierre Jaccoud, Geneva's senior lawyer, head of the Bar
Association and chief of the all-powerful Radical Party
in the town, and it was a real grand slam in scandals.

The story is this: on May 1st, 1958, an elderly man,
Charles Zumbach, was found shot and stabbed in his
house on the outskirts of Geneva. His wife, on returning
from a church meeting that night, was shot at and
wounded by the murderer whom she described as a tall,
dark man wearing a dark suit who had dashed out of
the house and made his escape on a black bicycle. It
was a headline story, but no headlines were black enough
for the sensational arrest of Maitre Pierre Jaccoud a
month later on the charge of murder.

The scandal developed swiftly. It was revealed that,
shortly after the murder, Jaccoud had gone to Stockholm
and had his hair bleached, that he had tried to take
poison during the police investigation, and that he had
had a mistress, Linda Baud, a secretary at Radio Geneva.
All this of one of Geneva's sons who had been nicknamed
'Calvin' at school because of his puritanical nature; of
a lawyer who had counted Aly Khan, Sacha Guitry and
I.G. Farben among his clients, of a Director of the
Conservatoire de Musique and of the Orchestre de la
Suisse Romande, of a Municipal Councillor and Deputy
of the Grand Conseil of Geneva – worse, of a man who
lived in a street that abutted on the rue des Granges!

It turned out that Jaccoud had met Linda Baud, then

in her twenties, at an official dinner when, as his lawyer claimed, 'he was ready to love like a schoolboy, never having loved as a schoolboy'. The affair lasted ten years, with passionate ups and downs. His wife knew all about it but did nothing for fear of offending the conventions, and, when it ended, Madame Jaccoud, worn down by those 'meals heavy with silence', took him back and the marriage was mended.

Unfortunately, in the summer of 1957, Linda Baud took another lover, a young technician from Radio Geneva called André Zumbach, to whom, out of jealousy, Jaccoud wrote anonymous letters. They were sordid ones:

> I have heard that you are a friend of Linda Baud and feel you should be informed of what is going on. After having been the mistress of a barkeeper, then of one of the employees of your organization, not to mention a number of other adventures, she has been the mistress of a married man for several years. I have just heard that she has relations with someone very dear to me. I saw them together on the 17th August and found by chance a most edifying photograph of the way they spend their time. I am enclosing this photo.
>
> [Signed] 'SIMONE B.'

The photograph was one of Linda Baud naked which, she claimed, Jaccoud had taken of her at pistol point one evening in the grimy little room they had used for their affair. André Zumbach accused Jaccoud of sending these letters and the prosecution maintained that Jaccoud, frightened by the accusation, had gone to Zumbach's home to kill André Zumbach and get the letters back. Surprised by the father, Jaccoud had shot him and, panicking, had also shot the mother.

The trial, in March 1960, lasted three weeks and was enlivened by the production of five hundred love-letters from Jaccoud to Linda Baud, the discovery of a Moroccan dagger, showing traces of blood and liver cells, at Jaccoud's home, and of a button, found on the scene of the crime, of an English raincoat parcelled up in Jaccoud's apartment to be sent to the Red Cross. To heighten the drama, the Public Prosecutor was a great friend of Jaccoud and they broke out into 'tu' in the court – the court where Jaccoud himself had so often pleaded. The judge also knew the accused, and the defence lawyers were old friends. The Public Prosecutor himself admitted acquaintance with Linda Baud, and the drama was intensified by the appearance of a famous Paris lawyer, Rene Floriot, for the defence, who spread mud still more widely over Geneva, to the fury of the inhabitants.

Finally, with the natural respect of the Genevese for authority, titles and high society torn to shreds, Jaccoud was convicted and sentenced to seven years, subsequently reduced to three.

Such cases – the Dubois espionage affair of 1957 was another one – burst upon the Swiss scene with all the greater impact because, though sordid crimes occur in every other country of the world, they really should not disturb a society that has 'Mon Repos' as its motto. These scandals have no more impact abroad than any other headline murder story, but, among the Swiss, it is as if a corner of the lid of the great pressure-cooker had lifted to emit a poisonous jet of steam – a whiff from the great cauldron of human chaos that is the supreme enemy of the symmetry that is Switzerland.

Much, far too much, I fear, of what I have written will seem critical of the Swiss and of their surpassingly beautiful country. Yet it is not my wish to be critical, but merely to examine, to look beneath the surface of a country that holds so much more mystery than those that wear their hearts and psychoses on their sleeve. I was partly educated in Switzerland – at the University of Geneva where I studied Social Anthropology, of all subjects, under the famous Professor Pittard. I was once engaged to a Swiss girl. I am devoted to the country and to its people and I would not have them different in any detail. But, as I said at the beginning, Switzerland has a Simenon quality, an atmosphere of still-water-running-deep, which is a great temptation to the writer of thrillers. If I have revealed a wart here and a wen there and poked mild fun at the reserved, rather prim face Switzerland presents to the world, this is because the mystery writer enjoys seeing the play from back-stage rather than from out front, in the stalls.

To conclude, I will draw the veil aside from one last Swiss secret that, amongst all, the world has perhaps found the most baffling: Swiss cheese has holes in it because, in the process of making Gruyere and Emmental, carbon dioxide is formed and, as the cheese solidifies, the bubbles remain.

## INCIDENTAL INTELLIGENCE

*Hotels*

Hotels in Geneva are usually top-heavy with conference delegates. This applies even to winter-time and even to conferences no one has ever heard of.

Luxury hotels are growing like mushrooms, but the *Richmond* and the *Hotel des Bergues* are particularly favoured by visiting high society and statesmen, while the newer *Hotel du Rhône* is more frequently chosen by business magnates and sheikhs.

For another type of luxury: quiet, remote lakeside setting and the atmosphere of a country manor, there is the less-known *Clos de Sadex*, near Nyon, twenty-five kilometres outside the town on the Route Suisse leading to Lausanne, and therefore only recommended to the motorised. The *Clos de Sadex* is run by English-speaking Mr and Mrs L. de Tscherner who have transformed their own home into a first-class residential hotel and who loan their own motor boat for lake excursions.

A picturesque but not inexpensive retreat in Geneva itself is the *Hotel Lamartine*. This is an 'authentic' chalet in its own garden at Champel, chemin des Clochettes; it is mentioned in the Guide Michelin and caters mainly for bed-and-breakfast customers.

Less money to spend? There is a pleasant pub-style

pension on the lakeside a kilometre or so outside Geneva at la Belotte, chemin des Pecheurs, the *Hotel de la Belotte*. A limited number of rooms and the inconvenience of Sunday invasions of lunchers who come *inter alia* for *perches du lac,* a fresh-water fish speciality.

## Restaurants

The gastronomic delights of Geneva are slightly over-shadowed by the vicinity – within fifty kilometres – of Le Pere Bise, one of France's three best restaurants, at Talloires, just after Annecy. Inside Geneva the *Béarn,* quai de la Poste, is the uncrowned king of local restaurants. After that the choice is vast and interesting, and advice will be tendered from every side.

For *fondue bourguignonne,* a local speciality, *Le Chandelier,* 23 Grande Rue, in the old city, ranks high. This fondue consists of portions of cut-up raw steak which you impale on a stick and cook yourself in boiling oil and butter at the table. It is served with a variety of sharp sauces.

Cheese fondue is rarely served in summer and it tastes better in any brasserie than in a restaurant. I always feel that this cheese-and-white-wine speciality takes the lime-light from an even tastier speciality: raclette. Raclette is merely toasted cheese. But what toasted cheese! The performance takes place at an open fire and the chef scrapes the melted cheese straight from the fire on to a numbered plate: yours. You are automatically served with a fresh portion on the same easily identified plate until you beg for mercy. Raclette should be eaten in the mountains before the fresh cheeses and the cows come down to the valley. In Geneva the *Café du Midi*, round the corner from the *Hôtel des Bergues*, has a cellar, or *carnotzet*, which specializes in raclette – if you can stand the heat.

It is cooler, less picturesque, and the raclette or fondue is just as good when served in a cafe called *Le Bagnard*, place du Marche, Carouge. The word Bagnard comes from Bagne cheese and not from a convict past in the café ownership.

I hope habitués will forgive me for giving away the name of a bistro which serves excellent meals and charges according to the size of the portion asked for: *Chez Bouby*, rue Grenus I.

At the other extreme, as a preliminary to night-clubbing, the only place where it is possible to dine to music and dance is the *Gentilhomme*, which belongs to the *Richmond*. (Incidentally all restaurants, including the *Béarn*, must be looked up in the telephone directory for booking purposes under the word 'café', for reasons unknown.)

*Night-life*

Night-clubs are numerous, cheaper than in England and as naughty as those in Paris, hope the Genevese.

The *Bataclan*, run by Madame Irene, is famous for its strip-teasers. The floor show here is one reason why German Swiss, less privileged at home, find business visits to Geneva quite essential.

*La Cave à Bob*, in an old town cellar, also has strip-teasers, chansonniers, and tries to be reminiscent of St-Germaindes-Pres. The *Moulin Rouge* usually has extremely good attractions from Paris and even New York.

With a star show, night-clubs charge an entry fee of up to ten francs. Otherwise a whisky or a shared bottle of vin blanc can last you till 2 a.m. at a cost of about 10s. per person. It is of course possible and easy to spend more.

# 12
## Naples

Oliosasso! Oliosasso! Oliosasso! The monstrous auto-strada hoardings, demonstrating, even more forcibly than the Italians' total lack of interest in their artistic and architectural treasures, that Italy is a race of Philistines, flip by with the kilometres. A tiny dot in the driving mirror becomes an Alfa or a Maserati. There is a searing screech from double wind horns, the Gatling crackle of twin exhausts from which the mufflers have been removed and, a few minutes later, nothing ahead but the white, empty ribbon of the autostrada vanishing into the glistening heat-mirage.

The sheer harshness of motoring in Italy shocked all the more after a night spent in one of the few bedrooms attached to one of the three greatest restaurants of France, the aforesaid *Père Bise* at Talloires on Lake Annecy. There, I am ashamed to say, an injudicious combination of the Pere's *pâté de foie gras chaud en croute* followed by *gratin de queues d'écrevisses* was too much for a stomach attuned for three weeks to the milder pabulum of *Wienerschnitzel mit grunem Salat*. But I had not allowed this disgrace to diminish the enchantment of one of my favourite beauty spots in Europe, and the slow meander through the High Savoy and over the Mont Cenis pass, opened ten days before, and the descent towards Italy through fields of gentians, alpine crocuses and white and sulphur anemones, were a beautiful transition from the douce north to the brazen south of Europe. Then Turin, Milan and the broad, silken ribbon of the Autostrada del Sole that hurtles the motorist down south to Florence. And there to be met by the full impact of international tourism combined with the appalling tumult of post-war Italy.

Florence was a rude shock, but Rome – in preparation for the 1960 Olympics – was worse. The city may not have been built in a day, but it has now been almost rebuilt in under two years, and we arrived in the last stages of the pandemonium. Bridges, bypasses, stadia and new housing settlements, being rushed to completion in a turmoil of dust, road drills and excavators, had converted the city into a maze of closed roads, badly marked detours and axle-smashing craters. Maddened and confused, the great ants' nest of anyway hysterical Romans scurried hither and thither amidst the welter of high-frequency horn and exhaust notes trying to get where they wanted before the great boot of the townplanners gave their nest another kick. In the circumstances, the foreign motorist could only make blindly for the Tiber and savagely cling to it until, sweating and exhausted, he reached the blessed darkness and peace of his hotel bedroom.

The whole of Rome, and of most other Italian cities, is a *zona di silenzio*. Frequent notices to this effect are, of course, a waste of lath and paint. The whole psychology of the Italian, particularly of the Southern Italian, is based on *far figura*, to 'cut a dash'. With the advent of the motor-scooter, this posturing, previously expressed through flashy clothes, exaggerated tones of voice, expressions and gestures, has now been vastly reinforced by the attachment, apparently to every Italian male, of a chattering two-stroke engine, an electric horn and an exhaust pipe. The use of these instruments, known as *sputnikare*, gives him an even greater illusion of importance and power. The amount of noise he can make with his vehicle, particularly via the exhaust pipe, has come in some obscure way to represent a virility symbol, and for the police to pray silence is as vain as to tell Italians not to lend grandeur and emphasis with their hands to the simplest of conversations.

Italy, in 1959, had nearly seventeen million visitors, of which the British furnished one and a half million. In 1960, I understand, bookings were considerably down on 1959, with Britain in particular sounding the retreat, and the authorities were understandably worried. Since Italy has now lost my own custom in the foreseeable future, perhaps I can give her a word of advice.

It is not that the ordinary Italian, while loathing and despising all tourists, milks him with the minimum of grace of the maximum amount of money, nor that prices are ridiculously high for the services, and particularly the food, available in most of Italy, but that sheer noise and ugly chaos are literally driving the ordinary tourist to distraction.

The problem is bad enough in most modern cities, but in Italy the frenzied hysteria in the towns is definitely injurious to the health of the northern visitor – to his senses and to his nerves. As for the spoliation of the architectural beauties of the country, I recommend the minister concerned with tourism to visit Siena and there to note that the perspective of the pink, shell-shaped piazza that has enchanted for five centuries is now utterly lost since, amazingly, the piazza has become a parking place for charabancs and motor cars. Against such vandalism, of which every visitor has his pet example, what can a small handful of archaeological custodians and museum curators in Rome hope to achieve in preserving the beauties of Italy? Only a lack of receipts at the turnstiles is likely to have any effect. It was a blessing to hack one's way out of the suburbs of Rome and on to the Appian Way for Naples – a beautiful road, through the Pontine Marshes, that meets the sea at Terracina. Ten miles farther down the new coast road you come, after Sperlonga, to the first of several road tunnels through the cliffs, and just before it, behind barbed wire, are the excavations of Tiberius's grotto, which my wife and I were determined to visit. You are supposed to have a letter from some high authority in Rome to gain access to the site, but the name of the *Sunday Times* worked with the guardian and we scrambled down through the clumps of wild love-in-the-mist, and scuttling green lizards, to the scene of the excavations and the hutments which house some of the rich treasure-trove of sculpture – alas, all in fragments – recovered since 1957 under the direction of Professor Jacopi.

The huge grotto that opens to seaward and that has now been completely cleared of rubble is splendidly romantic – a grandiose water-folly adjoining the foundations of what must have been a handsome belvedere standing back from the shore-line of the graceful bay of Sperlonga. In the floor of the deep grotto there is a twenty-foot-wide circular swimming-pool fed by a fresh-water spring. In the centre of the pool stands a square pediment that may have held an enormous group of Laocoon wrestling with his serpents. One single marble leg of this statue and bits of the serpents have been recovered, and the leg alone is seven feet high. Adjoining this circular pool are large fish-tanks fed tidally with seawater, and the custodian suggested, rather fancifully perhaps, that these had contained the giant Moray eels to which slaves were fed to improve the flavour of this famous Roman delicacy. The walk round the swimming-pool had been terraced with bright blue mosaic, and statues are thought to have been arranged as sculpture for the interior walls of the cave, while some may have stood guard at either side of the entrance and on the headland to the east. But these are nothing more than theories, for at some time the beautiful cavern with all its elegant eccentricities was smashed to fragments, perhaps with the advent of the Christians some hundred years after the date that has been provisionally given for the creation of the grotto.

I wonder if Tiberius really was such a monster as we have always heard. It seems that his memory aroused such loathing that even long after his death people were still savagely smashing the vestiges of the monuments he had left behind. Were Tacitus, Suetonius and Juvenal, who tore at him like maddened wolves, any more than high-class gossip writers? No doubt that is heresy. But the fashion of giving historical idols feet of clay makes me wonder if some of the traditional villains don't deserve the opposite treatment. Real monsters are even more difficult to credit than real saints. I was still musing on this weighty theme when we arrived in Naples.

To the hardened traveller the almost bestial harshness of Naples comes with nearly the same shock as one's very first visit to the Continent. Here there still thrives the true 'foreigner'. Here you are still cheated, jostled, burgled and generally intimidated by the inhabitants as you were at, say, Calais in your early teens. It is as if, as you arrive, the whole town licks its lips and says, 'Here he comes,' and you are then set upon with a relish and an ingenuity which never slacken until you have got away again with your life and the relics of your purse. During the war, Naples took on the whole might of the American Base Headquarters in Italy and skinned it like a rabbit. Submarine telephone cables across the Bay had huge sections cut out of them for the sake of the copper wire, heavy tanks, crippled in the taking of the city and temporarily abandoned, gradually melted away as if they had been made of ice-cream, and the ordinary G.I. was skinned, boned, consumed and spat out as if he had been one of those flannelly Neapolitan fish they force you to eat in their restaurants.

The chief operators in this process of eviscerating the foreigner are the packs of teenage *delinguenti* operated, Fagin-like, by older gangs, that infest the poorer quarters of the city. One particular trick they had with the errant G.I. has a macabre genius that will forever haunt me. The G.I., preferably a negro, on pleasure bent, would be enticed into some den and there sold a bottle of venomous hooch. When he had consumed this firewater and fallen unconscious, the ragamuffins would drag him out into an alley, put him on a hand-cart, and wheel him off through the back streets to where the Fagins would be waiting. The boys would receive some small change for their trouble and the body of the G.I., complete with clothes, wallet, wrist-watch, etc., would be put up for auction among the Fagin co-operative. Sold to the highest bidder, he would then be stripped of all his belongings and hustled off into the hinterland where, when he recovered, he would be put to manual work in some distant vineyard until, through undernourishment or some other cause, he became useless. He would then be banged on the head and left somewhere down by the docks for the military police to collect.

Little remains of those golden days except the black market in cigarettes, liquor, etc., still copiously fed from Tangier and Beirut, and a thriving market in pornography. Dirty postcards were offered me at 9.38 one morning – a record in my experience. There is also the narcotics traffic to America which is so cunningly and successfully manipulated that the Italian and American secret services can find nothing better to do than put the blame, by rumour and innuendo, on a gentleman called Mr Lucky Luciano.

Just before Raymond Chandler died, some eighteen months earlier, I arranged for him to visit Naples and meet Lucky Luciano in the hopes that Chandler, fast running out of a desire to write about anything, would have his imagination stirred by the man who was the last surviving fragment of the myth of the Al Capone era. Chandler came back to England convinced that Luciano had been framed by fellow gangsters and offered up as a hostage for their own safety to the Attorney-General, Mr Dewey. Chandler, to my delight, became very excited by this new view of Mr Luciano and sketched out to me the plot of what might have been a most exciting play on the story of a wronged gangster. But he thought that Luciano had been so harshly treated by fate that he decided to write to him to ask permission before embarking on his project; however, Luciano never replied to his letters. That finished the idea so far as Chandler was concerned, but when I planned to visit Naples I made arrangements through Mr Henry Thody, 'Our Man in Rome', to meet Lucky Luciano and come to my own conclusions about him.

This was not an easy thing to do. Lucky Luciano is leery of publicity, perhaps because he modestly realizes that he is famous only in a role which he would prefer to forget. He is also tired of being pursued, every time the American fleet is in, by gawking sailors who assure him fervently that the only things they want to see in Italy are him and the Pope. But the meeting was arranged and the day after our arrival Mr Luciano came to tea in the formal surroundings of the Hotel Excelsior.

Lucky Luciano is a neat, quiet, grey-haired man with a tired, good-looking face. Whether he deserves the notoriety attached to his name or not, he has certain physical characteristics which one associates with men of power and decision – unsmiling, rather still eyes, a strong, decisive jaw-line and a remarkable economy of movement and expression. We sat chummily in the corner of the vast lounge, my wife, Mrs Lee Thody (a brilliant free-lance photographer who, thanks to Luciano's trust in her, had been able to stage the tea party), Lucky Luciano and myself, and the polite handing round of sugar and milk and the dainty nibbling of biscuits amused me. Mr Luciano's general appearance of a minor diplomat or government official fitted in well with this civilized ritual. He was well dressed in casual grey tones, white silk shirt and dark tie, and he was expensively, though unobtrusively, barbered and manicured (by two barbers every morning, I understand). It was only when he talked that undertones of Runyonese gave evidence of his past in Chicago.

'There is this man which I told you tries to frame me, which is this man from the Narcotics Bureau. I have the evidence of this frame stamped by a judge of this court in Palma and in Catania which is where the retrial takes place. There is this mayor who is murdered which I am supposed to have done, together with a kidnap in Tangier and a lot of other stuff which is about people I never even heard of, and this son of a bitch' – (embarrassed pause) – 'if you'll pardon the expression, this person says I am involved in these things, things I never even heard of until I read them in the newspapers. Well, you know what happens? The Italian police get to look into this frame which has been dreamed up by the American Narcotics Bureau and I am asked to attend the trial. The judge which is looking after the case asks me if I know anything about these things, and when I say no he says then you may leave the court. And then the prosecution gets up and asks three years for this guy for perjury for trying to frame me, and the guy gets two and a half years. See what I mean? These American Narcotics people are always trying to frame me. For why? Which is because they can't think of anyone else to frame for all the narcotics going into the United States. They are always making fools of themselves these people. How do you suppose I can live peacefully here in Naples, where everybody knows everybody's secrets, if I am mixed up in things like that? I guess these guys is mad at me because I call them "the bicarbonate policemen", which is because they are always getting guys lined up on account they have been drug-smuggling, and they get an agent to go to these guys to buy dope, and these guys take the money and say thank you very much, and hand over a secret-looking packet, and when the Bureau opens it up why it's just bicarbonate of soda.'

We all sympathized. Then I asked wasn't it true that the bulk of the drugs getting into America came from Italy? No, said Lucky Luciano, that was old hat. Now, as he read in the papers, it was coming from Mexico. 'And do you know what, Mr Fleming? It's all the fault of the American Government. They are not handling this narcotics problem right, which is why it goes on getting worse every year. Washington is spending billions of dollars every year trying to stamp out the traffic, but that is not the way to stop it. You have to realize, Mr Fleming, that this stuff is expensive, you need maybe two hundred dollars a week to get the stuff and who has that kind of money? So the mainliners have to steal or murder to get the money to buy the stuff. So what ought Washington to do? They ought to set up clinics all over the country where you can register as a drug-taker like you do in England, and go and get your dose for nothing, for free. So every time you go to the clinic, which has plenty of entrances so you won't be recognized, you get tapered off a fraction, a very small fraction. So in the end you get cured, see? The point is, Mr Fleming, that if you can get your drugs for nothing, you won't have to rob or murder somebody for the money to buy the stuff. So the middlemen, the traffickers, will go out of business, and then you have no law enforcement problem and no smuggling. Ya see, Mr Fleming, it's just the way you spend the money – on setting up clinics, or on law-enforcement that cannot work and that only makes the problem worse.'

I agreed that this made excellent sense and asked

why he didn't put the whole thing down on paper and send it to the President. Lucky modestly shrugged his shoulders and excused himself on the grounds that he had not got all the figures and the details to back up his plan. I urged him to go ahead, and I still do so. The idea of the 'Luciano Plan' to beat the narcotics problem, in connection with which he was originally sentenced and extradited from the States, seemed to me just the gimmick to 'send' the beatniks and hop-merchants who are the main consumers in America.

I then inquired why it was that all the great American gangsters, with the exception of Legs Diamond and one or two others, were, and still are, of Italian origin, and whether the Mafia operated as briskly in the United States as it is alleged to do. Rather speciously, I thought, Mr Luciano lightly dismissed the whole idea. It was just, he said, that nowadays people in America seemed to have a down on the Italians. As for the Mafia, that was just something for the journalists to write about. Did it operate in Naples? Mr Luciano shrugged the whole existence of the Mafia away. It was all boloney, he said. It was just to make the stories better for the journalists.

I personally feel that this total denial of the darker side of the moon does not contribute to the dignified and highly respectable front that Mr Luciano presents to the world. He is, of course, right to try and forget everything connected with the youthful way of life with which he is credited, but to express ignorance of the daily face of Italo-American crime is surely an affectation.

But no doubt Mr Luciano is right in that an incautious word to a journalist, particularly anything critical of his present habitat, might lead to exaggerated headlines and a diminution of the genuine friendliness with which he is regarded in Italy, and particularly around Naples, where he is well known for an exemplary life and generous private gifts to charity. His one dream is to be allowed to get away from the Naples area where he is confined and settle somewhere else where, above all other amenities, there must be a golf course – a recreation he misses most of all. Here in Naples, since the death of a much-loved lady companion, he has nothing to occupy his mind except three miniature Dobermann Pinschers and watching his diet which, on medical advice, is exceptionally frugal.

I urged him to write his memoirs, but he said, sadly and truthfully, that nobody would read them unless they were all about the bad things in his life. Nobody wanted to read anything good about him, although the original case against him had now been proved to have been a frame and he had received complete exculpation from the courts.

When we walked out together for Lee Thody to take some photographs, I asked him for the name of the best restaurant in the town, and he said 'Angelo's'. When I asked him about one in the yacht harbour in front of the Excelsior, he said, 'Don't eat there. The food's O.K., but they've got a heavy pencil.'

I have no idea how to equate the nicely spoken Signor Luciano of Naples with the old-time Lucky Luciano of

Chicago, but I did take pains to check his present record in Italy and I found it so exemplary that it is reasonable to suppose that any teeth he may have had in America have been either drawn or self-extracted in exile. In March 1958, for instance, a magistrate's special commission in Naples considered a police request from Rome that Luciano should be exiled from Naples to a small island or mountain village, on the grounds that he was involved in the international drug traffic. The commission ruled that there was no case against Luciano, who was 'a free citizen as has been proved and conducts a perfectly regular life giving no grounds for censure'. The Public Prosecutor appealed against that decision, alleging that the evidence against Luciano had not been properly weighed, but the Italian Court of Appeals found 'not even elements of suspicion' against Luciano, and that he was 'totally above suspicion of illegal activities'.

Then, in March 1959, occurred the case which Luciano had described to me. The record says that the court found a certain Scibilia guilty of damaging slander against Luciano and did indeed sentence him to two and a half years' imprisonment. Scibilia admitted he had sold false information about Luciano to the American Narcotics Bureau in Rome 'to earn a few pennies'. This information was to the effect that Luciano had ordered the 'disappearance' of an Italian mayor because he had double-crossed him over a drug deal.

What will become of the man and the myth? Apparently Mr Quentin Reynolds has been writing a story round him for Universal Pictures. How splendid it would be if the story could end with the adoption by the United States of the Luciano Plan for defeating the drug-smugglers, and with his triumphal return to America where, to the accompaniment of those heavenly choirs Hollywood does so well, Mr Luciano could be seen graciously accepting honorary membership of the Seminole Golf Club! [Mr Luciano died, peacefully, in 1962. I.F.]

Before closing this little chapter, I must record, out of all context, a most extraordinary experience of our photographer, Mrs Lee Thody. We were talking about magic and superstition which, hand in hand with ardent Catholicism, are the mainsprings of the Neapolitan spiritual life. The dark belief in these things, which the Church is quite incapable of stamping out, is principally concerned with noting omens towards a winning number in the Lotto, or State Lottery, which is the passion of the Neapolitan. The sorcerer king of Italy is a famous soothsayer living in Rome called Francesco Waldman, and Lee Thody, who was interested in these things, had recently written an article about him. After finishing the article she went back to the soothsayer and said she would like to take some photographs of him. He was very reluctant to allow this, but when she pressed him he finally consented while warning her that the photographs would not be successful on that particular day. Mrs Thody, who, as I have mentioned, is a professional photographer of high repute, prepared her Leica with flash attachment, but though she tried again and again the flash would not work, though it had previously been in perfect order. She accordingly changed to her Rolleiflex and took several pictures.

The next morning she took the two cameras to her developer who, first of all, checked the flash attachment to the Leica. It worked perfectly. He then proceeded with the development of the Rolleiflex plates. They were completely blank! Utterly bewildered, Mrs Thody returned to the soothsayer, explained what had happened and asked for another sitting. He reminded her that he had said it would be no good photographing him the day before, but said that it would be all right now. She took photographs of him with both cameras and they came out perfectly.

From Naples southwards there is not only daemonology in the air, but also an atmosphere of almost medieval savagery and barbarism, well illustrated, I think, by this brief story of a recent occurrence in the deep south.

A young farm labourer, Salvatori Funari, on his way to the fields, always took the same path past a farmhouse inhabited by four brothers and a younger sister, Antonina Guirlando, aged twenty-five. Salvatori used to wave to the girl as he went by in the morning and came back at night, and one day went so far as to call out 'Buon giorno'. Weeks later the girl summoned enough courage to call 'Buon giorno' back. Then the youth took to stopping by the garden fence and exchanging a few words of village gossip, and this innocent habit went on for two years without any closer relationship, except that the girl began to wear her long black hair tied severely back, a local indication that she was engaged.

One evening the girl was not in sight and Salvatori, on an impulse, knocked on the door. She opened the door, upon which he playfully kissed her and went off happily home.

The girl reported the kiss to her brothers. They spoke darkly of family honour and at once called upon Salvatori, the four of them, and told him that he had dishonoured their sister and must marry her.

Salvatori protested that he had done nothing dishonourable. It had just been a playful kiss and he was not yet old enough to marry. The brothers bought a revolver and gave it to their sister, and when Salvatori passed next day and shouted 'Buon giorno', she shot him dead.

She protested to the police that Salvatori had dishonoured her, but the police doctor confirmed that she was still a virgin and she was duly committed for trial on a charge of murder, though I am ignorant of what sentence she received.

Countless authors and sociologists have written about the stark, savage country south of Naples where all vestiges of the twentieth century, apart from an occasional Jolly hotel, have petered out, and we suffered no temptation to explore farther than Paestum. Instead we took the well-beaten sightseeing route from one five-star spectacle to the next, and on these I will briefly report.

Capri: This island of dreams, vanities and myths is still, though probably not in summer, a place of enchantment and eccentricity, though the bathing on the minute, pebbled beaches flecked with black fuel oil is as hellish as ever. It is an enchanting place to do absolutely nothing whatever in except contemplate your navel, or other people's, while trying to achieve a fashionable *tintorella* (sunburn). There are only five possible excursions – to the north, south, east and west or round the island in a boat – so, apart from getting sunburnt, people have nothing to do but squeeze on to the tennis-court size piazza and make, or fail to make, love. The failing – the refusals, broken unions, tears, recriminations – are the one source of energy on the island and the one topic of conversation. (Happy affairs are without interest. Only bad news makes gossip!) Thirty years ago, when I was last there, Capri was a great place for homosexuals, but the Homintern has now, lemming-like, left the island to seek greater privacy on Ischia and the more southerly and smaller islands north of Sicily. The only other perceptible change is the establishment by Miss Gracie Fields of a luxury restaurant and swimming-pool at the Piccola Marina of which she is the queen. Here, her privacy infested by every Tom, Dick and Ethel from England, she holds friendly court, and she was kind enough to invite us to luncheon.

Capri has always had at least one 'notable', a famous person, nearly always a foreigner, whom every visitor wants to see.

Gracie Fields has assumed the cloak of Axel Munthe and Norman Douglas and, apart from Emilio Pucci, the fashionable couturier, she is today the local star – a fame which this handsome, kindly, humorous woman from Lancashire wears, as her admirers will guess, with casual equanimity. She is happy there from May to October, but complains of being bored to death in winter when she takes flight for her old theatrical stamping grounds. In the winter, she laments, there is nothing to do in Capri but watch the television. 'Boris [her charming and intelligent Russian husband] and the cook are thrilled by it. I like watching but I don't know what the hell they are saying. Boris begins to explain to me and by that time the people on the screen are saying something else and I say what the hell, it's a short life, and then we all go back to watching again. No, I don't do much singing here. Occasionally we have a wing-ding when Sophie Tucker or someone else comes along, but there's plenty of excitement. Sometimes a smart yacht puts in with friends. They come ashore and so-and-so gets me alone and starts crying on my bosom and saying her husband is trying to kill her. You know what people on yachts are! Well, I am probably having dramas over something here, the neighbours or rival restaurants or something, and someone is trying to slay *me,* so I say to my girl friend, "It's the same thing all the world over, dear. Some man is always trying to strangle some woman. Don't you worry about it."'

Boris gave us wine from their own vineyard to drink – perhaps one of the few bottles of true Capri wine on the island, for what is sold in the shops is nearly always a blend. He personally supervises the vintage and I said I had always been curious to know if the wine really was trampled by beautiful girls. He said definitely not.

It was a tradition in Italy that to use women was very dangerous. During their menstruation periods, they are believed to kill all growing things they approach. Even in Italian agricultural colleges, he said, girls were not allowed to attend lessons on the farms or in the fields when they were in this condition. It was men who did the stamping of the wine. They soak their feet in a solution of leaves and herbs that each family keeps secret. This is an astringent preparation that closes the pores. At the end of the day they have to soak their feet in hot water to get the circulation going again.

I asked him how their fine establishment on the beach was doing and he said very well, though there were too many Germans who brought picnic luncheons and ate them all over the place. They also were constantly arguing about the entrance fee. There had been one extraordinary man that week who had created a frightful row at the entrance. He had insisted on coming in, but had refused to buy a ticket on the grounds that the Germans were much better soldiers than the Italians and had lost thousands of lives fighting for Italy! Boris had been called to settle the row and had told the German that he could be Boris's guest. This favour the German angrily rejected. He would not buy a ticket nor would he accept any favours from Boris. He just insisted on getting in for nothing on the grounds that the Germans were better soldiers than the Italians. When Boris had roared with laughter at this fantastic attitude, the German had stumped off, muttering darkly.

We later encountered crowds of the Herrenvolk on

the near-by island of Ischia – ex-stormtroopers who had gone to fat which they were trying to reduce by digging themselves graves in the radioactive beaches and covering themselves up with the volcanic sand so that nothing showed but rows of purple, sweating faces. The Italians are, on the whole, pleased to see them because, thanks to their frugality, they fill up the smaller pensions and rooms-to-let, and from the war-time experience of the two peoples they know a good deal of each other's languages.

A far more real pest of these regions is that new menace, the blaring transistor radio strung over the shoulder while the vacant-eyed carrier moons along hoping to *far figura* with his or her dreadful one-man band. In fact he is sounding the modern leper's bell – 'Keep away from me, I am the world's chaos and malaise.'

Pompeii is still, despite hordes of tourists, pimps and guides a very great marvel. We nearly killed ourselves there by refusing to hire a guide or buy a guide-book. We had forgotten how big it is and how quickly the giant cobbles, rutted by chariot wheels, murder one's feet.

There was one local phenomenon, at the door of the far-famed Lupanar – a totally unbribable custodian. He refused entry to my wife and she had to stand outside the little stone hovel with the wife of a Frenchman while he and I were allowed to enter the house of pleasure with its six tiny little bedrooms and the childish pictures high up on the walls to show you how to make love

– if you were the right shape and extremely athletic. The Frenchman was indignant that his wife was not allowed to view the vaunted mysteries of this antique bordello. He continued to argue while the custodian endeavoured to shock us by translating some of the vulgar graffiti on the walls, and explaining the much-flaked little pictures. 'You see,' he said, his eyes gleaming, 'that is the woman and that is the man!' 'Pah!' shouted the Frenchman. 'You think I have come a thousand miles from Paris to see that? Why, I was doing it myself when I was sixteen!' 'But this, Signor, and this!' beseeched the guide. 'Infantile!' shouted the Frenchman. 'These stupid Romans had no idea how to make love. And you mean to say you won't let my wife see this nonsense!' 'Ah no, Signor, troppo pericoloso.' 'Merde alors,' said the Frenchman, and we returned to our indignant wives.

Far more beautiful than anything in Pompeii itself is the nearby Villa dei Misteri, only recently completely excavated. This large and very handsome dwelling was apparently dedicated to the mysteries of Dionysus or Bacchus that had to be practised in secret because of the scandals associated with them. Here the pavements and friezes are astonishingly well preserved, the latter, representing the initiation of a virgin into the secret rites, being far finer and fresher than anything in Pompeii. It is said that these enchanting paintings, so light and graceful, are copies of far greater originals that have been lost – no doubt the victims again of the coming of the Christians. This beautiful shrine is off the tourist track, but visitors to Pompeii would do well to cut short their rambles amongst those haunted ruins and spend some time at this exotic and haunted place.

After this, Herculaneum held little interest except perhaps for those for whom the first plumbing, central heating and double-storied dwellings in history have a message. I found the ruins gaunt and melancholy, but the further excavations which have now been authorized may produce something more beautiful than the Neptune pavement in the women's baths which is all that impressed me.

Paestum, its splendid temples standing mutely and sadly beside the shore, filled me, since I do not greatly admire huge ruins however ancient, only with melancholy, but we were lucky to have luncheon at a small, out-of-the-way seaside *albergo* – the Olympia – and it was there, bathing on the vast, deserted beach, that we witnessed a most bizarre natural phenomenon, the life-cycle, or most of it, of two dung-beetles (?*Scarabaeus stercorarius paestanus*).

I was sitting on the edge of the dunes, when two medium-sized black beetles appeared, laboriously pushing a ball of animal dung, about the size of a ping-pong ball. It seems that these were two female beetles, for suddenly a much larger beetle erupted from the sand, dashed down, wrested away the ball of dung, told one of the females to buzz off and proceeded to roll the ball furiously along the sand followed by his chosen wife. He didn't push the ball with his nose, but, standing on his fore-legs, propelled it along backwards with his hind-legs – a most uncomfortable posture.

Fascinated, we watched this operation for about two hours as the beetles scurried down towards the sea, their tiny tank tracks leaving a spidery, Tachiste sketch in the *soft* dry sand. The couple had many adventures – falling down sandy ravines, scrabbling up great mountains and around obstacles, and, all the while, through friction from the spiky feet and the sand, the ball of dung was getting infinitesimally smaller.

I explained to my wife that the whole picture was a clear representation of our own existence. There was I, laboriously forwarding my career towards some unseen destination, while she fussed around in my wake and occasionally got in the way. The allegory was all the more exact in that Mr and Mrs Beetle stopped every so often and appeared to engage in a bout of fisticuffs or possibly love-display before Mr Beetle got his head down again and took up his sisyphean task.

The sun was going down, but we still could not leave without witnessing the end of this titanic pilgrimage. For it was titanic. The two beetles had covered nearly a mile of beach – equivalent, presumably, to a human being crossing all Europe on the run. But now, perhaps because the setting sun had lit up the line of sand-dunes and acacia clumps and provided the horizon that so many insects rely on to assist their sense of direction, the father beetle turned at last inland and hurried back towards the dunes.

Once there, all became clear. He heaved the ball of dung up the shifting slope to a clump of grass, and there, carefully balancing his ball on a small ledge of sand, began furiously to dig under the grass roots. At one moment the ball looked like slipping down the slope, but the faithful Mrs Beetle, waiting at the entrance to the growing hole, scrambled to the ball and held it steady. After about ten minutes' digging, Mr Beetle came back outside, collected his ball and accurately rolled it through the mouth of his home. Then he vanished after it, followed by Mrs Beetle, and the sand fell down and closed the entrance.

We could only assume that now the two beetles would make love and bear children, and that the ball of dung represented the hoard of food on which the baby beetles would be nurtured until they could grow up and go out into this great sandy world in search of another ball of dung and another spouse – and so *ad infinitum.*

Our last bit of sightseeing was to Cumae, just north of Naples and adjoining Lake Avernus, into which, you will recall, the descent is so facile. Here is the grotto of the sibyl, and it was hereabouts that Aeneas approached the infernal world over the Styx. (I had not thought about these things since, as a youth, I had had to write out hundreds of lines of Virgil as a punishment.) The grotto, hardly visited by tourists, is a most doomful and awe-inspiring sculptured cave of Minoan origin. It is a hundred yards long, more than six feet wide and some eighteen feet in height, and leads through various ante-chambers, lit by great windows to seawards, to the circular inner chamber with a connecting bedroom where the sibyl, no doubt a simple peasant girl with the gift of second sight, was kept by her priests. Along the walls of the grotto are curious and unexplained channels in the sandstone and these were perhaps acoustic devices to carry the voices of the priests through the secret inner draperies when they had some sibylline prophecy to announce to the crowds outside. Other slots and holes in the walls were presumably for curtain rods and draperies.

The atmosphere of this dark and ancient place is powerful but not inimical. One feels that many mysterious things were indeed enacted here, but that they were for good and not for evil. Apparently the Christians, when they came, were also sympathetic and treated the shrine with respect. Otherwise one suspects they would surely have destroyed it.

A couple of hundred yards from the hillock, on which stand the ruins of the Temple of Apollo and the Temple of Zeus and beneath which is the shrine, is a large tunnel through the mountainside leading down to the neighbouring Lake Avernus. This tunnel was used as an ammunition store by the Germans, who blew up the central section during their retreat.

The whole area is amazing and made me wish for the first time in my life that I had bent my head more faithfully to my *Aeneid*.

One final word to the visitor to Naples – don't bother to go up Vesuvius, or at any rate not by the motor road. There is absolutely nothing at the top but a few muddy bubbles and wisps of steam coming from the fumaroles in the crater, and anyway the volcano was due to erupt again that year – an even stronger reason for leaving it alone. But the reason I particularly counsel against it is that lava – that beautiful word that is almost the name of a girl – is harsh, brittle, smelly, black and, above all, immensely dull. It is true that my wife found a rare orchid on the lower slopes under the young umbrella pines, but the great pile of dead lava that is Vesuvius oozes a kind of mental depression that requires many drams of Lacrimae Christi, the wine grown at the foot of the mountain, to repair.

I have tried to analyse the dismal effect Vesuvius had on both of us and I think it comes from the fact that lava is totally lacking in 'anima', the quality that seems to inhabit all terrestrial materials down to the comparatively friendly clinker of coal. There may be friends of lava whom I have offended by this indictment, and there may be varieties of the stuff that can be put to some lowly purpose, such as pumice stone for taking nicotine stains off your fingers, but in my experience lava is the bottom stuff in the world.

The fact that Naples is largely paved with this hellish material and that the town, inundated from time to time with fire and brimstone, stands at a major gateway to the underworld, perhaps explains why this exciting, rewarding, vivid city yet verges so nearly on the infernal.

It is, of course, only coincidence that Al Capone, on January 15th, 1899, first saw the light of day at Afragola, a suburb of Naples, almost exactly half-way between the centre of Naples and the crater of Vesuvius.

## INCIDENTAL INTELLIGENCE

## NAPLES

*Hotels*
Five-star: *Hotel Excelsior, Hotel Vesuvio, Hotel Royal,* all on the waterfront overlooking the Bay of Naples. *Royal,* the newest with attractive, brightly furnished, studio-type rooms and windows.

Two-star: *Hotel Torino* (Via A. Depretis 123), and *Hotel Nuova Bella Napoli* (Piazza Garibaldi), by the central railway station. Pensione-type, low-priced accommodation not recommended in Naples.

*Restaurants*
The American travel guide, Fielding, summed up Neapolitan cuisine: 'It ranges,' he wrote, 'from high mediocre to just plain lousy.' I cannot improve on that.

Every visitor to Naples ends up at one of the three Santa Lucia quayside restaurants, the *Transatlantico, La Bersagliera,* or *Zi Teresa.* There's nothing to choose between them. Food is indifferent, waiters rude, strip-lighting hideous, and musicians play non-stop, except for a pause to push a plate in your face. As good food as any in Naples, including sea-food specialities, such as pasta with clam sauce (*spaghetti alla vongole*) and *fritta mista* (mixed fried fish dish), is to be found in restaurants of the three big hotels, *Excelsior, Vesuvio* and *Royal,* with the *Royal* especially recommended.

If you have transport, it's worth the fifteen-minute drive to *Le Lucciole* restaurant at Capo Posilipo. Lovely seaside position, excellent seafood. If you are looking for a real Neapolitan *pizza*, try *D'Angelo* – lovely view above Bay of Naples.

## Night-clubs

Best advice about average Naples night-spots is – stay away from them. Safest places are the *Royal Club* (winter) and *Royal Roof* (summer) in the *Royal Hotel*, and the club in the *Hotel Vesuvio*. The *Caprice Club* is also a normal night-club run on international lines.

## Things not to miss

It is in every guide book, but some visitors unfortunately still miss a visit to the Naples National Museum. Unlike many of Naples, attractions, this is first class. Contains finest of the treasures excavated from Pompeii and Herculaneum.

Afterwards go for a real black Neapolitan *espresso* coffee or an ice-cream in one of the cafes in the glass-roofed arcade, the Galleria. Here is real, living Naples, but watch your wallet and your handbags.

Colourful, too, is a visit to the fishermen's quayside at Mergellina, a seaside suburb, where sea-food is eaten from open-air stands as aperitifs – clams, mussels, sea-urchins, with Capri white wine.

## CAPRI

In good weather in the summer months Capri may now be reached in twenty-five minutes by helicopter (seven services a day, £3 day return), or hydrofoil boat, the *Aliscaft,* in thirty minutes, single 18s. (ninety-minute boats, 3s. 6d. single).

*Hotels*
Five-star: *Hotel Quisisana, La Ptneta;* at Anacapri, *Caesar Augustus* (April to October), built on sheer cliff-edge with fabulous view over the Bay of Naples. All one- and two-star Capri hotels are comfortable enough for a short stay if the larger hotels are full.

*Restaurants*
*La Pigna, Da Gemma.* Best restaurant, and you won't find it in most guidebooks but some of the best cooking south of Rome, is *Da Pietro,* managed by a colourful Scottish emigrant, Gloria. A stone's throw from Gracie Fields' *La Canzone del Mare,* where food is good but very, very expensive. At *Da Pietro* food and wine are good, reasonable; specialities, cheese pancakes, sea-food salads, fresh grilled fish and lobsters.

*Night-clubs*
*Number Two,* a damp, dank, jazz-smoke-filled cellar, nearest thing to a Paris bôite in Italy.

# 13

# Monte Carlo

'Neuf. Rouge. Impaire et Manque.' The moment's silence, the rattle of the losing chips being raked across the baize, the buzz of comment and then the sharp French voices firing their next bets at the cold, patient croupiers, and the echo from the croupiers to confirm the bets and help them remember. 'Finale quatre par cinq louis.' 'La derniere douzaine par cinq mille.' 'A cheval', 'Transversale pleine', 'Carre' . . . all the noisy abracadabra of one roulette table among six others. And then the hubbub from the chemin-de-fer, and the baccarat, and a whisper of music from somewhere in the distant background. And yet the grey-haired, donnish-looking man I was watching never looked up or seemed to pay any attention to what was going on around him. He sat very quietly and calmly at an empty chemin-de-fer table with his back to the room and stared with a chess-player's concentration at a huge sheet of paper spread out in front of him and occasionally jotted something down on it or consulted a chronometer which stood beside it.

As I watched him, a woman in black satin, anywhere

between fifty and a hundred years old, with badly dyed hair and a care-worn face, broke away from the nearest table and came and stood beside him. He did not look up as she opened her bag and put a handful of one- and five-hundred-franc chips on the table beside the chronometer. She stood there obediently while he made a series of calculations with a ballpoint pen. Minutes passed. The man made some more calculations. He consulted the chronometer. He selected some chips from the pile beside him and said a few words without looking up. She took the chips and walked swiftly to the nearest table. I followed her. She put six chips of a hundred francs *à cheval* on 6/8, 10/11, 13/16, 23/24, 27/30, 33/36. Or rather she said, 'Tiers du cylindre sud-est,' to the croupier. He didn't look up, but took the chips and placed them. He knew her voice. Sixteen came up. She was paid 1,700 francs on her 13/16 *à cheval* and lost five hundred on the others. She picked up the chips and her stake and went back silently to the man with the chronometer. I moved away from the table so that I could have a last look at them and fix them in my mind. They suddenly looked tragic and dedicated, like people who think the earth is flat.

I was screwing up my courage to go and talk to them when a girl's voice containing in equal proportions sarcasm, curiosity, envy, and pleasure at finding a friend from England, brought me back to earth.

'Well, I suppose you've broken the bank.'

'No,' I said shortly, although I was pleased to see her, 'I haven't.'

'Why don't you shoot out the lights with your .38

Police Positive with the sawn barrel? Then we could grab some chips and make a dash for the door.'

I pretended not to hear. She followed my eyes. 'What's that old man doing over there?'

'He's working on a system,' I said. 'It's based either on astronomy or the movement of the earth on its axis. He's not interested in what came up on the last throw. He just backs a third of the board according to the precise time of day. He thinks the turn of the steel cylinder is affected by magnetic fields, or gravity or something. He won handsomely on the only coup I watched.'

'He must be mad,' said my friend. 'All one needs is capital. It's hopeless playing with only ten mille.' (It was the age of the old francs.)

'Ten mille is a hundred even-chance bets at the hundred-franc roulette table,' I said prosily. 'Nowadays all English people moan about not having enough capital to gamble with. It's just a question of what units you bet in and how much you want to make. You're just a scattercash.'

'I suppose James Bond's got an infallible system,' she said frostily. 'Why don't you let other people in on his secret? Tell me, or I'll never speak to you again.'

This is the gist of what I told her – what I believe to be the only way of gambling with a capital of ten pounds with a reasonable prospect of making the price of a good dinner, with the pleasure of staking a bet at many turns of the wheel and with the excitement of joining in that technical expertise which is part of the attraction of a casino.

The first rule, I told her, is to get a seat at the roulette table. This is achieved by getting to the casino early, say at nine o'clock in the evening, or in the afternoon. The formalities of getting into the casino need not deter you. All you need is your passport and a respectable suit or frock (except at Deauville and the Casino de la Foret at Le Touquet where you may have to wear evening clothes, in which case there is Trouville, or the Casino de la Plage). Do not approach casinos with timidity or reverence. They are simply fruit-machines tended by bank clerks and mechanics. Be relaxed and confident. They are very pleased to have you come in and will be sorry to see you go. You are one of the few people who take trouble and you are going to win and stop when you have won. You are a person of free will and iron self-discipline who will beat the machine.

You enter the casino and sit down at a roulette table. (If there is no seat available, give one of the uniformed attendants a hundred or two hundred francs and ask him to find you a seat, and one will be found.) Remember: a seat at the table is essential. Most people lose money in a casino because their feet get so tired they decide to fritter away a few chips and go to bed. If possible get a seat opposite the even chance, red or black, which you favour (because your hair or your eyes are red or black, or for any other reason). Settle yourself. Take out a card and a pencil and write the figures 1, 2, 3, 4, 5 down the page. You have been to the caisse just inside the swing-door and in your pocket or your bag you have ten pounds in chips of one hundred francs each. More than a hundred of them. Comparative wealth, with the minimum stake at a hundred francs. Pay no attention to the strident voices, gestures and emotions of the other players. Observe the chaos with interest and indulgence, secure in the knowledge of the symmetry of your own deadly system.

Suppose, I explained to the girl, you have chosen red. (You can choose any of the six even chances and alter your choice at any moment if you wish, but personally I prefer to espouse either red or 'impair', or 'passe', and stick with it all the evening.) Your first bet, which you place firmly on the big red diamond a few inches away, is the sum of the top and bottom numbers on your list – 5 plus 1, six chips of one hundred francs each. If you win, you cross out the 5 and the 1 on your list, and your next bet is the sum of the remaining top and bottom numbers of your column – 4 plus 2. Whenever you lose, the amount of the loss is written at the end of the column. Your next and subsequent bets are always the sum of the top and the bottom numbers you have *not* scratched out. When (and if) all the numbers are scratched off, your win will amount to the sum of all the numbers in your original five-figure column – fifteen hundred francs or one good dinner.

After successfully completing one round of the system you can, of course, play it again if you want to spend longer in the casino, but you should remember that the casino will beat you in the long run and that the sooner you can collect your profit of fifteen hundred francs and walk out the better. Since, I said to the girl, you are a gambler of free will and iron discipline it should be simple for you to resist temptation and go home to bed and dream of the menu of the excellent dinner the casino has just paid for.

Above all, you must be patient, have courage when the going is hard and stick rigidly to your system and not fritter away chips on single numbers which are the date, or the number of buttons on your dress, or a message from another world. You are a professional gambler out to make a profit and get away with it.

I said to the girl, 'But of course no system at roulette is infallible, and all of them, including this one, can be just ways of losing your money slowly. But on this system, even with a small capital, you will only be defeated by long adverse runs, which are uncommon, or by the downright bad luck of an unusual preponderance of the other colour during the session.

'The main point about it is that, with this system, you get your money's worth. If you lose, you shouldn't lose quickly. Its best recommendation is that it is used by the little resident gambler in French casino towns where the locals are allowed to play. It's really nothing more than a variation of the martingale or progression system – a very gradual form of doubling up. It's called the Labouchère system.'

Later that evening the girl came up to me. Her eyes were shining. 'I've won a fortune,' she said. 'Come and have a drink.'

'I told you it was a good system.'

'You and your system!' she said scornfully. 'I hacked

away at it for an hour. I backed red and too many blacks kept on coming up. Your system's just another way of losing money, only it's much harder work. Typical of James Bond to dream it up. He just wants the agony to last longer.'

'Well, what happened?' 'I was down to my last thousand francs and I said to hell with it and put the thousand francs on my birthday. And it came up. What has clever Mister James Bond got to say to that?' she said scornfully.

'He might be unkind and suggest that you backed a number right down at the end of the last dozen,' I said curtly.

The night of this slightly fictionalized account of my first evening in Monte Carlo I myself did badly. I had taken all the necessary precautions – noting the number of my hotel bedroom, remembering the date of my wife's birthday and, most essential of all, rubbing the horse's knee of the equestrian statue of Louis XIV in the hall of the Hotel de Paris (all the bronze veneer has been rubbed off by generations of the superstitious and the knee now gleams like gold), but nothing had availed me. I put my misfortune down to a state of spiritual derangement caused by a group of noisy and mannerless Italian businessmen who had put me off my psychological stride at chemin-de-fer, and by the significant fact that, on sitting down to dinner, the two knives to the right of my plate had been crossed – a sure message that I would be out of luck that night.

I am not by any means a passionate gambler nor a

very audacious one, but I greatly enjoy the smoke-filled drama of the casino and the momentary fever of the game. The casino at Monte Carlo is not my favourite. For me the casino at Beaulieu has the greatest charm, followed by Le Touquet, with, at the bottom of the list, Enghien les Bains outside Paris, which has the unenviable distinction, for a gambler, of making the highest annual profit of any casino on the Continent. The Monte Carlo casino is rather too much of a show-place and there is a railway-station atmosphere about the vast gaming rooms that, despite the glorious vulgarity of the decor (note, in the inner *salon vert,* the naiads on the ceiling; they are smoking cigars), is slightly chilling. The intimate surroundings of the Sporting Club, decorated, as the casino hand-out charmingly puts it, 'par les peintres Warring et Gillows', are far preferable, but this select enclave has strict winter and summer seasons and was closed at the end of May.

Part of the trouble with the Monte Carlo rooms is that they were built in an age of elegance for elegant people, and the gambling nowadays has the drabness of a Strauss operetta played in modern dress. The Italians, Greeks and South Americans, who are by far the richest post-war gamblers, are almost totally without glamour and, if they support beautiful cocottes in the true casino tradition, they leave them at home so as not to be distracted from what used to be a pastime but has now become a rather deadly business of amassing tax-free capital gains. Monte Carlo and its casino were designed for flamboyants – for Russian stories putting the casino in a rosy light are still fostered, such as that the casino recently lost more than sixty million francs in three days; that in 1952 an English couple won thirty million francs in a week and were never seen again; and the history of Charles de Ville Wells who inspired the music-hall song 'The Man who Broke the Bank at Monte Carlo'. The story of Sir Frederick Johnston also finds its place in the authorized version, though it sounds highly improbable. This Milord, in 1913, when they still played with louis d'or, was wearing a blazer with brass buttons. One button broke off and rolled under the table. 'Don't disturb yourself, Milord,' cried the chef de parti, 'where does the louis go, on red?' 'Always red,' laughed Sir Frederick, not knowing what it was all about. He then left the table and moved to another room only to be sought out by a huissier with the news that he now had the maximum on red and that it must be withdrawn in order not to hold up the game. Milord had won 25,000 francs with a button!

Monte Carlo is full of these tales which find their way again and again into books and articles about the casino. The only one I could have verified (but forgot to) is to the effect that, in the English church, they only sing hymns with a number higher than thirty-six since otherwise the congregation, it is said, quit the church at the first organ note in order to dash to the casino and back the number of the hymn.

I have always had a desire to examine the mechanics of a casino and, with the help of Mr Onassis's staff, I gained access to the engine-room, so to speak, of this famous gaming house.

To the left of the imposing main entrance to the casino there is a small door with nothing written on it, and through this you go down flights of stone stairs into a maze of underground passages and rooms that remind one of the back of a theatre. The largest of these rooms is the atelier where the roulette wheels are constructed and where all the gambling equipment is repaired. The chef d'atelier was an attractive, youngish man with great enthusiasm for his work, though he was totally uninterested in gambling and said, proudly, that he had never hazarded a single franc. That day he had three roulette wheels for repair and these were draped in green baize while they 'slept'. He undraped one and lifted it from its spindle on to its die and explained to me the extraordinary number of things that can go wrong with a *cylindre*. Everything to do with a roulette wheel is subject to minute wear, the spindle obviously, but also the aluminium slots, the brass bosses, the top rosewood level where the ball spins, and the ivory ball itself, which, with use, gets smaller and smaller. All these points and many others come under daily review when at 9.30 a.m., half an hour before gambling begins, the chef and his team verify every single piece of equipment in the gaming rooms – the croupiers' rakes, the chemin-de-fer shoes, the diameter of the roulette balls and of, course, the level of each table, which can be adjusted at the base of the feet.

I asked about the croupiers' school, and the chef

explained its functioning. Apparently examinations for the school are held at irregular intervals. A candidate must first pass a strict medical and then come before an interview board which reviews his personal life and that of the whole of his family, which must be above reproach. He is then put through tests for general intelligence, which must be above the average, and for memory, which must be exceptional. He should be between twenty-three and forty, have long, supple fingers and be extremely agile in his movements. His speech must be correct and without significant accent and he should have some knowledge of at least one foreign language – generally either Italian or English.

As an additional and supreme safeguard, no candidate is considered unless he has served for two years with the Société des Bains de Mer, either as a secretary, commissionaire, watchman or fireman, for instance.

Having passed these preliminary examinations, he is put to practical schooling under senior croupiers for six or eight months, with intermediate examinations at the end of each month. At the end of this period he is put through a 'disaster course' – a horrifying experience during which every conceivable complication and unexpected incident is thrown at him. He then has a second medical examination, and after this a final trial in the public rooms. This, apparently, is the most anguishing experience of all. The candidates, already wrought to a high pitch of nervous tension and knowing that they are under surveillance from half a dozen watchful pairs of eyes, occasionally faint at the table and nearly always sweat so heavily that the equipment, particularly, the ivory ball, slips in their fingers. If they pass this final inquisition with success they are appointed croupiers and probably continue in the métier, working six hours a day, until they are sixty or sixty-five, when they are retired on a pension. They work on a fixed salary and receive a percentage of the tips which, on an average, doubles their monthly wage.

There are various conventions that the experienced gambler will have noticed. The croupier must refer to the roulette as 'le cylindre', and frequently uses the term 'louis' when announcing bets, although this piece of money has been out of currency for more than forty years. He must also remember that there are in theory no women at the table, and that it is always, 'Messieurs, faites vos jeux.' This tradition dates from the time when it was considered inelegant to associate women with the passion for gambling.

It is almost impossible for a croupier to cheat. The last successful cheat was before the war when two Italians bribed a croupier to mark the cards at a chemin-de-fer table with dots of an ink that was invisible except through specially tinted glasses worn by the Italians. The cards were marked with tiny dots representing their face value and this allowed the Italians, when they held the bank, to know the total held by the punter – a knowledge that, from time to time in the game, can be of decisive value. The conspiracy was successful for several weeks but was then uncovered by a suspicious chef de jeu who became mystified when the Italians

Cousteau, who incidentally surveyed the Persian Gulf offshore wells for the British Petroleum Company, is technical adviser for all underwater aspects of this six-hundred-billion-franc pipeline plan. Amongst smaller projects, he is now experimenting with a collapsible ship made of nylon coated with plastic. The prototype is sixty-three feet by twenty-three feet and is powered by two 600 h.p. diesels. This deflatable vessel will be used in conjunction with the diving saucer for short-term marine exploration wherever it is needed, the entire equipment being transportable by air at short notice.

Unfortunately Cousteau's writing never catches up with all his various projects and it is only now that he is considering a sequel to *The Silent World* (*The Living Sea*, published in 1963 by Hamish Hamilton). Meanwhile he has formed his own film company (after experience of 'show biz' in connection with his film of *The Silent World,* he has called it Requins Associés, Sharks Ltd.) which is to produce a television series of fifty-two films.

His company recently won a Hollywood Oscar for Cousteau's film *The Golden Fish*. This is the story of a small Chinese boy who wins a goldfish in a lottery. In his small room he already has a canary in a cage and when he goes off to school each day the goldfish in its bowl and the canary make friends. A hungry black cat hears the canary singing for joy over the acrobatics of the goldfish and we see him climb in through the window just as the boy is leaving school. As the boy saunters home, the cat tries to get at the canary and, prepared to sacrifice himself for his friend, the fish jumps out of the bowl on to the table. The cat leaves the canary and slowly stalks the fish. Will the little boy be in time? No, he can't be! Hurry! Hurry! The cat picks up the fish in his mouth! Disaster! But, as the little boy walks into the room, the cat reaches up and drops the goldfish back into his bowl.

Cousteau's famous research ship, the *Calypso*, is now in Greek waters, but the days of treasure hunts and archaeological discoveries are, alas, over, and Cousteau's whole research programme is devoted to scientific work. But whatever he touches he infects with so much brilliance and enthusiasm that a morning spent in his company is a wonderful refreshment for the spirit – particularly when it is jaded by the life of too many cities, however thrilling, in too short a time.

And then it was time to take off on the last lap along the screaming hubbub of the Cote d'Azur, up through the olive groves of Provence, and the mysterious maze of the Auvergne, to the soft Loire. Then the long straight hack across north-west France to the bustling little aerodrome of Le Touquet.

One last delicious meal at the airport restaurant (five stars in my personal good-food guide), the pangs of jealousy as the other cars come off the planes to begin their holidays, and then the melancholy flight back across the Channel. How many excitements and alarums, how many narrow squeaks, how many thrilling sights and sounds in those six weeks! What fun it all was! What fun 'abroad' will always be!

IAN FLEMING PUBLICATIONS

Ian Lancaster Fleming was born in London on 28 May 1908 and was educated at Eton College before spending a formative period studying languages in Europe. His first job was with Reuters news agency, followed by a brief spell as a stockbroker. On the outbreak of the Second World War he was appointed assistant to the Director of Naval Intelligence, Admiral Godfrey, where he played a key part in British and Allied espionage operations.

After the war he joined Kemsley Newspapers as Foreign Manager of *The Sunday Times,* running a network of correspondents who were intimately involved in the Cold War. His first novel, *Casino Royale,* was published in 1953 and introduced James Bond, Special Agent 007, to the world. The first print run sold out within a month. Following this initial success, he published a Bond title every year until his death. His own travels, interests and wartime experience gave authority to everything he wrote. Raymond Chandler hailed him as 'the most forceful and driving writer of thrillers in England.' The fifth title, *From Russia With*

*Love,* was particularly well received and sales soared when President Kennedy named it as one of his favourite books. The Bond novels have sold more than 100 million copies and inspired a hugely successful film franchise which began in 1962 with the release of *Dr No,* starring Sean Connery as 007.

The Bond books were written in Jamaica, a country Fleming fell in love with during the war and where he built a house, 'Goldeneye'. He married Ann Rothermere in 1952. His story about a magical car, written in 1961 for their only child, Caspar, went on to become the well-loved novel and film, *Chitty Chitty Bang Bang.*

Fleming died of heart failure on 12 August 1964.

www.ianfleming.com

🐦 TheIanFleming

📷 Ianflemings007

f IanFlemingBooks